Mythmakers
of the
West

SHAPING AMERICA'S IMAGINATION

by John A. Murray

NORTHLAND
PUBLISHING

For Brad Melton

Cover: Georgia O'Keeffe (Courtesy Palace of the Governors, Museum of New Mexico), Geronimo (Courtesy Denver Public Library, Western History Collection), Jim Morrison (Courtesy Maverick Recordings), Annie Oakley (Courtesy Denver Public Library, Western History Collection), Edward Abbey (Courtesy Jack Dykinga), John Wayne (Courtesy Warner Bros.), and Monument Valley (Courtesy Gene Balzer). Photo illustration by Lois Rainwater.
Page iv–v: The Teton Range as seen from the Oxbow Bend on the Snake River. Courtesy John Murray.

Art Director: Lois A. Rainwater
Designer: Lois A. Rainwater
Editor: Brad Melton
Copy Editor: Kathleen Bryant
Production Supervisor: Lisa Brownfield
Editorial Assistant: Kimberly Fox

www.northlandpub.com

FIRST IMPRESSION, 2001
05   04   03   02   01   5   4   3   2   1

Composed in the United States of America
Printed in Hong Kong

Library of Congress Cataloging-in-Publication Data

Murray, John A., 1954–
    Mythmakers of the west : shaping America's imagination / by
    John A. Murray.
      p. cm.
    Includes bibliographical references and index.
    ISBN 0-87358-799-5 (hc) — ISBN 0-87358-772-3 (softcover)
      1. West (U.S.)—Civilization. 2. Legends—West (U.S.) 3.
    Landscape—West (U.S.) 4. Regionalism—West (U.S.) 5. West
    (U.S.)—Intellectual life. 6. West (U.S.)—In mass media. I. Title

F591 M93 2001
978—dc21
                                          2001030112

I was all alone on a broad plain now
with my feet upon the earth,
alone but for the spotted eagle guarding me.
I could see my people's village far ahead,
and I walked very fast, for I was homesick now.
Then I saw my own tepee,
and inside I saw my mother and my father,
bending over a sick boy that was myself.
And as I entered the tepee,
someone was saying: "The boy is coming to;
you had better give him some water."
Then I was sitting up; and I was sad
because my mother and my father didn't seem
to know I had been so far away.

—The Oglala Sioux holy man Black Elk,
writing of his vision as a young man,
circa 1873 (from BLACK ELK SPEAKS*)*

CONTENTS

PREFACE VI

INTRODUCTION
LIGHTING OUT
The American West as Mythic Province 1

CHAPTER ONE
WHEN I PAINT MY MASTERPIECE
Visual Artists and the Landscape of Legend 11

GEORGE CATLIN
Images of a Vanishing People 14

ALBERT BIERSTADT AND THOMAS MORAN
The Pantheistic Sublime. 16

FREDERIC REMINGTON
AND CHARLES RUSSELL
The End of Something. 20

THE TAOS SOCIETY OF ARTISTS
Inside the Gates of Eden 23

CARL RUNGIUS
Across the High and Wild. 26

MAYNARD DIXON
Visions and Revisions 29

ANSEL ADAMS AND EDWARD WESTON
The Search for One Pure Image 32

IMOGEN CUNNINGHAM
New Directions 36

GEORGIA O'KEEFFE
Inner Landscapes. 39

T. C. CANNON
Native Son 41

RUSSELL CHATHAM
Radiant Darkness 45

CHAPTER TWO
OF FILMS AND FABLE
Motion Pictures as Mythmakers 49

JOHN FORD AND JOHN WAYNE
Eden Invaded 51

TELEVISION WESTERNS
The Big Sky on the Small Screen 54

MARILYN MONROE
Innocence Betrayed. 56

CLINT EASTWOOD
The Pursuit of Justice. 59

ROBERT REDFORD
Heroes and Anti-Heroes. 62

KEVIN COSTNER
Requiem for the Past 65

CHAPTER THREE
THE LIGHT OF THE WESTERN STARS
The Western Writer as Fabulist 69

LEWIS AND CLARK
Paradise Found 72

WASHINGTON IRVING
AND FRANCIS PARKMAN
The Birth of the Literary West 74

JOHN BOURKE, O. O. HOWARD,
COCHISE, AND GERONIMO
How It Was. 78

MARK TWAIN
The Comic West. 84

THEODORE ROOSEVELT
Last Light Breaking 86

JOHN MUIR
Nature's West. 89

WILLA CATHER AND MARI SANDOZ
O Pioneers! 91

MARY AUSTIN
Days in the Field. 94

ZANE GREY
Pulp Fiction 96

JOHN STEINBECK
The Realistic Southwest. 98

A. B. GUTHRIE AND WALLACE STEGNER
West of the Hundredth Meridian 100

EDWARD ABBEY
Mother Nature's Son 104

LARRY MCMURTRY
Yesterday and Today. 107

CHAPTER FOUR
MUSIC, SWEET MUSIC
Popular Song in the Service of Myth 111

BALLADS AND LAMENTS
The Romance of the Cowboy 113

BOB WILLS AND HIS TEXAS PLAYBOYS
As Free as the Wind. 116

WOODY GUTHRIE
The Dark Side of the Dream 118

BUDDY HOLLY AND THE CRICKETS
The Power of Optimism. 120

PACIFIC COAST MUSIC
The Far West as Creative Wellspring 123

Los Angeles: Endless Summer 123

San Francisco: Somebody to Love 130

Seattle: Purple Haze. 132

JOHN DENVER
Rocky Mountain High. 134

WILLIE NELSON
The Outlaw Life. 137

SELENA
Down by the River 139

CHAPTER FIVE
A COUNTRY OF THE MIND
The Province of the West in Popular Culture 143

FOLK LEGENDS
The Call of the Wild 145

MORMONISM
Exodus to the West 148

THE FRED HARVEY COMPANY
AND THE SANTA FE RAILWAY
Visions of El Dorado 151

DUDE RANCHES
*Mama, Don't Let Your Babies Grow Up
To Be Cowboys* 153

COMMERCIAL ADVERTISING
The Selling of the West. 156

ARIZONA HIGHWAYS
The Transcendent Landscape 159

ROUTE 66
"Get Your Kicks, on Route Sixty-Six!" 161

AFTERWORD
ONLY THE EARTH ENDURES 164

A CHRONOLOGY OF THE WEST 168

SELECTED BIBLIOGRAPHY. 174

INDEX. 177

PREFACE

The purpose of this book is to explore, with words and images, the mythmaking forces that have shaped perceptions of the American West as a cultural region. The narrative focuses, in roughly chronological fashion and within five categories (art, film, literature, music, popular culture), on those individuals and entities who have played the most active roles in promoting the historic myths of the region. The book tells the story of the enduring fables that have grown from the history and landscapes of the West, examines the relationship between myth and reality, and inquires into the manner in which the West, as a land of space and sun, has become a metaphor for corresponding provinces of the spirit and imagination. The book is a chronicle of the legendary West. It examines the fictional or imaginary world of the West, as each successive American generation has, with inquiry, vulnerability, movement, and expectancy, reengaged—and, in a sense, reinvented—the landscape and the people of the region.

Why read this book? Because, more than any other province of the country, the West is a realm rich in myth: the age of the fur trappers, the Santa Fe and Oregon Trails, the battles of the Little Bighorn and Apache Pass, the historic cattle drives, the building of the railroads, the era of the homesteaders, the Butterfield-Overland Stage, the marshals of Tombstone, the birth of the desert gambling towns. More so than the dry facts of history, the mythical stories of the West give us personal, immediate insight into who we are, what we believe, how we think, and where we want to go in the future as a people. England may have its myth of King Arthur and his Knights of the Round Table, Italy may have its legend of Aeneas, and Greece may have its hoary fable of Troy, but in America we have something quite different, something quite a bit more recent, something very original. The West is our own private dream-world, the spacious, sun-washed repository of some of our most cherished myths.

What follows is the story of the mythological West—past, present, and future—and some of its most influential mythmakers. It is told through their lives, their visions, and the journeys they made. It explores a landscape as different from the East and the South as the New World is from the Old World. The smell of the sage, the song of the coyote, the towering saguaro cactus, the gray horn of the Grand Teton, the great falls of the Yellowstone—all are part of the world you are about to enter. The book is meant to be read in sequence, as an extended story with a cumulative lesson. The chief character in the plot is the landscape itself—the deserts and mountains, rivers and forests, canyons and mesas. Without the gift of its open space and freedom, there would be no myths at all. In the end we are left with a sense of a cultural heritage unlike any on Earth, as we see how people flow through time like a river, carving their channels and pooling up in their curious backwaters, always moving forward with the force of myth and truth.

How exactly are we to define the West? Is it somehow restricted to those areas where wild horses and wily coyotes, slick rock and sagebrush, prairie dogs and prickly pear are found? Or is it something larger and more comprehensive, a sprawling region of earth and light and sky? For the purposes of this book, the West will be defined as that region residing west (give or take a few hundred miles either way) of the 95th Meridian. Scattered along that imaginary line from north to south can be found such geographic sites as Pipestone National Monument near Sioux Falls, Homestead National Monument near Omaha, Fort Scott National Historic Site near Kansas City, and Davy Crockett National Forest near Houston—in other words, the beginning of a landscape substantively different than the East. The West described in this manner is not as narrow as that offered by some (west of the 100th Meridian and east of the Sierras), nor is it as large as that proposed by others (everything west of the Mississippi River). The West in this book does not include Alaska, which is more Asian than North American in landforms, fauna and flora; nor does it include western Canada or northern Mexico, both of which are similar in some respects (photographically), but different in others (historically and culturally).

The American West can be broadly delineated by what the East lacks—open space and public land. By these terms, the West ranges from the corn silos and rolling sunflower fields of central Iowa to the quiet harbors and salmon trawlers of coastal Oregon, from the wheat fields north of Great Falls to the orange groves south of Tucson. It includes the palm-lined boulevards of Las Vegas, as well as the wind-swept streets of Lubbock. It takes in the rain forests of the Olympic Peninsula, as well as the scorched expanses of Death Valley. It is the fabled domain of Jim Bridger and Jim Morrison, Henry Fonda and Peter Fonda, George Catlin and Georgia O'Keeffe. It is the place where

the sun goes down every night, the place we travel to when everything behind us has been lost, the place that beckons forever to the restless at heart. To paraphrase Whitman on another subject, it is a province that is as beautiful as it is full of contradictions, a realm that, in its immensity, comprehends multitudes.

I owe many thanks. First to the dear friends who have accompanied me over the last six years on my rambling excursions across the West: Katy Bosch, Fen Ying Hao, Aliette Frank, Christine June, and Natalya Ryabova. Thanks as well to the Yellowstone Institute for providing a venue for me to teach my courses. Thanks also to Klaus Kranz, Robert G. Rainwater, Jack Dykinga, the Medicine Man Gallery, Photofest, Darlene Dueck of the Anschutz Collection, Mitchell Brown Fine Art, the National Museum of Wildlife Art, the Ansel Adams Trust, Metropolitan Museum of Art, the Smithsonian, The Albuquerque Museum, The Heard Museum, The Denver Public Library, The Imogen Cunningham Trust, the Taos County Historical Society, Joyce Cannon Yi, Russell Chatham, Terrance Moore, Denver Art Museum, Arizona Historical Society, Northern Arizona University, the Library of Congress, Bookman's, and McGaugh's Newsstand, all of whom were instrumental in adding to the book's rich imagery. I would like to express my gratitude to my editor Brad Melton for his continual inspiration and counsel, and to art director Lois Rainwater for her creative passion and vision. Finally, a deep word of appreciation for my son, Naoki, and for my father, Charles, for their daily love and support.

William R. Leigh, GRAND CANYON, *1908.*
Courtesy The Anschutz Collection.

LIGHTING OUT

The American West as Mythic Province

The most brilliant colors are there,

I believe, and the most beautiful

and extraordinary land forms—

and surely, the coldest, clearest air which

is run through with pure light.

—N. Scott Momaday
THE NAMES

AS MUCH AS IT HAS BEEN INSPIRED BY A LOVE for the American West, this book traces its genesis to two events.

In October 1997 I had the opportunity to view an exhibition of the paintings of William R. Leigh (1866–1955) at the National Museum of Wildlife Art in Jackson, Wyoming. Among the works featured was a large (thirty-six-by-sixty-inch) canvas entitled *Grand Canyon, 1908*. Leigh, who studied for twelve years at the Royal Academy in Munich, Germany, used a Southwestern palette of soft pink and muted purple, with earth-toned pigments of terra rosa, ochre, and sienna. Viewed up close, the extent of his artistry became apparent: the lingering traces of individual brush strokes, the delicately textured ridges of pigment, and the bold application of impasto in places to emphasize form and compositional line. Leigh had put the elements down deliberately but always freely, and color was emphatically used to convey an array of visual effects, from the atmospheric haze of obscure depths to the exacting brightness of sharply defined heights. Viewed farther back, the work evoked as much a transcription of a literal canyon as it did a vision of the human spirit, with its correspondingly diverse geography.

The canvas is so large—fifteen square feet—that a viewer feels he or she can almost rise up and disappear, Keats-like, into the timeless world of the imagination, an effect which was part of the artist's aesthetic plan. In the foreground is a minor side canyon, dropping steeply away from a shelf of junipers and sage. The eye enters the painting at this point and travels north for several miles, deeper into the abyss. On the right, or east, is a steep ridge layered with parallel bands of sandstone and topped with a castle of weathered limestone. In the middle ground are the far canyon walls that lead toward the North Rim, thirty miles distant. Nowhere in the painting is the ultimate creator of the scene, the Colorado River,

More than other works I've viewed, this painting captured the elusive mythological essence of the West.

visible, but everywhere the effects of its passage are evident. Dominating the background on the left, or west, is a passing summer storm, the clouds gray with moisture. Transparent blue threads of virga drift toward remote ponderosa forests. Across the canvas the proportions and values are faithfully rendered—Leigh was a careful naturalist and conscientious about such fidelity—and the colors, though slightly softened to avoid a photographic appearance, are entirely true to nature.

More than other works I've viewed, this painting captured the elusive mythological essence of the West: the boundless perspective of space and time, the striking interplay of rock and sky, the combined effect of contemplative peace and penetrating vision. Leigh starkly expressed the rich mixture of spirit and matter that defines the human experience of the province, a region whose elementary, often stark features continually awaken a sense of the sacred. The scene, depicted with honesty and directness, invites spiritual communion, encourages renewal, and suggests the promise of liberation. As with all successful realistic paintings, there is also a strong element of abstraction, of metaphor, that transcends the visual source of inspiration. The artist makes it clear, in his choice of subject and technique, that we might also be viewing a self-portrait, a rendering of the human spirit, or a landscape of the mind. From such moments, such representations, all myths are born.

The second incident occurred several years ago while traveling in southern Utah. I was on a little-traveled highway in the Cedar Mesa country, headed south toward Monument Valley. Along either side of the road were low rolling hills with pinyon and juniper, interspersed with the occasional dry watercourse or old grass pasture turned to sage. The asphalt pavement went on, straight and narrow, for miles, and the only radio station came from Window Rock on the Navajo reservation—a group of men chanting to the beat of a single drum. From the south the sky was brighter than in any other direction, and that brightness was the reflected light of Monument Valley, which is largely exposed stone. I had planned to spend the day photographing the Mitten Buttes, but on passing the trailhead to Grand Gulch, a five-hundred-thousand-acre archaeological preserve, everything changed. I am one of those souls who cannot resist an opportunity to hike into the backcountry, particularly on a sunny spring morning, and so I parked the car and filled the pack and set off. Northern Arizona would have to wait until tomorrow.

The trail began on the west side of the road and dropped by degrees into the upper portals of a canyon. In places the sage and junipers were shoulder high, and the main trail was easily lost among the cattle trails. Once in the canyon the converging trails became a single narrow path. The stone walls rose up toward the sky and the air became still and cool, with the intimate quiet of a contained space—a place of worship, a library retreat, a museum exhibit space. A mile farther there was a cattle guard. I opened and closed the gate and quietly stepped into that other world, the one from which all livestock and machinery are excluded. Instantly there was the feeling of exhilaration that always attends one's entry into the wilderness, as if one is returning through a wormhole to the lost, innocent world of childhood. Deeper and deeper the canyon carved into the plateau, curving like a serpent with sinuous bends and darkly streaked overhangs and quiet alcoves set in the stone. At first the stream was dry, but shortly there were dripping springs and standing pools and spurting waterfalls. Here and there, rising above the trail, were balanced rocks the size of rail cars.

After four miles the side canyon opened into a larger canyon, and it was there, above a grassy triangular bench, that I came upon the remnants of an Anasazi village. The houses, granaries, and kiva were not on the flats, where the fields would have been, but were perched high in the rocks, in the manner of cliff-swallow nests. The highest structures could only have been reached by rope, for two stories of vertical rock separated them from the ground. In those protected nooks the resident Anasazi would have stored their seed caches of maize, melons, beans, and sunflower in stone cists or clay pots, safe from rodents and birds. Most of the dwellings were clustered at ground level in an overhang that formed a shallow cave. The cave faced south in such a way that the residents would have been warm and sun-washed in the winter and cool and shaded in the summer. Aesthetically, the Anasazi homes fit into the landscape in a way modern frame homes do not, for they were built directly from the earth, using sandstone and mud.

I spent the day exploring the village and the central canyon, which is in its full length sixty miles long. There was much of their world to see—room after shadow-haunted room, pottery sherds with geometric designs painted on them, scattered piles of nine-hundred-year-old corn-cobs, pipe fragments and reed baskets, well-worn grinding stones, chipping rocks and unfinished arrowheads, a child's straw sandal at the bottom of a kiva. Not far from the ruins, nearly lost among the cottonwoods, was a rock panel with petroglyphs scratched into the darkly varnished wall surface. Despite the inherent limitations of the artistic technique, the images had unusual spirit and strength: a pair of deer, tense and alert, their heads raised at some disturbance. The distorted image of a man. A strange spiral. A coyote. A serpent. A star. A half-moon. Handprints, perhaps the artist's attempt at a signature. The spare, visionary style evoked images found in other dry and dusty parts of the world—the desert mountain ranges of North Africa, the ancient canyonlands of Central Asia, the high plateaus of South America. The impulse to create mythic worlds is cross-cultural and global and is not bound by any particular time or place, for it is part of each human being's spiritual endowment.

Evening came early to the bottom of the canyon: a little brown bat with translucent wings flittering among a cloud of mosquitoes, a gathering violet to the sky, one faint star to the east. I headed back up the dark side canyon, reluctant to leave, but deeply appreciative for what I had seen. The Anasazi village, and accompanying

Despite the inherent limitations of the artistic technique, the images had unusual spirit and strength: a pair of deer, tense and alert, their heads raised at some disturbance.

Anasazi rock art in southern Utah. Courtesy John Murray.

rock panels, had provided me with a penetrating glimpse of how a group of human beings could live in fundamental communion with the natural landscape. The ancient ones have much to teach us of the West. From them we can learn how to look at the landscape, how to walk through it, and perhaps most important, how to let the spirit of one place—its gentle life, its surprising secrets, its elusive presence—quietly come to us. We see in the end, too, that their myths—the Thunderbird, Coyote, Raven, hunting magic, vision quests, creation, the afterlife—are not so very different from our own.

Myths pervade our world. From the time we are born we hear them—legends and fables that fictionalize reality in small and great ways, whether at the level of the family or at the scale of society. Myths can broadly be divided into two categories, the good and the bad. A good myth would be one that, at worst, is harmless and that, at best, is in some way helpful to its teller or its listener. All of us, for example, have experienced romantic love at one time or another. Almost all love affairs have a creation or origin myth, the sacred tale of how the blessed union began. These fables can involve an accidental meeting, a passing conversation, an embarrassing event, a humorous personal ad, a mutual project at work, a blind date, a friendship that evolves, a persistent courtship. Couples take these real events and polish them, embellish them, and naturally treasure them. The actual event may have been incidental and entirely mundane, but the modified fictional version—the full-blown myth—persists until it becomes a monumental form of truth.

In the American West we think of the good myths, quite often, as being the modest ones—as when the young New Yorker Theodore Roosevelt, feeling out of his element in the Dakota Territory, decided he would pretend to be fearless and that after a time (even though he was as human as anyone) he would appear to be so. His personal attempt at mythmaking apparently worked, for his larger-than-life image is now carved into Mount Rushmore in South Dakota. Another example of this form of myth would be the film career of John Wayne.

Raoul Walsh's THE BIG TRAIL (*Fox, 1930*) *introduced the world to mythmaker John Wayne. Courtesy Photofest.*

Although he was a mild-mannered, straight-A student in college, when Wayne began to act in movies he had to unlearn his polished, polite ways and, among other things, be taught to say the word "ain't"—in other words, to pretend to be something he wasn't. Within a few years, the former president of the high school Latin club had been transformed into the rugged hero of *The Big Trail* and other Hollywood productions. Another myth of the good variety would be represented in the career of John Muir—the lost man who finds himself in the wilderness and then fights, Moses-like, for the preservation of that which saved him.

A bad myth would be one that perpetuates a hurtful or evil lie, an Iago-like distortion or patent invention that intentionally inflicts harm upon an innocent person or people. We are all familiar, for example, with what happens when one group of people—on a sports team, in the workplace, in a nuclear family—feels threatened by the success of another. The members of the faction begin to fabricate stories—unkind exaggerations or outright fabrications—about the other person. They live by the axiom that if you tell a lie long enough, it becomes the truth. Eventually the object of their enmity, more often than not, faces an injustice—a loss or injury—as a result of the myth. The history of the American West, unfortunately, records many more egregious instances of this form of destructive mythmaking.

In the nineteenth century, for example, we see the often-racist portrayal of Native Americans by journalists, military commanders, business-men, and civic leaders as part of the same hateful mythmaking process. Artists such as George Catlin and writers such as Helen Hunt Jackson vigorously fought this pernicious mythology in their respective works and activities. Others, like the Reverend John Chivington, labored just as hard to perpetuate it. (Chivington led the troops at the Colorado Sand Creek Massacre in 1864, which left 105 Cheyenne women and children and 28 Cheyenne men dead; all had been peacefully encamped under the American flag.) More recently, a similar mass propaganda machine resulted in thousands of innocent Japanese-American citizens being interned in Western detention camps during the Second World War. Because of their ancestry, they were perceived as a threat, when in reality they posed no more of a danger to national security than Italian-American and German-American citizens who had also lived in the country for many generations. To their credit, both as responsible members of the artistic community and as compassionate human beings, photographers Ansel Adams and Dorothea Lange devoted their considerable talents to documenting this injustice and to actively countering, as myth-debunkers, the sad hysteria of their times.

The West has proven itself to be particularly fertile ground for mythmakers because the region was originally an undeveloped territory, both as a geographic place—an immense tract of wild land—and as a cultural landscape inhabited by a very unique people, the Native Americans. It was as ripe a province as ever existed for the human imagination—aspen-splotched mountains, canyons that sprawled twenty miles from

and Hopi, and the Pueblo communities of the upper Rio Grande) with their own highly refined forms of government, art, literature, and tradition. The myth, though, was that the West was a virgin paradise, essentially unoccupied, and this fog-like fiction would serve to support and appear to legitimize the eventual colonization of the region.

The second period, from around 1850 through 1890, represented the time of most intense conflict, as the military conquest of the colonial region was undertaken. Here the myths focus on the heroic or epic aspects of the national struggle, while the historical reality was that the annexation of the West was an illegitimate,

rim to rim, lumbering grizzly bears, a people who lived in teepees made of buffalo hides. As we look at the history of mythmaking in the West, three distinct periods stand out. For each of these periods there is also a corresponding cluster of mythmakers—writers, artists, photographers, musicians, and later, filmmakers—who worked within the same contemporary framework of beliefs.

In the first period, which extends roughly from 1804 through about 1850, several myths were born that persist to this day. Even in the early government surveys, for example (Lewis and Clark, Pike, and Long), the West was portrayed as a fertile Eden or vacant Promised Land in the Christian mythological tradition. Paintings from this era by artists such as Karl Bodmer and Alfred Jacob Miller further supported this impression. The reality was, of course, that the region had been occupied by human beings for at least twelve thousand years, and that it contained a number of cultures (including the Sioux and Mandan, the Navajo

haphazard, and violent usurpation of land and people. This era, the age of Manifest Destiny, reached its mythic culmination in the Battle of the Little Bighorn on June 25, 1876. On that day Lieutenant Colonel George Armstrong Custer, trying to make the Black Hills safe for gold prospectors (the Black Hills had previously been ceded to the Sioux), attacked a peaceful village of Sioux and Cheyenne. His defeat, and the subsequent return of the northern Plains Indians to their reservations, marked the high point (or low point) in the twilight struggle to bring the West under governmental control.

The myth of Custer—as a heroic fool who was betrayed by Major Reno or as a racist war criminal who got what he deserved (or both)—has been painted (Fritz Scholder's *Portrait 1876–1976*), written about (Evan Connell's *Son of the Morning Star*), and made into several films. Later, in 1890, the massacre of nearly three hundred men, women, and children encamped at Wounded Knee was a logical extension of the same dark mentality that motivated Custer and the other imperial mythmakers of his century. Wounded Knee served as the natural conclusion of the mythic frontier period, which had begun with the mountain men, passed through the age of the Oregon Trail, and ended with the building of the railroads, the mass slaughter of the buffalo, and the arrival of the Texas longhorns.

Ever since, the artistic community has been trying to make sense of the mythological West, past and present. Two modes of creative response

CANYON DE CHELLY, ARIZONA, *by Timothy O'Sullivan. Courtesy U.S. Geographical Survey.*

have predominated in this third period of myth-making. The first looks deeply into the past and returns to the region's primal myths—agrarian utopia, landscape of the future, realm of hope and regeneration—whether in film, novels, paintings, or popular song. One thinks of the nostalgic canvases of Charles Russell and Frederic Remington, the retrospective Monument Valley films of John Ford, the elegiac historical novels of A. B. Guthrie and Mari Sandoz, and the ballads and laments of folk and country-western music. Even when they are unflatteringly realistic—as in, for example, Guthrie's *The Big Sky* and *The Way West*—these ever-popular representations tend to portray the frontier past as a golden age of grand events, yet-undiminished landscapes, and epic men and women.

The other approach has been to focus on the present, and to either actively demythologize the region (as in the works of Larry McMurtry) or, conversely, to examine the old myths in new ways. In the film *Tender Mercies* (1993), for example, we see two of the oldest myths of the West—the regenerative power of the open spaces and the centrality of the family—pre-sented in a contemporary context. Similarly, the paintings of T. C. Cannon look deeply into the faces and landscapes of the modern Native American Southwest, while still evoking the Indian legends of the past. Elsewhere, the songs of Buddy Holly built upon the optimism, good cheer, and deep faith that were the defining Christian mythos of the early pioneers, while troubadour John Denver exploited the same wilderness myths as did John Muir a century earlier. Regardless of the mode (old or new), the traditional mythic archetypes persist: the solitary frontiersman, the vigilant scout, the intrepid cavalryman, the noble Indian, the good-hearted prostitute, the indefatigable homesteader, the evil bully, the stalwart defender of justice.

A MYTH CAN PRODUCE considerable good or terrible evil. No chronicle of the American West can be complete without a full accounting of its myths—simple and sometimes elaborate fictions that have had as much of an effect on the people as the rivers and mountains, bliz-zards and droughts, floods and tornadoes, skir-mishes and battles, mass migrations and vagaries of history. The West will forever be a mythic ter-ritory, the legendary province of the future, hold-

John Denver's songs embraced some of the West's oldest myths. Courtesy Photofest.

ing out the promise of freedom, justice, and good fortune. "But I reckon," as Mark Twain wrote in *Huckleberry Finn*, "I got to light out for the Territory ahead of the rest, because Aunt Sally she's going to sivilize [sic] me and I can't stand it. I been there before."

Although much has changed since the first prehistoric people ventured into the territory ages ago, much still remains the same. Each morning the Mitten Buttes still throw long blue shadows over the red sands of Monument Valley, each afternoon the sun still blazes down on the high peaks and snowfields of the Sierras, and every evening the local star passes silently beneath the cobalt horizon of the Pacific. The geographic features of the Western landscape are the ultimate mythmakers, continually inspiring humankind to make of this wonderful land something different, something better, than what they have known elsewhere.

The mountains of northern Montana have inspired artists (Carl Rungius, Maynard Dixon), writers (A.B. Guthrie, Tom McGuane, Norman Maclean) and filmmakers (Robert Redford's THE HORSE WHISPERER*). Courtesy John Murray.*

Maynard Dixon, LIMIT OF DESERET.
Courtesy Medicine Man Gallery, Tucson, Arizona.

WHEN I PAINT MY MASTERPIECE

Visual Artists and the Landscape of Legend

I loved it immediately.

From then on I was always

on my way back.

—GEORGIA O'KEEFFE

on first seeing northern New Mexico in 1917

HIKERS IN THE CANYONS OF THE FOUR CORNERS REGION often observe, among the petroglyphs chipped into the desert rock, the image of a man with a flute. This figure is commonly found as far north as the canyon of the Green River in Dinosaur National Monument and as far south as the middle Colorado River. The drainage of the San Juan River is particularly rich in this representation. Further east, near the village of La Cienega in New Mexico, there are several exposed rocks bearing his familiar form. The flute-player is known as Kokopelli. His mythic image is thought to have represented human fertility. More often than not, the Anasazi flute-player is portrayed with a bag of seed on his back. His image appears regularly in what might be called natural "art galleries,"—sheltered canyon alcoves and rock walls. In these quiet sanctuaries, ideal for contemplation and craft, the ancient ones would come in the heat of the summer—those long dreamy days when the desert turtles sleep in old fox dens and the deep windless canyons are filled with solstice light—and chip away at the darkly varnished red sandstone. What they left behind for posterity was the first art of the American West, as well as a visual rendering of one of the oldest myths in the human experience, the myth of fertility.

Art in the more recent historical period of the West was at first little more than visual documentation, the methodic rendering of landscape and wildlife by scientist-artists. The purpose was to prepare an exhaustive catalog of the natural features and life forms in what was then a terra incognita. We as a civilization are doing much the same today as we systematically map and photograph the surface of Mars, naming river valleys, studying unusual features, preparing for exploration and colonization. This dry, clinical approach is best seen in the illustrations that accompanied the official expedition journals of Captains Meriwether Lewis and William Clark (1804–1806), Major Zebulon Pike (1805–1807),

Thomas Moran, CHILDREN OF THE MOUNTAIN.
Courtesy The Anschutz Collection.

and Major Stephen Long (1819–1820). Everything is there, from the pocket gophers of Kansas to the grizzly bears of Montana, from the windswept Missouri Breaks to the lower valley of the Arkansas River, but in a sense much is also missing, as the interpretive faculties of the human imagination are almost wholly absent.

This exacting realism persisted in the works of the first formally trained explorer-artists—Alfred Jacob Miller, Karl Bodmer, and George Catlin. Even given their self-limiting format, however, certain myths were beginning to take shape. The West was seen by these pioneering artists as an undisturbed paradise of nature, a province that offered a pristine vision of the world before the arrival of civilization. The West was seen by them, and their viewers, as a landscape of the future and the past, as a place to become lost or to be found, and as a realm of idle daydream and penetrating vision. Art visually supported this Edenic myth by portraying a prelapsarian abundance of life, a wealth of natural landscapes distinguished by their beauty and grandeur, and perhaps most importantly, a freedom-loving people—the Plains Indians—living in all the informality and innocence of nature.

The next phase involved more active interpretation and more ardent mythmaking with the arrival, in successive generations, of such influential figures as Albert Bierstadt and Thomas Moran, Frederic Remington and Charles Russell, Carl Rungius and William R. Leigh. In just a matter of a few decades, a whole series of myths—the exotic, the romantic, the dramatic—were energetically developed by these gifted artists. The popular culture became immersed in these new images and mythologies as Western drawings and paintings filled their newspapers, magazines, books, calendars, posters, galleries, and museums. The sometimes-ethereal paintings of Bierstadt and Moran portrayed the West as a realm of sublimity and epiphany. Remington and Russell introduced ordinary or heroic people into the landscape—and usually in a proportion much greater than the setting. Both artists were actively engaged in exploring (some would say promoting) the whole mythology surrounding the cowboy and Indian. Later artists such as Carl Rungius and William R. Leigh saw the West in a more balanced, contemporary context, as a realm where fact and symbol could be as important as myth.

By the early twentieth century many artists had become disenchanted with the artistic scene in Europe and on the East Coast. As a result, they began migrating to the West and forming creative colonies. Chief among these was Taos, New Mexico, where there was already a five-hundred-year tradition of Indian arts and crafts (pottery, weaving, jewelry making). These emigrant artists began creating a rich new form of Western art that portrayed indigenous landscapes and people with modernist art techniques (most notably, those of Postimpressionism). The Taos artists worked primarily within the utopian mythic system, portraying northern New Mexico as a secret paradise.

During the 1930s the American West found itself in the midst of two catastrophes—the Dust Bowl and the Great Depression. These twin events, one environmental and the other economic, greatly influenced artists like Dorothea Lange and Maynard Dixon, who held an unflinching mirror up to their times, and in so doing examined the dark side of the agrarian myth. At the same time, figures such as Imogen Cunningham, Edward Weston, and Ansel Adams revived the old "pantheistic sublime" of Bierstadt and Moran in their highly detailed, large-format photographs. More recently, artists like Russell Chatham and T. C. Cannon have found new ways of imagining and rendering the timeless landscapes and ever-changing people of the West.

We stand now at the beginning of a new century, a new millennium, for the West. Even today, some artist is applying the first brush strokes to an empty white canvas that will one day depict the Grand Tetons, or is setting up a large-format camera on the South Rim of the Grand Canyon to capture the first light of the Arizona sunrise, or is chiseling away at a dark granitic riverstone that is destined to become a swimming otter. The history of art in the American West is the history of an extended love affair between a group of people and the myths that have grown around a landscape unlike any other on the planet. Though much has changed in the world since the Anasazi first began scratching images into the desert varnish of the Four Corners Region, much has remained the same. One thing has not altered—the need of all human beings for the comforting world of myth, and for the enduring images of art. And what is the West, after all, these artists seem to ask, but a series of beautiful myths?

One thing has not altered—the need of all human beings for the comforting world of myth, and for the enduring images of art. And what is the West, after all, these artists seem to ask, but a series of beautiful myths?

GEORGE CATLIN
Images of a Vanishing People

LET US IMAGINE for a moment a time when there were no roads—not one—in the entire drainage of the Missouri River, a time when a person could be born, live, and die and never hear one syllable of this strange new alien tongue called English. A time when there were no clocks, no calendars, but for the passage of the sun or the moon, the coming of the yellow cottonwood leaves, the falling of the snows, or the arrival of the first geese in the spring. A time when herds of buffalo moved darkly over the summer prairie like the shadows of the clouds, and the passage of a single dusty herd took not hours but days. A time when there was no such thing as coins or currency, contracts or corporations, wills or estates, only wolf furs and grizzly bear claws and buffalo hides and half-wild horses for trade. A time before the Oregon Trail and the homesteaders, before the railroads and the Little Bighorn, before Sand Creek and Wounded Knee, before dams and power stations and underground missile silos. A time when all the grassland that is now divided into states and counties and townships belonged not to the United States of America but to Native American tribes like the Pawnee and Sioux, the Crow and Blackfeet, the Omaha and Ponca, the Arapaho and Cheyenne, the Mandan and Arikara, the Oto and Assinboine, the Shoshone and Gros Ventre, the Kansa and Iowa.

It was into this world that a thirty-six-year-old lawyer-turned-artist named George Catlin came on a primitive riverboat steamer in 1832. His grand adventure had begun in Philadelphia six years earlier, when he observed a visiting delegation of Indians from the Far West. So impressed was Catlin with the beauty and intelligence of the representatives at that encounter that he resolved to devote his life energies to providing a visual history of the endangered people of the West. He later wrote:

> In silent and stoic dignity these lords of the forest strutted about the city for a few days, wrapped in their painted robes, with their brows plumed with the quills of the war eagle, attracting the gaze of all who beheld them.... I wanted to use my art and so much of the labor of my future life as might be required in rescuing from oblivion the looks and customs of the vanishing races of native man in America.

After corresponding and meeting with General William Clark (who had co-led the Lewis and Clark expedition of 1804–1806) in St. Louis, Catlin secured a berth on the American Fur Company's steamer *Yellowstone* on its first voyage up the Missouri River to Fort Union. (The fort is now a national monument in North Dakota.) During his three month stay on the Upper Missouri, Catlin painted nearly two hundred canvases, including images of buffalo hunts and various tribal ceremonies, such as the buffalo dance and the manhood rites of the Mandan (a tribe that was shortly decimated by a smallpox epidemic). Catlin is most known now for his detailed portraits of the Native Americans he met along his journey. In paintings such as *Buffalo Bull's Backfat, Head Chief, Blood Tribe,* or *Mint, A Pretty Girl* he preserved forever the original faces of the American West in their native garb, with the chief clothed in a handsome dark-stained elkskin shirt and the young maiden in a lovely blouse of what appears to be rabbitskin.

Elsewhere, his landscapes (as of the Indian-set prairie fires) and action paintings (as in the buffalo hunts) provide environmental historians and anthropologists with helpful renderings of what life was like in the American West before the Union Pacific and the Homestead Act. Nor was Catlin without great regret as to what was happening during his time. He later wrote:

> I have viewed man in the innocent simplicity of nature, in the full enjoyment of the luxuries which God has bestowed upon him ... happier than kings and princes can be ... and I have seen him shrinking from civilized approach, which came with all its vices, like the dead of night.... I have seen the grand and irresistible march of civilization ... this splendid juggernaut rolling on, and beheld its sweeping desolation.

In his paintings, and in passages like this, Catlin was consciously promoting the myth of the West as a once-pure Eden that had fallen into the vulgar hands of a barbarous nation—his own.

George Catlin was the region's original artistic mythmaker, the great-great-grandfather of all those who followed. Not only did he preserve the people and scenes of the West, he also promoted them, hiring visiting Indians, for example, to perform dances and ritual shows in his traveling gallery (which included trips to England, Ireland, and Scotland). From such humble beginnings did such later dramatic renderings of the West as Buffalo Bill's Traveling Wild West Show and John Ford's retrospective films arise. Most importantly, in terms of the future of the West, was Catlin's then-controversial proposal in 1841 that the nation form a "nation's Park"—the world's first—somewhere at the head of the Missouri River:

> What a beautiful and thrilling specimen for America to preserve and hold up to the view of her refined citizens and the world, in future ages! a *nation's Park*, containing

George Catlin; BUFFALO BULL'S BACK FAT, HEAD CHIEF, BLOOD TRIBE, *1832. Courtesy National Museum of American Art, Washington, D.C./ Art Resource, NY.*

man and beast, in all the wild and freshness of their nature's beauty! I would ask no other monument to my memory, nor any other enrollment of my name amongst the famous dead, than the reputation of having been the founder of such an institution.

Fifty years later, in 1872, President Grant established Yellowstone National Park and made Catlin's youthful dream a reality. Such was the immortal legacy of this incredible man, artist, writer, ethnographer, and mythmaker of the American West.

ALBERT BIERSTADT AND THOMAS MORAN
The Pantheistic Sublime

IN THE THIRD QUARTER of the nineteenth century, a generation after Catlin had documented the Plains Indians, two gifted artists—Albert Bierstadt and Thomas Moran—arrived in the American West. Their paintings captured a morning-fresh sense of excitement and amazement at the splendor of the Western landscapes. Even by Victorian standards, Bierstadt and Moran's output of field sketches, watercolors, prints, illustrations, and paintings was enormous. Between the two of them, they forever changed how people of the East—especially political leaders in Washington—viewed the American West. Both artists viewed the American West through a translucent romantic lens, as a misty, mythic realm where the spirit of nature infused all things—peaks, canyons, waterfalls, forests, rivers, and streams—with a sublime majesty. Neither artist believed in literal transcription—in an exact rendering of what they saw. Their paintings often took considerable liberties with the landscape, as they both eschewed pure realism and aimed for a more abstract reality achieved through inspiration.

Thomas Moran once observed that "My general scope is not realistic; all my tendencies are toward idealization. Topography in art is valueless … except as it furnishes material from which to construct a picture." Mythmakers Bierstadt and Moran were consciously creating an alternative world in which the beauty of the West was taken to a whole new level—a rich mixture of the Alps, the Scottish highlands, and brooding canyons such as might have been found in the imagination of Samuel Taylor Coleridge.

Albert Bierstadt and Thomas Moran were both formally trained artists by the time they arrived in the region, far more so than their predecessor George Catlin. Before immigrating to the United States, Bierstadt had studied art in Düsseldorf with Achenbach and Lessing, two leading German artists of the mid-nineteenth century. After a brief stint as a painting teacher in Massachusetts, his lucky break occurred in 1859, when he was asked to join General Frederic Lander's expedition to survey a wagon route to the Pacific Ocean. (Lander,

Wyoming, is named for General Lander.) Bierstadt later developed the field sketches and photographs from this trip into large-scale landscape paintings. In 1860 he exhibited these first canvases of Western mountain scenery at the National Academy. He returned to the Rockies several more times, making his last trip in 1863. Thereafter he enjoyed growing fame as a landscape master and maintained a studio on the Hudson River. Bierstadt's popularity declined in the late 1880s, when his mid-century style was considered outdated. By then Impressionism had taken over as the dominant school of art in Europe and America. At the time of his death in 1902, Bierstadt had lapsed into quiet obscurity, only to be resurrected as a forgotten master half a century later.

Most of Albert Bierstadt's major paintings were monumental affairs, large both in canvas and conception. This view was consistent with

Albert Bierstadt, THE ROCKY MOUNTAINS, LANDER'S PEAK, *1863. Courtesy The Metropolitan Museum of Art, Rogers Fund.*

the larger-than-life spirit of Manifest Destiny that then pervaded the American West. Quite often Bierstadt's more epic paintings incorporated a number of scenes that the artist had sketched or photographed in the field. From these separate images he then worked to create a composite scene that was infused with a pantheistic sense of the sublime. A classic example would be his painting *The Rocky Mountains—Lander's Peak*, which was painted in 1863. Anyone who has ever hiked in the Wind River Range of Wyoming, where this painting is supposedly based, will immediately recognize that there is no scene in that mountain range that even remotely resembles what is portrayed in Bierstadt's painting. On the other hand, the artist has created an alternative version of the range that, in a sense, has as much reality, as much validity, as the physical range that inspired it. The canvas presents a grand, Wagnerian picture of the Rockies that supports the romantic myth of the West the country was in love with at the time.

Like Albert Bierstadt, Thomas Moran was also a highly trained artist and had already mastered wood engraving, watercolor, and oil by the time he joined the Hayden Expedition to explore the Yellowstone River headwaters in 1871. The trip proved a watershed in his life, and his vibrant watercolors of the forests, waterfalls, geysers, hot springs, and lakes show the region clearly made a deep impression upon him. His Yellowstone paintings, displayed before Congress the next year, helped excite political interest in preserving the area as the world's first national park (a bill signed into law by President Ulysses S. Grant in March 1872). The government later honored Moran's influential work by naming a prominent twelve-thousand-foot peak Mount Moran in the Teton Range near Jackson, Wyoming. Moran's popularity continued to grow, and he remained an industrious painter, living at the Brown Palace Hotel in Denver, well into his eighties (he died at the age of ninety in 1927). The short (five-foot-five) artist proved himself a giant mythmaker in the American West, as several of the areas he drew and painted became national parks.

Moran is best known for his two immense national park paintings—one of the Lower Falls of the Yellowstone River in Wyoming and the other of the Grand Canyon in Arizona. The first, undertaken in 1871, was painted on a seven-by-twelve-foot canvas. It depicted what is today known as Artist's Point—that place on the southern cliffs of the Grand Canyon of the Yellowstone River where the Lower Falls are fully visible. Although not as loose with reality as Bierstadt's version of Lander Peak, the painting still plays somewhat with the scene, as the forest trees are made to tower unnaturally (one to the height of a sequoia) over the party of observers. In truth, the trees are but a fraction of that height. The geology of the scene, though—the intricately weathered cliffs of volcanic ash—are faithfully rendered, as are the surface features in Moran's other park epic, *The Chasm of the Colorado* (1873–1874). In both cases, the Western landscape became a visual metaphor for the myth of sublimity.

Even as Albert Bierstadt and Thomas

Moran worked on such canvases, a new form of art—landscape photography—was taking root in the American West. With the extraordinarily detailed, large-format images of such early masters as William Henry Jackson and Timothy O'Sullivan, a new realism was beginning to challenge old mythic views of the region. So, too, were new artists—most notably Frederic Remington and Charles Russell—beginning to feature people more prominently in their representations of the West. The twentieth century was being born, and with it would come many changes to traditional views of nature and art, as well as to perceptions of the American West. Nevertheless, the achievements of Bierstadt and Moran continue to remind us of a time when America was fascinated with the grand notion of sublimity, the westward march of empire, and the colossal paintings that turned mountains into myths.

Thomas Moran, THE CHASM OF THE COLORADO. *Courtesy National Museum of American Art, Washington D.C./Art Resource, NY. Lent by the U.S. Department of the Interior, Office of the Secretary.*

FREDERIC REMINGTON AND CHARLES RUSSELL
The End of Something

THE MYTHS that have accreted around the cowboy are at the core of the human experience of the American West. No consideration of the region can be complete without giving account to the myth of the cowboy, which has inspired folk legends, stories, novels, paintings, sculptures, country-western songs, documentaries, and feature films for over a century. It is at its heart one of the oldest myths of all—the belief that through hard work and self-reliance an individual can live outside society and be at one with the natural landscape. The myth has its intellectual roots in sources as diverse as the political and philosophical writings of Thomas Jefferson, Henry David Thoreau's *Walden,* and the Utopian movement and social experiments of the 1840s. In some ways the myth of the cowboy is the purest expression of the restless and independent democratic spirit of America.

The first Western cowboys were the Spanish vaqueros who worked the ranching country of northern Mexico and coastal California as early as the seventeenth century. Such words as mustang, lariat, hacienda, and rodeo have all come down to us from this colorful period. The history of the cowboy in the heartland of the American West dates back to the 1840s, when Anglo cattle ranches began to proliferate in central Texas. After the Civil War, there was a great demand for beef as homesteaders and railroads expanded west onto the plains. Reservation Indians also needed to be provided for. Buffalo herds were rapidly collapsing by then, and so the government turned to the nascent Texas cattle industry. Beginning in the 1870s Texas longhorn cattle were pushed north along now famous trails—the Chisholm, the Goodnight-Loving, and the Pecos. The brief golden age of open grassland ranching persisted into the 1880s, when a series of devastating winters followed by summer-long droughts decimated the free-ranging herds and helped to break up the gigantic early ranches. In the 1890s two gifted artists set out to chronicle the ephemeral heyday of the cowboy on canvas and in bronze.

The careers of Frederic Remington and Charles Russell, like the careers of George Braque and Pablo Picasso, or Paul Gauguin and Vincent van Gogh, are often considered together. Both artists dealt with similar thematic material and with the same core mythologies. Their world was the last days of the frontier, especially the cowboy period. They painted few landscapes. The story of the cowboy was their central domain. As people, they could not have been more different. Remington was from the east, played football at Yale University, and maintained a studio in New York and later Connecticut. He was friends with Theodore Roosevelt and other luminaries of the age. Affluent and famous, he lived a comfortable existence in the same eastern artistic milieu as Winslow Homer and Thomas Eakins. Russell, by contrast, was a working class hero, a man who turned his back on a bourgeois St. Louis family and toiled for years as a ranch hand, wrangler, and cowboy on the sage steppes of eastern Montana. One winter (1888) he was so destitute he lived with the Blood Indians in southern Canada. At thirty-two he married a girl nearly half his age, and she became his best friend and astute business partner. Until the end of his life he called Great Falls, Montana, his home, and remained close to a small group of old and cherished cowboy buddies. Both artists were self-taught, were considered illustrators more than artists for much of their careers, went on to become accomplished bronze sculptors, and then died suddenly while in their maturity. Remington passed away at forty-eight from a ruptured appendix, probably related to his weight (three hundred pounds) and obsessive eating patterns. Russell died at sixty-two from a heart attack caused by years of heavy smoking and constant work.

What most characterizes both artists is their distinctive narrative style, popular at the turn of the century, the notion that a painting should tell or imply a story. Frequently both artists also portrayed the last of the Plains Indians, who shared the high plains for many years with the first cowboys. In Remington's *Return of a Blackfoot War Party*, the viewer is presented with four Blackfoot warriors on horseback returning to camp with two Indian prisoners on foot. The time of year is midwinter. One can feel the cold in the frosty breath of the men and the horses, and in the fiercely blowing snow. The faces of all six men are tired, drawn, resigned. The third Blackfoot warrior to the rear raises a leather whip to force a prisoner along. The Blackfoot leader holds up a fresh scalp for those in the valley to see. On the cottonwood flats below are the buffalo-skin teepees of the Blackfoot encampment, where others await the arrival of the party. The effect of the canvas upon the viewer is melancholy,

What most characterizes both artists is their distinctive narrative style, the notion that a painting should tell or imply a story.

Frederic Remington, RETURN OF A BLACKFOOT WAR PARTY. *Courtesy The Anschutz Collection.*

Charles Russell,
THE SCOUTS.
*Courtesy The
Anschutz Collection.*

painting like *The Scouts*, a large western documentary in the classic Russell style. The painting captures, in a loosely photographic style, a momentary scene near sunset on the Montana prairie. A group of horse-mounted Indians have reached a sage-covered rise and have paused momentarily to consider the country before them. The clouds are lit with the last light of day. The leader, wearing a war-bonnet of eagle feathers and holding a lance, is gazing at something in the distance. The warrior to his left is speaking and motioning with his right hand. The painting preserves an intimate scene of the wild prarie before the arrival of cattle and fences, the whole set beneath a glorious sunset no doubt plucked from Russell's memory and frozen in time forever.

oppressive. One is left to wonder: What will be the fate of the prisoners? Will they be kept to trade for other prisoners held by the enemy tribe? Or will they meet a worse fate? This is classic Remington—a canvas that captures a lost frontier world marked by violence and hardship, and in so doing relates, or infers, a legendary story from the mythic past.

Unlike Remington, Charles Russell painted exclusively in one relatively small geographic area—the prairie hills north of the Missouri River and its tributary Marias River and south of the Canadian border. This is the heart of the Montana cattle country, the old buffalo prairie, in which Russell worked as a range cowboy from the age of sixteen to thirty-two. His familiarity with the subject is evident in a

Charles Russell lived long enough to see the first silent Western films of William S. Hart, Harry Carey, and others, and to witness the birth of another phase in the mythologizing of the Old West. By the time of his death in October 1926, much of the world he had known in his youth was gone, but in his and Remington's paintings and bronze sculptures, that lost frontier world was given a permanent life. Today Russell and Remington's legendary creations are held in major collections at the Charles Russell Museum in Great Falls, Montana; the Buffalo Bill Museum in Cody, Wyoming; the Gilcrease Museum in Tulsa, Oklahoma; and elsewhere around the West. Their works of art tell the timeless story of the winning of the American West, and in so doing perpetuate some of its most appealing myths.

THE TAOS SOCIETY OF ARTISTS
Inside the Gates of Eden

TAOS IS A VALLEY with a long and wonderful history. First there were the Indian pueblo-builders, more than five hundred years ago, who raised the massive four-story adobe pueblo, the tallest still standing in the Southwest today. Next came the Spanish explorers and settlers following the Coronado expedition in 1541. Three centuries later the legendary Taos trappers—Jim Bridger, Kit Carson, and others—wandered into the valley and made the town their summer headquarters, trapping north in Colorado and Wyoming during the winter months. From the beginning, Taos has captured the human imagination and played to a mythological sense of the region as an earthly paradise. As the frontier has faded more and more into history, Taos has increasingly come to represent a pristine vestige of a Southwestern past that never really was—a time when Hispanic, Indian and Anglo cultures lived in peaceful harmony with themselves and the desert landscape. The myth of Taos is one of the enduring fables of the region, that there is a place in the far West where the fields are ever-fertile and the valleys ever-peaceful, a sun-washed utopia where gentle people make beautiful art—pottery, jewelry, rugs, paintings, drawings, sculptures, photographs—with the same devotion that workers in other parts of the country and world manufacture computers or automobiles.

The story of the Taos art colony begins with Joseph Henry Sharp, an Eastern-born, Paris-trained artist who made his first visit to the region in 1883. So impressed was Sharp with the lovely upper Rio Grande country that he subsequently journeyed west every summer to paint in the area (as well as in northwestern Montana among the Blackfeet). Like George Catlin half a century earlier, Sharp felt a responsibility to record Native American life before it was further contaminated by Anglo cultural influences. Sharp painted in the Impressionist style that predominated in the nineteenth century, employing confident, fluid brush strokes, bold compositional designs, and natural earth-tones. It was in 1885 that Sharp told fellow artists Ernest Blumenschein and Bert Phillips about the secret Shangri-la of Taos and persuaded them to come out for a visit. Blumenschein later recalled his first view of Taos:

> The color, the reflective character of the landscape, the drama of the vast open spaces, the superb beauty and severity of the hills, stirred me deeply. I realized I was getting my own impressions from nature, seeing it for the first time with my own eyes, uninfluenced by the art of any man ... I saw whole paintings right before my eyes. Everywhere I looked I saw paintings perfectly organized, ready to paint.

Blumenschein eventually became one of the leaders of an art colony known as the Taos

The myth of Taos is one of the enduring fables of the region, that there is a place in the far West where the fields are ever-fertile and the valleys ever-peaceful, a sun-washed utopia where gentle people make beautiful art.

Society of Artists. The original members of the group included Joseph Henry Sharp, Bert Phillips, Ernest Blumenschein, Oscar Berninghause, E. Irving Couse, and W. Herbert Dunton. In later years, other artists were added, including Victor Higgins, Walter Ufer, and E. Martin Hennings.

The group flourished until 1927, when it disbanded. Of the approximately one dozen artists who were associated with the Taos art colony, Blumenschein stands out as a creative figure in several ways. He was, in a sense, the Ansel Adams of his time, a visual artist who, like

TOP *(left to right):*
Walter Ufer,
Herbert "Buck" Dunton,
Victor Higgins,
Kenneth Adams.
MIDDLE*:*
Joseph Henry Sharp,
E. Martin Hennings,
E. Irving Couse,
Oscar Berninghaus.
BOTTOM*:*
Bert Geer Phillips,
Ernest Blumenschein.
Courtesy Taos County
Historical Society.

Adams, was also a classically trained musician. (Blumenschein played first violin under conductor/composer Antonín Dvořák in 1894.) Like Adams, Blumenschein also utilized musical rhythms, harmonies, counterpoints, and patterns in his work. Blumenschein's paintings are representative of the best achievements of the Taos pioneers. His Taos home and studio are today maintained as a fascinating museum and provide an intimate sense of daily life in the early years of the colony.

Like the other Taos artists, Blumenschein is known both for his landscapes of the local mountains and canyons and for his portraits of the resident Pueblo Indians. His paintings of the latter subject are particularly distinguished. Blumenschein depicted Native Americans in ordinary activities—dancing, hunting, planting the fields, harvesting the orchards, making bows or pottery, moving livestock, horseback riding, undertaking religious activities (the Taos Indians were Christianized by the Spanish), working around the Pueblo—in a way that supported the sense of a primal, mythical realm. In paintings such as *Moon, Morning Star, Evening Star*, which depicts a ritual gathering, or *Sangre de Christo Mountains*, which focuses upon a self-contained adobe village, Blumenschein sought to immortalize traditional scenes of northern New Mexico. Other of his paintings were thematically more contemporary, such as *Jury for Trial of a Sheepherder for Murder* or the extraordinary portrait *Star Road and White Sun*.

In retrospect, it is clear that the pastoral art of the Taos colony, representing an idealized natural landscape in which nature and humanity are perfectly integrated, was a response to the rapid industrialization of the time. Art, for them, offered an opportunity to create a pictorial realm of order and harmony undisturbed by the unpleasantness—the urban anxiety and materialism—of the early twentieth century. Their work was not merely a romantic escape into Edenic nature, but was a conscious attempt to create a new mythic world for the region and the country. One senses in their vibrant paintings a spiritual exultation, a pantheistic vision of nature that is deeply rooted in the earlier work of Moran and Bierstadt. As a result of their legacy, the Taos region has become to the United States what Provence is to France— a fabled realm of sacred blue mountains and quiet meadows where artists may come and find paintings waiting to be completed in the warmth and brilliance of the southern sun.

Their work was not merely a romantic escape into Edenic nature, but was a conscious attempt to create a new mythic world for the region and the country.

E. L. Blumenschein, STAR ROAD AND WHITE SUN. *Courtesy The Albuquerque Museum.*

CARL RUNGIUS
Across the High and Wild

THE CAREER OF GERMAN-BORN wildlife artist Carl Rungius (1869–1959) can be seen both as the culmination of a long line of traditional Western mythmakers and as the beginning of a new strain of modernism in Western American art. On the one hand, Rungius—like Bierstadt, Moran, Remington, and Russell—uncritically extolled the sublime beauty of the mountains and prairies. His was a sensibility and imagination deeply wed to the romantic myth of wilderness and to maintaining the aesthetic purity of the Old Frontier landscapes. He embraced the American West and its wildlife, as well as its cowboys and cattle-ranching culture, with what can only be described as an enthusiastic and very pure love.

On the other hand, Rungius was also a sophisticated European-born artist with a gallery in New York City and, eventually, Banff, Alberta. He was keenly aware of contemporary movements, such as Cubism (after 1911), that were based on innovative, sometimes radical, ways of interpreting nature. Although formally trained at the Berlin Royal Academy of Arts, Rungius was determined to transcend conventional landscape and wildlife painting and incorporate fresh techniques wherever he could.

When Carl Rungius first came west, he hunted here in the Wind River Range of Wyoming (pictured is the Cirque of the Towers). Courtesy John Murray.

This is most evident in his Cezanne-like use of geometric shapes and patterns to emphasize and/or balance key aspects of the composition, as when wildlife is strategically placed in burned-over pine forests among the stark and sharply angled dead trees.

Rungius first saw the American West in 1895, at the age of twenty-six and just one year after he had arrived in the United States from Germany. Like many outdoorsmen of that period (this was the golden age of Theodore Roosevelt and Frederic Remington), Rungius made an autumnal pilgrimage to the Rockies for the big-game hunting season. The rugged landscape of the Wind River Range in northwestern Wyoming was unlike anything the young artist had seen before in northern Europe or in the eastern United States—soaring thirteen-thousand-foot granite peaks, spacious alpine valleys, grand prairie vistas, tremendous waterfalls, clear cirque lakes, brimming snowmelt streams and wildlife everywhere in natural profusion.

The value of the experience for Rungius as an artist was that he had seen the wild Edenic landscape of his personal and creative future. The trip struck him with the force of a revelatory event, and would forever change both his painting and the mythology of Western art. Everywhere the young artist went among the big mountains he carried his sketchbook and camera, carefully recording scenes of camp life, wildlife, and wilderness that he would later reproduce on canvas in his studio. Equally important to Rungius as a painter was the task of skinning out and preparing the meat of the animals that were killed (elk, mule deer, moose, bighorn sheep, black and grizzly bear, antelope). This invaluable process provided him with an intimate familiarity with the anatomy of his future subjects. Rungius saw firsthand exactly how the muscles are laminated to the leg bones, how the central organs swell in a mass below the ribs, how the skull is contoured beneath the skin, and all of this prepared him to introduce a striking new naturalism to wildlife portraiture.

Each year thereafter Carl Rungius made a trip out to the northern Rockies to hunt, sketch, paint, photograph, and observe. Although initially his forays were confined to the high country of Wyoming and Montana, Rungius eventually wandered further afield, in 1904 to the Yukon Territory with conservationist Charles Sheldon (father of Mount McKinley National Park in Alaska), and then to the southern Canadian Rockies in Alberta in 1910. It was during this time that Rungius began selling his paintings at a gallery in Banff, as well as in New York City. In 1913 he was elected an associate of the National Academy of Design. Six years later his position in the prestigious organization was elevated to that of full academician. By the 1920s, Rungius had become recognized as the premier wildlife artist in North America (much as another former art student from Berlin, Wilhelm Kuhnert, had established himself as the master wildlife artist of southern

Carl Rungius, AN OLD FIGHTER. *Courtesy National Museum of Wildlife Art.*

Africa). Rungius' art was in constant demand, and even during the Great Depression of the 1930s, the artist and his wife Louise lived comfortably by selling his drawings, paintings, and etchings to wealthy collectors and museums.

One of Rungius' most representative paintings—*An Old Fighter*—was for many years exhibited in the now-closed Museum of Western Art in downtown Denver. A small canvas for Rungius (twenty-four inches by thirty-two inches), the oil painting depicts a mature bull moose poised at the edge of a small woodland pond, with thick coniferous trees looming darkly all around. It is a late autumn day, for the aspen trees are yellow and orange, and even the water reeds (the last to turn) have lost their summer green to the frost. The front hooves of the moose (and it is a Yellowstone, or Shiras, moose) have broken through the purple ice of the shallows and he is about to drink, but he has turned and is looking over his right shoulder in the direction of the viewer, who may be another bull moose or perhaps a hunter. The bull's position is alert, for it is mating season and he is "an old fighter." The effect of the entire dark-toned canvas is cold, tense, suspenseful. It is a classic Rungius work, focusing as it does upon a mature male animal during the height of the breeding season in an intimate wilderness setting. The canvas captures all the old romance of the high autumnal West, when men were men and trophy animals had every reason to be nervous.

Carl Rungius, who lived to be ninety, killed his last bighorn sheep (with horns forty inches around the curl) in the northern Rockies in 1950, at the age of 81. This achievement is even more remarkable when one considers that bighorn sheep live at high altitude and in remote, mountainous areas that are difficult even for young people to hike and climb in. Rungius was the last of a kind, a tough-as-anvil-iron artist whose life and career witnessed the

death of the frontier and the birth of something quite different, both in the American West and in art. Through it all he remained faithful to his vision—the romantic myth of the high and the wild—and his craft, which has become synonymous with artistic excellence.

Today Rungius' paintings can be viewed at the finest Western museums, including the National Museum of Wildlife Art in Jackson, Wyoming (an entire gallery is permanently devoted to Rungius' work), at the Buffalo Bill Museum in Cody, Wyoming (with major paintings of wolverine, antelope, and bighorn sheep), and at the Glenbow Museum in Calgary, Alberta (the collection includes many of his etchings). Rungius' influence continues to be seen in the work of a number of successful Western artists. The current list includes such luminaries as Tucker Smith of Green River, Wyoming; Luke Frazier of Provo, Utah; Ken Carlson of Kerrville, Texas; Bob Kuhn of Tucson, Arizona; and Clyde Aspevig of Loveland, Colorado. Each emulates Rungius' bold, fluid brushwork and quiet fidelity to nature, though in very different ways. Each also would likely acknowledge that Carl Rungius is the greatest painter of wildlife ever to work in the American West.

MAYNARD DIXON
Visions and Revisions

AS A SIXTEEN-YEAR-OLD BUDDING ARTIST in southern California, Maynard Dixon mailed his portfolio to Frederic Remington, who wrote back to him on September 3, 1891, in a now famous letter:

> Your letter and books are here and I have quite enjoyed your sketches.... You draw better at your age than I did at the same age—if you have the "Sand" to overcome difficulties you could be an artist in time.... Be always true to yourself—to the way and the things you see in nature—if you imitate any other man ever so little you are "gone." Study good pictures, but do not imitate them ... above all—draw—draw—draw and always from nature.

Dixon took this sage advice to heart and assiduously devoted himself to studying nature and developing his craft. Over the next ten years Dixon (as Rembrandt had in his youth) traveled widely, often on foot or horseback, through the backcountry of the American West, especially the Southwest, always drawing, sketching, and painting.

Although Dixon went on to work for some time as a magazine and book illustrator (and illustrators at the turn of the century were some of the most ardent champions of traditional Western mythology), he eventually transcended the accepted iconography of the region and invented a radically new visual vocabulary. His distinctive style involved depicting conventional Western themes—cowboys, Indians, landscapes—with striking color schemes and simplified forms, acknowledging the cubist influence. Over time Dixon became disillusioned with purely commercial work, writing in 1912 that "I'm being paid to lie about the West. I'm going home where I can do honest work." Eventually he did just that, walking away from the lucrative trade work based on empty Western clichés that he had done for such widely-circulated publications as *The San Francisco Examiner*, *Harper's Weekly*, *Cosmopolitan*, *Sunset Magazine*, *Century*, *Scribner's*, *Collier's*, and *McClure's*.

From that point forward Dixon devoted himself as an artist strictly to the real people—particularly the native people—and the natural landscapes of the Southwest. No one had ever painted the region the way Dixon did. His portraits of

Maynard Dixon, STUDY FOR THE EARTH KNOWER. *Courtesy Medicine Man Gallery, Inc., Tucson, Arizona.*

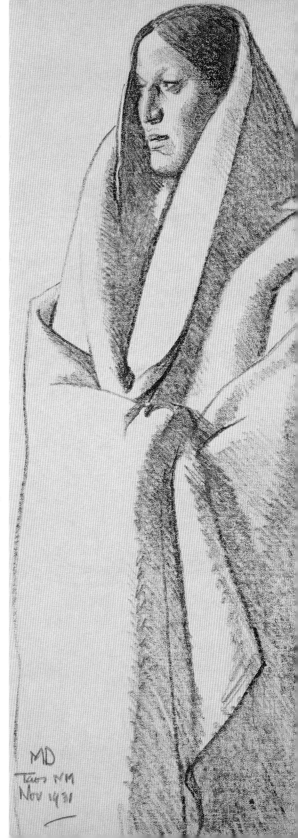

Maynard Dixon,
SILENT HOUR,
Courtesy Mitchell
Brown Fine Art,
Inc., Santa Fe, NM.

Native Americans, such as the widely admired *Earth Knower* (1932), revealed the lingering influence of Paul Gauguin's work in Tahiti, as Dixon deliberately mixed the Postimpressionist European influence with the modern West. Elsewhere, Dixon painted colorful landscapes of the Painted, Mojave, and Sonoran Deserts as Cezanne might have, had the French master been born in California instead of France. Maynard Dixon was quite intentionally recording and, in a sense, creating a new visual West that would stand in opposition to the frontier mythology of the Old West.

Given his love for the open range and big skies of the Southwest, it is not surprising that Maynard Dixon gravitated toward larger canvases and, eventually, to murals. His vision of the region was of a monumental and inspirational landscape with soaring peaks, vast deserts, and especially, towering cloud formations. The turning point for him occurred in 1917, when he received a commission from the Great Northern Railroad to prepare a group of paintings that focused upon Glacier National Park and the Blackfoot Indians. From that year until his death in 1946, Maynard Dixon continually refined his craft, while never departing from the clarity of form, sharp lines, and fresh colors that so distinguished his unique vision of the West.

One of his most representative canvases, *Desert Southwest* (1944), depicts a typical landscape of open, arid country, distant hardscrabble mountains, and expansive sky in the Mojave Desert of Nevada or California. This is a classic work from Dixon's mature period, when the artist sought particular images that conveyed the beauty and the power of the Southwest in a way that was deceptively simple. The sky in *Desert Southwest* is of particular note. Other artists might have been tempted to fill the majority of the canvas with clouds, but Dixon had the courage and vision to leave the sky completely empty, forcing the eye to face, and the brain to absorb, a vast negative space. Elsewhere, deep blue shadows fall from the massive granite range in the background, with the sweeping sand playas still fully illuminated by the late afternoon sky. Through the center of the painting an unpaved road heads west—as into the core mythology of the region—through a sage steppe, a scattering of black rock outcrops, and a sand dune field. The effect of all this is to depict a spiritual territory that could be, alternatively, purgatory or paradise. The geographic location could be Death Valley, or any one of a hundred other valleys in that vast region south of the Great Basin Country, east of the Sierra Nevadas, west of the Grand Canyon, and north of the warmer subtropical deserts along the Colorado River. The scene could also be, for that matter, a landscape from the human spirit, a striking visual metaphor for the dry hinterlands of the soul.

No discussion of Maynard Dixon would be complete without mention of his second wife, Dorothea Lange, who was one of the most accomplished members of the f/64 Group of photographers. Dorothea Lange, like songwriter Woody Guthrie and novelist John Steinbeck, was a farsighted humanitarian, and set out to document, as well as to interpret artistically, the

Given his love for the open range and big skies of the Southwest, it is not surprising that Maynard Dixon gravitated toward larger canvases and, eventually, to murals.

enormous human suffering associated with the Great Depression years. Her photographs from the Dust Bowl country of Oklahoma, Kansas, and Texas never crossed over into socialist propaganda or melancholy sentimentality. They were clear, unblinking documents of what she saw and felt during the 1930s. They remain some of the greatest art produced in the twentieth century. Her ten year marriage to Dixon (1925 to 1935) was a creative collaboration as much as it was a loving relationship, and Lange had considerable influence on Dixon's painting during this period, when he often focused on the stark realities of the Depression.

What Maynard Dixon brought to the mythology of the West was a refreshing new simplicity, a rendering of complex physical forms into their most basic geometry. His paintings helped younger artists leave behind the empty conventions and faded mythology of the past and create a new art that reflected the West of the twentieth century (seen currently in the paintings of Phoenix artist Ed Mell). Dixon imitated no one, and as Remington suggested, used nature as his sole source of inspiration. It is not surprising that when Dixon died in 1946 he had his ashes scattered on a mountaintop not far from Zion National Park in southwestern Utah, the perpetually sunny, forever sprawling province of the American West he most loved.

ANSEL ADAMS AND EDWARD WESTON
The Search for One Pure Image

ANSEL ADAMS LIKED TO TELL the story of his visit to northern New Mexico in 1930. At the time, the gifted twenty-eight-year-old was still debating, Hamlet-like, whether to devote his life energies to music (he was a classically-trained concert pianist) or photography. It was a difficult time for him. Adams later wrote of this transitional period: "I was wracked by indecision because I could not afford either emotionally or financially to continue splitting my time between them." While in Los Gallos, New Mexico, to develop a book on Taos Pueblo, he had a friendly dinner with Georgia O'Keeffe, a noted artist and the wife of New York gallery-owner Alfred Stieglitz, and Paul Strand, a distinguished photographer. The following after-noon Strand shared a collection of his four-by-five negatives with Adams, who was awestruck: "My understanding of photography was crystallized that afternoon, as I realized the great potential of the medium as an expressive art. I returned to San Francisco resolved that the camera, not the piano, would shape my destiny."

Strand's pioneering images also had an epiphany-like effect on the career of Edward Weston (1886–1958). These two energetic Californians—Edward Weston and Ansel Adams—would work in the 1930s, often together, to radically reshape photography in the American West. Within two years they would form f/64 Group, an artistic movement that was as important to modern photography as the Salon exhibitions of the Impressionists had been to nineteenth-century painting. It was Ansel Adams who prepared a "visual manifesto" for the eleven members of f/64 Group. The manifesto included the following statement:

> The Group will show no work at any time that does not conform to the standards of pure photography. Pure photography is defined as possessing no qualities of technique, composition or idea, derivative of any other art form.... [Above all we] must always remain independent of ideological conventions of art and aesthetics that are reminiscent of a period and culture antedating the growth of the medium itself.

Their new sharp-edged realism, reflecting the scientific consciousness in the popular culture, would come to dominate photographic interpretations of the American West for the rest of the twentieth century.

The chief myth celebrated by these California photographers—the West as natural paradise—was actually not that dissimilar from the "pantheistic sublime" embraced by earlier mythmakers, such as Thomas Moran and Albert Bierstadt. The f/64 Group photographers, in their emphasis on perfectly realized landscapes, advanced a "classical sublime" ideal. In each case, the visual source, the magnificent scenery of the American West, remained the same: Yosemite Valley, the Grand Canyon, the Tetons, the open deserts of the Southwest. The only difference was in the interpretation of the myth of wild beauty. Adams and Weston, the most successful members of this anti-romantic group, strove for an identical artistic goal that involved a wealth of visual detail (achieved by using the smallest aperture—f/64—to obtain the greatest depth of field) and a maximum of contrast between black and white tones on the image (produced during the printing process). For both photographers, the realization of this elusive aesthetic and technical task took on the form of a religious crusade, with Weston working tirelessly from his home on Wildcat Hill at Carmel and Adams doing the same from his studio in Yosemite (later in Carmel as well).

Many people around the world today base their view of the American West upon the images of Ansel Adams and, to an extent, those of Weston. Adams' classic photographs have changed forever the way people regard the Sierra Nevada Range, the Mojave Desert, the Big Sur country, and many other locations around the region. His signature photograph, *Moonrise Over Hernandez,* sums up much about his role as a mythmaker in the American West. The photograph was taken during the height of his most productive period, in the autumn of 1941, when he was on an extensive tour of the Southwest. (An astronomer later calculated by the position of the moon that the photo had been taken between 4:00 and 4:05 P.M. on October 31, 1941.) On this particular afternoon Adams had spent the day in the Chama Valley to the north of Hernandez, New Mexico, and was returning south when he saw the moon climbing over the Sangre de Cristo Mountains

Adams and Weston strove for an identical artistic goal that involved a wealth of visual detail and a maximum of contrast between black and white tones on the image.

to the east. He pulled to the side of the road, hurriedly set up his bulky tripod and eight-by-ten view camera, made adjustments for shutter speed and aperture, and captured forever this famous (and very ephemeral, given the position of the moon and fading light) image.

"This photograph," Adams later wrote, "has undoubtedly evoked more comment than any other I have made, and represents an unusual situation of content and effect." It is also his best-selling print, with originals made by Adams currently commanding in excess of thirty thousand dollars at auction. By artificially darkening the sky during the developing process (Adams did not begin doing this until the early 1970s), he produced an image of unusual tonal contrast and power. *Moonrise Over Hernandez* embodies the best of Adams' aesthetic system—the sense of lifting sky and of a quiet, austere landscape rendered with exacting purity and clarity. It captures, like many of the paintings of Montana artist Russell Chatham, a melancholy moment near dusk and in the autumn of the year. There is in the photograph a deep sense of peace, of spent fertility and loss, and of a Vergilian calm upon the land. Many believe the season of the harvest moon is the most beautiful time in the West—a time of golden aspen and bugling elk, last warmth and first cold, quiet magic and ancient myth. In this image Adams immortalized that time of year.

If Edward Weston has a signature work, it is not a single image but, rather, the ensemble of photographs he gathered along the California coastline from the fabled vistas of Point Lobos to the legendary dune fields at Oceano. This unique region, where the sea meets the land in often-dramatic scenes, is renowned around the world for its striking natural beauty. The Pacific coast was Weston's favorite place in the American West and remained a continual source of inspiration for him (and later for his photographer-son Brett) throughout his career. The angular and heroic rock formations, the fertile tidepools, the crashing waves, the stark dune fields, the weathered Monterey pine and cypress were for Weston powerful symbols that starkly evoked a myriad of resonances—the creative energy of birth, the often challenging struggles of life, the sudden border with the vast sea of eternity.

Weston also worked for years with Tina Modotti and Charis Wilson making outdoor figure studies, a genre later brought to perfection by f/64 Group member Imogen Cunningham. Weston's work with his wife Charis produced many images of virtuosity, in which he, like Cunningham, sought to blend the human form into nature. Some of his best work was done in Death Valley near Stovepipe Wells and in the dune fields of Oceano north of San Diego. Charis's posthumous 1998 memoir—*Through*

Another Lens, My Years with Edward Weston—is a unique work in the history of western art, insofar as it provides the model's point-of-view on the creative relationship between the muse and the artist: "Edward was ... a robust lover of life ... a man who found the world endlessly fascinating. With his camera he pored over it, probed it, sought to comprehend it, and to render for others its beauty, complexity, and inexhaustible mystery."

In the end, these two restless creative spirits, Ansel Adams and Edward Weston, brought about an artistic revolution the results of which are still being felt. They changed fundamentally how we view the landscape of the American West and produced a legacy of immortal works.

Edward Weston, DUNES OCEANO, 1936. Courtesy The Denver Art Museum Collection: General Service Foundation Purchase Fund, 1976.7. © Denver Art Museum 2001.

Along the way they rejected all of the old myths from the nineteenth century, as did contemporary painters such as Maynard Dixon and Georgia O'Keeffe, and successfully created a New Art to accompany a New West. Although they were rationalists and realists—and their photographic work certainly reflects this—they were also men of feeling and extraordinary sensitivity. It was, after all, Ansel Adams who once observed that "we all continually move on the edges of eternity, and are sometimes granted vistas through the fabric of illusion." Their photographs were windows into that timeless other world, that natural paradise that can be found at the end of so many roads in the American West.

IMOGEN CUNNINGHAM
New Directions

AS A YOUNG WOMAN at the University of Washington, Seattle, Imogen Cunningham (1883–1976) worked for a time in the studio of Edward Curtis, one of the old-style mythmakers of the nineteenth century. Curtis photographed Native Americans in carefully posed, often heroic, settings. His romantic—some would say sentimentalized—portraits gave expression to the lingering nostalgia for the Old West that developed after the frontier, as a geographic and historical fact, was declared officially dead in 1890. Curtis' work, which covered eighty tribes of the American West, resulted in forty thousand photographs, which were then gathered into twenty folio books and collectively entitled *The North American Indian.* Imogen Cunningham's early exposure to Edward Curtis' antiquated mode of mythmaking and artificial style of photographing was important to her own art in the years that followed. Seeing firsthand the inherent shortcomings of Curtis' aesthetic philosophy in terms of the twentieth century, she ultimately rebelled against both that backward-looking school and the soft-focused pictorial movement. Like the other photographers in the f/64 Group, Cunningham believed in seeking out simple images that captured with powerful clarity the abstract essence of the landscape, the still life, or the human form.

One of the most persistent myths of the American West is that the province is a sort of Garden of Eden, a bountiful paradise on Earth placed here for the use of humankind. The outdoor figure studies of Imogen Cunningham can be thought of as a visual commentary upon this appealing and multifaceted myth. Her human subjects are cast, quite literally at times, as prelapsarian souls freely inhabiting a wild Rousseauian utopia, latter-day Adams and Eves. Her camera actively explores the resonances between their forms and the natural forms of the landscape, finding the deeper visual harmonies that unite all life and providing further expression to the nature-as-refuge myth. Imogen Cunningham's landscape nudes can, in this way, be interpreted as miniature essays or

Blakean poems on the myth of lost innocence, both in the physical and the spiritual sense. Although some have tied her work in this regard to the contemporaneous figure studies done by Edward Weston and his two chief models Tina Modotti and Charis Wilson, Imogen Cunningham actually relied more on several pioneering women photographers for guidance and inspiration, most notably the work of Californian Anne Brigman. Cunningham's work in the genre predated Weston's, though later they came to share common beliefs on the subject and amicably cross-fertilized each other's work, as artists often do.

Imogen Cunningham actually relied more on several pioneering women photographers for guidance and inspiration, most notably the work of Californian Anne Brigman.

Imogen Cunningham, HELENA MAYER, CANYON DE CHELLY, *1939. Courtesy The Imogen Cunningham Trust © 1978.*

During the 1920s, following her marriage (in 1915) to artist Roi Partridge, Imogen Cunningham began to attract increasing attention as one of her generation's most compelling photographers. This included a presence in the influential *Film Und Foto* exhibition, supervised by Edward Weston, in Stuttgart, Germany, in 1919, followed by solo exhibitions in 1932 at both the Los Angeles County Museum and the de Young Memorial Museum in San Francisco. That same year she became a member of f/64 Group. Six years later she largely abandoned the four-by-five large-format camera favored by several members of f/64 Group for a more flexible medium-format camera, the 2 1/4-by-2 1/4 German-made Rollei with Zeiss lens (a camera still popular today). It was with this camera that she took her famous series of outdoor photographs of Mills College professor and Olympic fencing medalist Helena Mayer at Canyon de Chelly in 1939.

For the rest of her life Imogen Cunningham was regarded as one of the preeminent American photographers of her time. All that follows a commitment to artistic excellence was hers: election to the American Academy of Arts and Sciences, shows at the finest venues (Art Institute of Chicago, San Francisco Museum of Art, Seattle Art Museum), and an honorary doctoral degree (from the California College of Arts and Crafts). Her various later projects included studies of pregnant women in the 1950s, a series of forays abroad, and her final project, a study of people over the age of ninety when she herself was over ninety years of age.

Imogen Cunningham's photographs remain perennially popular. They speak, as all great art does, to what Pablo Picasso once called, in his seminal essay "Art as Individual Idea" (1923), "the eternal present." In Spring 2000, a major exhibition of Imogen Cunningham's photographs (as well as those of her son, Ron Partridge) was held at the distinguished Camera Obscura Photographic Gallery in Denver. The photographs in that retrospective show summed up the magnificence of Imogen Cunningham's unique achievement: the early close-up flower studies of iris, false hellebore, and magnolia blossoms that so influenced Georgia O'Keeffe (and likely inspired O'Keeffe's signature painting, *Oriental Poppy,* 1927), the nude studies (including her legendary image *Triangles,* 1929), and the ever-modern still lifes (such as *Birdcage and Shadows,* 1921).

Imogen Cunningham placed the human body back into its original home—the outdoors. Each person she photographed became a metaphor for the human race. Each fragment of nature captured within her lens became a microcosm of the universe. She quietly reminded us that we all came from nature, and that we each would ultimately return to that realm, no matter where or how we lived. Her images, in that sense, are both uplifting and cautionary. They remind us of the oldest myth both in the American West and in western civilization— that we, as a race, have been expelled from the garden, but that through the purity of art, which eschews all that is wordly, we can reenter paradise and be at one with it, again.

GEORGIA O'KEEFFE
Inner Landscapes

THE ABSTRACT LANDSCAPES and supernatural still lifes of Georgia O'Keeffe are, quite literally, like no other representations of the American West. While other artists followed traditional mythological systems—cowboys and Indians, the wilderness Garden of Eden, the West as landscape of the future—O'Keeffe created her own West, her own personal mythology, a uniquely private realm rich in form and color, symbol and truth, imagination and paradox. Her daring visual images—deer antlers floating over a desert, folding and unfolding flowers, water-polished river stones, sun-bleached vertebrae beneath a ridgeline, a black tree against the night stars—are now familiar around the world. They evoke a very different American West from that which we saw earlier in the paintings of Albert Bierstadt and Thomas Moran. Although a revolutionary modernist in every sense of the term, O'Keeffe created a legacy that, paradoxically, is now regarded as entirely within the conservative center of our culture, and is as much a part of the mythological West as the paintings of Charles Russell and Frederic Remington.

Georgia O'Keeffe (born 1887) received a considerable amount of formal art education (Art Institute of Chicago, Art Students League of New York, University of Virginia, Columbia Teacher's College). Her two most important influences were Columbia professor Arthur Dow, who introduced her to Asian art (so evident in her later work), and New York gallery owner/photographer Alfred Stieglitz, who actively promoted her work and became her husband in 1924. A native easterner, O'Keeffe actually saw the West for the first time in 1912, when she worked in Amarillo, Texas, as supervisor of art education in the public schools. She was particularly struck by the shapes and hues of nearby Palo Duro Canyon. It was in the sun-washed canyons and on the windswept plains of west Texas that this world-class artist was born as a creative spirit.

Although at that time O'Keeffe worked primarily in small-scale watercolors, she later gained more confidence and turned to the more demanding medium of oil (which can take up to a week to dry) and to large stretched canvases (which require greater physical effort and advanced compositional planning). In 1929, the artist began spending summers in northern New Mexico. (The rest of the year she remained with her husband in New York.) The high-altitude light and the open desert landscapes intensely inspired O'Keeffe, and her most productive period followed. Within a few years O'Keeffe purchased Ghost Ranch near Abiquiu, New Mexico, and spent increasing time there. It is important to note that the artist battled mental illness during the middle period of her life (and was hospitalized at a New York mental facility for some time), as well as breast cancer. Her relocation from the

Georgia O'Keeffe found most of her inspiration through direct, daily contact with the desert. Courtesy John Murray.

East to the Far West can, in this context, be seen as a life-saving journey toward light, space, and health. This movement is consistent with the traditional myth of the West as the landscape of the future and as a place of hope and rebirth.

Although O'Keeffe is known for her many distinctive paintings, one of her most celebrated and suggestive works is the iconic canvas *From the Faraway Nearby* (1939). It is a large work (thirty-six inches by forty inches), currently owned by the Metropolitan Museum of Art in New York as part of their extensive Alfred Stieglitz Collection. The painting, which was executed when O'Keeffe was at the height of her powers, portrays the multiple antlers of a single mule deer (symbolic of the male presence on the Earth, and of nature's vitality and fertility) floating above a pink, white, and gray landscape (representative of the female presence on the Earth—the so-called "mother earth" myth). The clay hills in the foreground are soft, contoured, and deeply weathered. The sky ranges from a mixed ultramarine/cobalt blue, through a light cerulean, to a chalk-like pink, as if the dust has been lifted into the desert sky by the wind. The mountains on the farthest horizon, instead of fading with recession into lighter hues are—one of O'Keeffe's humorous paradoxes—actually darker than the clay hills closer to view. One has the sense in this painting that the canvas represents a mythic puzzle—a visual statement that is also a philosophical question, a colorful hallucination that is also a penetrating epiphany, an empirical fact that is also a playful fable. It actively engages the viewer and forces him or her to look at landscapes both interior and exterior, and to come to terms with a whole range of compelling possibilities.

O'Keeffe existed in a vibrant milieu of other Western artists and photographers, including Maynard Dixon, John Marin, Ansel Adams, and Edward Weston. What separated her from her peers was that they explored primarily the physical, external aspects of the Western landscape, whereas she was fascinated by their interior, subjective content. Like that other great twentieth-century artist, Pablo Picasso, Georgia O'Keeffe eschewed affiliation with any particular school of art and preferred to work alone, following her own instincts and vision. (Her rugged individualism is consistent with that other great myth of the West, self-reliance.) No one school—expressionism, realism, surrealism—could claim her. Slowly, over the years and decades, she formed her own unique form of art.

For lack of a better term, her aesthetic system could be called synthetic symbolism—synthetic because it absorbed the best of so many other artistic schools and symbolist because the viewer always had the sense that objects were being deliberately manipulated by the artist for very specific effects and purposes. O'Keeffe is, arguably, the single greatest artist of the American West, the one individual, both as a mythmaker and as a painter, who more than any other captured the elusive paradox of a riddle of an enigma that is the American West.

T. C. CANNON
Native Son

THE SECOND HALF of the twentieth century saw the emergence of what is now referred to as the "Indian Renaissance," a dramatic efflorescence of Native American art in the American West. Much of this new Native American art revisited the classic mythology of the West, presenting contrary and often critical perspectives on regional history and popular cultural legends. The artists in this group included Fritz Scholder, Billy Soza War Soldier, and T. C. Cannon. In their anti-mythic paintings, drawings and lithographs, the artists created a very different picture of their province: The intrepid cavalry so celebrated by Charles Russell and Frederic Remington became the bad guys, and the Indian-warriors faithfully defending their homeland became the good guys (as in Fritz Scholder's unflattering centennial portrayal of General Custer, *Portrait 1876–1976*), the Western landscape was transformed into a pure realm of inspiration and spirit, rather than a playground for adventure and exploitation, and the flow of time, including Western history, was represented not so much as a traditional linear sequence but as a fluid organic process (as in T. C. Cannon's eight-foot-by-twenty-foot epic painting entitled *The Mural*).

By far, the most accomplished artist in this group was T. C. Cannon, who was born on September 27, 1946, at the Indian hospital in Lawton, Oklahoma. Cannon's father Walter was a member of the Kiowa tribe, and his mother Mamie was of the Caddo tribe. Growing up on the Kiowa Reservation, T. C. Cannon lived among a traditional people of the southern plains renowned for the high quality of their art, as well as for their celebratory costumes and tribal songs. From a rudimentary start in the so-called "ledger art" (colored pencil and crayon drawings done in traditional paper ledger books) of nineteenth-century reservations, the Kiowa had then rapidly advanced to become exceptional painters and muralists (notably the legendary Kiowa Five).

Cannon showed artistic promise from an early age. While still a teenager, T. C. Cannon spent time with Lee Tsatoke, son of Kiowa Five painter Monroe Tsatoke, and learned much about the basics of drawing and painting from him. Surviving sketches and watercolors from this period evidence a precocious talent. After high school, Cannon attended the Institute of American Indian Arts in Santa Fe. While there he met the gifted Indian artist and teacher Fritz Scholder, whose course in art history introduced Cannon to three European artists who would profoundly influence him: Paul Gauguin, Vincent Van Gogh, and Henri Matisse. It was during this period, inspired by these and other artists, that Cannon painted one of his most extraordinary canvases: *Mama and Papa Have the Going Home Shiprock Blues* (84 inches by 59 1/2 inches, 1966, Collection of Institute of American Arts, Santa Fe). The eclectic, post-modern painting had an electrifying effect on Native American artists, liberating and empowering them as creative spirits. Its impact on the Native American artistic movement can be compared to that of Marcel Duchamp's iconic painting *Nude Descending a Staircase*, which catalyzed the Cubist movement in 1913. Cannon had established a motif he, and others, would employ often over the next decade: portraying traditional Native Americans, subjects of so many myths, in contemporary settings (in this case, a Navajo couple on a bench waiting for a bus and wearing sunglasses, which are representative of Euroamerican culture).

T. C. Cannon's training as an artist was interrupted in 1967, when he was drafted into the U.S. Army. In Vietnam he served as an aide to the commanding general of the 101st Airborne. During the 1968 Tet Offensive he distinguished himself during the defense of the 101st Airborne headquarters complex at Bien

Hoa when it was overrun by North Vietnamese troops. Cannon received two Bronze Stars and the Vietnamese Cross of Gallantry for heroism during this battle. After returning from the war he married Barbara Warner (of the Ponca tribe) in Oklahoma and then moved to Santa Fe to attend art classes. The Vietnam experience would persist for years, both subtly and not, in his paintings, as he was deeply conflicted between his humanitarian nature and his pride at having served in the Kiowa warrior-tradition.

Throughout the early 1970s Cannon's reputation steadily grew, as he presented shows in Santa Fe galleries and, eventually, in New York galleries. The most important event, in terms of exposing Cannon to a wider audience, was the 1972 Smithsonian spring exhibition entitled "Two Painters," which featured the work of T. C. Cannon and his former teacher Fritz Scholder. The Washington D.C. show included fourteen oil canvases by Cannon. Each was done in classic Cannon style—rich colors and bold designs combined to produce startling images of Native American history and mythology. The paintings eventually toured Europe, appearing in Berlin, London, Belgrade, Skopje, Istanbul, and Madrid. As a result, one of the best-known art dealers in New York, Joaquin Aberbach, offered T. C. Cannon a contract of representation in his gallery. Aberbach provided Cannon with access both to influential art critics and wealthy collectors, and the young artist came to know financial security for the first time in his life.

What followed was one of the most creative periods in the history of American art. Working at a furious rate, painting sometimes several canvases a week, Cannon produced, in six short years, more exceptional works than many produce in a lifetime. One of the finest portraits he composed during this period was *Chief Watching*, a large canvas (48-inches by 36 inches) in oil and acrylic. The painting represents a classic Cannon rendering of nineteenth-century warriors. The grim-faced leader is represented to the viewer frontally, with a Colt .45 Peacemaker in hand (the name a subtle irony). He is dressed in bright ochre-and-crimson leggings and red-spotted purple shirt, and is wrapped in a flowing red-and-white blanket. Around his neck is a large peace medal and a bright red, green, and yellow bandana. Red cloth wraps adorn his hair braids. The bold colors of red and purple are found on the wall behind him and on the rug at his feet. His stoic presence fills the canvas, and is meant to convey an image of power and determination.

Just when T. C. Cannon seemed poised at the verge of greatness—of joining the ranks of the most esteemed members of the guild—he was tragically killed in a car crash near Santa Fe on May 7, 1978. He was thirty-two years old. Like Buddy Holly and Jimi Hendrix, Cannon would know many things, but not longevity. With his death the West lost one of its most inventive and influential mythmakers and Native American artists lost their brilliant leader. The loss had a personal meaning to me, as my parents, longtime aficionados of Southwestern art, owned two of T. C. Cannon's beautiful

Working at a furious rate, painting sometimes several canvases a week, Cannon produced, in six short years, more exceptional works than many produce in a lifetime.

T. C. Cannon, CHIEF
WATCHING. *Courtesy
Joyce Cannon Yi.*

lithographs. To this day, they hang in the living room of the family home, reminding us all of the rare person that T. C. Cannon was, and of the extraordinary gifts he left behind.

One way to measure the greatness of an artist is by the influence he or she exerts on posterity. In the case of T. C. Cannon, the influence has been widespread. Visit the galleries of Santa Fe and Taos or open the pages of a popular art magazine such as *Southwest Art*, and you will find echoes of Cannon everywhere: bright colors, intense single-subject studies, innovative treatments of Southwestern themes and landscapes.

One of the best artists now working in the Cannon tradition is the Texas painter Cesar Martinez. For the past quarter-century, Martinez has been actively engaged in documenting the people of the U.S.-Mexican borderlands in striking portraits. His paintings are distinguished by their bold styling, intense colors, and a unique visionary quality akin to that found in Cannon. Like Cannon, Martinez prefers to darkly underpaint a large canvas, and then add brilliant fields of color. The effect of the underpainting is to give the surface colors an underlying shadowy quality. This brooding undertone is in keeping with Spanish-Christian myths about the fundamentally dark and evil nature of the world.

As the twenty-first century unfolds, the rich synthesis of cultural influences (Native American, North American, Western European) seen in the work of Cannon and his followers will continue to create new forms and schools of art, and new methods of interpreting the conventional and emerging myths of the American West. Cannon's ultimate legacy is that he, like other great mythmakers (Moran, Remington, O'Keeffe), inspired a revolution that has led his guild, and society, into an entirely new direction.

RUSSELL CHATHAM
Radiant Darkness

THE STORY OF HOW Russell Chatham first gained recognition as an artist is as much a legend of the modern West as is the traditional Western myth of natural beauty his paintings have come to embody. The year was 1975, and director Arthur Penn was filming *The Missouri Breaks* (a movie about a gang of late-nineteenth-century horse thieves) near Livingston, Montana. The cast included an Oscar-winning actor on his way down, Marlon Brando, as well as an Oscar-winning actor on his way up, Jack Nicholson. Each night after shooting, a few members of the cast would retire to the colorful cowboy bars that line the main street in Livingston. One evening a screenwriter on the film, Tom McGuane (who also had a quarter horse ranch in nearby Paradise Valley), introduced actor Jack Nicholson to a local artist named Russ Chatham, a thirty-six-year-old man who was struggling to support his family. Nicholson asked to see some of Chatham's paintings, loved them enough to immediately make a purchase, and soon introduced Chatham to other affluent buyers, who also recognized

Russell Chatham, THE SEA AT PACIFICA. *Courtesy Collection of Yvon Chouinard.*

founded by his great-grandfather in 1860, encompassed over five thousand acres and took in much of the southern slope of Mount Toro in Monterey County. It was here—among the oak woodlands, wildflower meadows, and clear trout streams—that Chatham began to absorb the colors and forms, moods and mysteries, peace and vitality of nature. Soon the restless young man began to paint with oil and brush on board and canvas. Like his grandfather, Chatham would develop a tonal style and would focus primarily, in subtle and often symbolic ways, upon pastoral and wild landscapes. Chatham received little formal training, and is largely a self-taught artist, although his work clearly incorporates the influence of the Dutch landscape painters of the Renaissance, the French and Dutch landscape painters of the Impressionist and Postimpressionist periods, American tonal artists such as James Whistler and Edward Hopper, and to a degree Bierstadt and Moran.

Two works exemplify the geographic and aesthetic poles of Chatham's world: *The Sea at Pacifica* (1986) and *Summer Fields Near the Yellowstone River* (1977). Both are included in his retrospective collection *One Hundred Paintings* (Clarke City Press, 1990). The first canvas, which is large even for Chatham (eighty inches by seventy-two inches), depicts a scene along the northern Pacific coast near the landscapes of the artist's youth. The flat purple light, filtered by afternoon clouds, falls uniformly on the tranquil western sea, viewed from sheer cliffs and high meadows. The limited palette and the washed-out sky colors brought

Chatham's rare genius. Nicholson's generous spirit saved a hardworking painter from unmerited poverty and also helped to give the West a formidable artist and mythmaker.

Russell Chatham was born in San Francisco on October 27, 1939, the grandson of noted California artist Gottardo Piazzoni (1872–1945). One of Chatham's strongest memories of boyhood was the family ranch in Carmel Valley, where summers were spent. The ranch, down upon the sea and land help to unify the canvas and produce a deep, Franciscan-like tranquility. The second painting, which is more modest in size (twenty-eight inches by thirty-six inches), depicts a representative scene from the other half of Chatham's world—the upper Yellowstone River near Livingston, Montana. Here, too, the mood is quiet and melancholy, as the sun-bleached fields in the Yellowstone Valley yield, down a long gentle slope, to the mixed cottonwoods and alders beside the river. Scattered groves of trees can be followed all the way to the other side of the valley. No sky is visible. The whole painting is suffused with a single orange-yellow light. There is a sense in this painting, as well as in the first, of emptiness and of loss, of an elemental natural scene that is also a metaphor for a landscape within the artist's soul.

Chatham, like Montana's other favorite artist, Charles Russell, received public recognition relatively late in life. As with Russell's work, there is a distinctive maturity and worldliness about Chatham's canvases. They reveal a large, knowing spirit that has been purified by struggle, humbled by adversity, and enlarged by long seasons spent in solitude close to nature. His work is suffused throughout with a deep appreciation for the beauty and the power of the Western landscape. He avoids the narrative tendency of Russell and Remington, and also disdains to work with the superficial clichés of mountain and ranching country or of the Pacific coast, as is seen so often with more commercial artists. One senses throughout his work, and especially on meeting him in person, a van Gogh–like understanding of the oneness of humanity and nature.

Chatham has devoted his life to capturing the essences of particular Western places that are dear to his heart: the mountains and valleys of western Montana and the seacoast of northern California. In doing so, he has become one of the American West's most influential modern mythmakers. He has had over four hundred one-artist shows, and his paintings have been exhibited in major museums across the United States, Europe, and Asia. He is regarded as one of the world's foremost lithographers. His paintings have appeared on the covers of books by such esteemed Western writers as Jim Harrison, who has a home in Tucson, and Rick Bass, who lives in northwestern Montana. Chatham's work is owned by such cultural luminaries as Harrison Ford, Warren Beatty, Jane Fonda, Peter Fonda, Tom McGuane, Robert Wagner, Don Henley, Tom Brokaw, Ed Bradley, and many others. No other Western artist in the modern era has been more successful at craft or career. Chatham's popularity, and ultimate legacy, is intimately related to the Western landscape myths that his paintings so richly explore and express.

As with Russell's work, there is a distinctive maturity and worldliness about Chatham's canvases. They reveal a large, knowing spirit that has been purified by struggle, humbled by adversity, and enlarged by long seasons spent in solitude close to nature.

Slim Pickens as Major T. J. "King" Kong hands out attack orders to a crew member in Stanley Kubrick's DR. STRANGELOVE *(Columbia, 1965). Courtesy Photofest.*

OF FILMS AND FABLES

Motion Pictures as Mythmakers

Alan Squire (played by Leslie Howard):

Have you ever read The Hollow Men? Well, don't.

It's very discouraging, because it's true.

It refers to the intellectuals who thought

they'd conquered nature. They dammed its waters

to irrigate the wastelands, they built streamlined

monstrosities to penetrate its resistance,

they wrapped it up in cellophane and sold it

in drugstores. They were so certain they

had it subdued and now—do you realize what

it is that is causing world chaos?

You don't, eh? Well, I'm probably the only

living man who could tell you. It's nature.

She's fighting back.... Nature's proving that she can't

be beaten up by the likes of us.

—from THE PETRIFIED
FOREST (1935)

THERE IS A SCENE IN THE 1964 STANLEY KUBRICK FILM *Dr. Strangelove* in which the commander of a B-52 nuclear bomber, Major T. J. "King" Kong (played by Slim Pickens), receives an order to attack his primary target, a Soviet ICBM base in eastern Siberia. The Major proceeds to the rear of the cockpit, opens a safe containing navigational instructions and aerial maps, and removes a white cowboy hat. "Boys," he exclaims to the crew over the intercom, "it looks like we're about to face nuclear combat toe-to-toe with the Rooskies, with the likelihood of promotions and citations for every man." So pervasive is the myth of the Western cowboy that even in this Cold War satire it plays a prominent, almost defining role. (Major Kong eventually rides the nuclear bomb, bronco style, down to its target.) Since the beginning, movies have proven to be one of the most effective vehicles for promoting many of the foundation myths of the American West. As a mythmaking tool, film offers several advantages, not the least of which is that it powerfully transports the audience into an alternative world—partly truth and partly fiction— through a completely self-contained illusion of both sight and sound.

Central to the Western film has been the retrospective celebration of the Old Frontier—its ironies and tragedies, ambiguities and mysteries, legends and fables. Much of this mythmaking process has involved the creation of larger-than-life heroes or anti-heroes. For example, in the 1929 film *The Virginian*—based on the classic novel by Owen Wister — there is a memorable scene in which Gary Cooper, playing the sheriff, is called a "son-of-a——" by the villain Trampas (played by Walter Huston). Cooper responds with a resonant line: "When you call me that, smile." In the Hollywood version of the American West, the hero always prevails, always upholds what is right, and always has the necessary come-back line, from "Not likely" by John Wayne (as bounty hunter Rooster Cogburn in *True Grit* [1969]) to "Go ahead, make my day" by Clint Eastwood (as San Francisco police officer Harry Callahan in *Sudden Impact* [1983]).

Much of the cinematic mythology of the American West is part of a much older world of mythology, that of law-giving. Strong and independent men (and women) rise up to defend a just and ordered society from all those who would diminish or destroy it. This theme of law-bringing has been one of the most persistent in Western film, whether we are watching Alan Ladd as the laconic gunfighter protecting virtuous homesteaders from the local bullies in *Shane* (1953), or Steve McQueen and company (Yul Brynner, Charles Bronson, Robert Vaughn, James Coburn, James Gardner, Brad Dexter) as the misfit gunslingers hired to defeat the bandits terrorizing a Mexican village in *The Magnificent Seven* (1960)—with that remarkable musical score by Elmer Bernstein. Even in a film as ostensibly anti-Western as *Chinatown* (1974), we are presented with an essentially decent character, an L.A. private eye played by Jack Nicholson, fighting a sinister presence (John Huston) in a complex story focusing on a classic Western theme: water rights. The film explores the experiences of an ordinary person who is drawn into one of the most ancient conflicts on earth: good versus evil.

Similarly, the 1935 film *The Petrified Forest* casts Humphrey Bogart as Duke Santee, the kind-hearted outlaw looking to reunite with his true love and escape to Mexico. Betrayed in the end by the woman he loves, Duke goes down shooting, another tragic victim of broken trust. The good guys have won and the bad guy has departed the territory, permanently. Civilization has once again prevailed over that which stands in opposition to it. The same is true of *High Sierra* (1941), in which Bogart played

Gary Cooper as The Virginian and Walter Huston as Tampas in Victor Fleming's classic western THE VIRGINIAN. *(Paramount, 1929). Courtesy Photofest.*

a California killer on the run named Mad Dog Earle. In this influential picture, the West is cast as a region where right and strength ultimately prevail over wrong and weakness.

In almost every Western film, nature—the vast, empty, and often austere landscapes of the American West—reigns supreme over the human drama, from the Wyoming Tetons of *The Big Sky* (1952), to the Montana ranch land of *The Horse Whisperer* (1998), to the Arizona desert of *Fort Apache* (1948). Whether the films are glorifying Manifest Destiny (*How The West Was Won*, 1962) or haranguing against it (*Dances With Wolves*, 1990), building heroes (*True Grit*, 1969) or demolishing them (*Butch Cassidy and the Sundance Kid*, 1969), they always prominently feature the landscape as an iconographic presence. Epic, timeless, and far removed from the petty quarrels of humankind, the landscape lives on forever as both the inspiration for and the residence of all Western myth.

Director John Ford is one of the most influential Western mythmakers of all time. Courtesy Photofest.

JOHN FORD AND JOHN WAYNE
Eden Invaded

LATE IN HIS CAREER, when asked by an interviewer which American filmmaker he most respected, the venerable director Orson Welles (*Citizen Kane*, 1941) replied "The old masters. By that I mean, John Ford, John Ford, and John Ford." Indeed, a reasonable argument could be made that John Ford was the most influential Western mythmaker of all time. In film after film (fifty-four Westerns in all!), Ford helped to preserve, and at times embellish, some of the fables and legends that have so sharply defined the West as a unique province of the human imagination. Ford brought to the medium a natural gift for storytelling, as well as an innate sense of how to turn a moving image into a thing of beauty. Together with his favorite actor and close friend John Wayne, he created a body of work that—rightly or wrongly— portrayed the Old Frontier as a realm of heroism and violence, adventure and danger, loneliness and adversity, open space and stark grandeur. To this day, many people around the world only know the American West through the dramatic stories of John Ford. The director's vivid cinematic myths have, for those viewers and perhaps for posterity as well, become an alternative form of historical reality.

The old masters. By that I mean, John Ford, John Ford, and John Ford.

—Orson Welles

Like so many who have made their living artistically in the West, Ford was born elsewhere. After a childhood in Cape Elizabeth, Maine—the thirteenth son of a saloon keeper—Ford moved to Hollywood in 1913, following his older brother Francis Ford. (Francis later became a noted actor, screenwriter and director.) For several years John Ford toiled at whatever entry-level jobs he could find in the industry, working variously as a stunt-man, propman, set laborer, and minor actor (appearing as an extra in *The Birth of a Nation* in 1915). Every successful movie career must have its lucky break, and Ford's occurred in 1917, when Universal Pictures hired him to direct several now-forgotten silent films. Five years later Fox Pictures entrusted Ford with the task of directing *The Iron Horse*, a historical epic that focused on the post–Civil War construction of the Union-Pacific Railroad. Filmed on location in Nevada, the complicated, lengthy production—which involved everything from hundreds of extras to large herds of buffalo—demonstrated that Ford was in possession of both uncommon artistic abilities and rare leadership skills.

It was during the 1920s that Ford met and began working with a young actor named John Wayne. (Legend has it when the two first met, they almost got into a physical altercation over some trivial misunderstanding.) Originally from Winterset, Iowa, John Wayne was raised in southern California and attended USC on a football scholarship. Summers found the six-foot-four undergraduate working as a laborer and propman on the Fox lot. By 1928 Wayne had begun to find regular, if secondary, work in the films of John Ford and other young directors. His break occurred in 1930, when he was given a major role in Raoul Walsh's *The Big Trail* (1930), a film shot on location around Jackson, Wyoming, with the Grand Tetons in the back-ground. Over the next decade, Wayne starred in over sixty B-grade films. He was finally rescued from this cinematic purgatory by John Ford, who cast him as the Ringo Kid in the Oscar-winning film *Stagecoach* (1939).

The rest, as they say, is history. Together, John Ford and John Wayne would make over a dozen movies together, including several classics shot in Ford's favorite location: Monument Valley, Arizona (*Fort Apache* [1948], *She Wore a Yellow Ribbon* [1949], *Rio Grande* [1950], *The Searchers* [1956]). Ford shaped Wayne into the ultimate leading man of the mid-twentieth century. As the pair grew and matured, so did the force and power of their films. Perhaps their greatest collabora-tion occurred in *The Searchers* (1956), a noire film

John Wayne as The Ringo Kid and Claire Trevor as Dallas in Ford's STAGECOACH *(UA, 1939). Courtesy Photofest.*

that examined a Civil War veteran's obsessive quest to find his niece (played by teenager Natalie Wood) in the Indian country of the Old Frontier. Ethan Edwards, played by John Wayne, is portrayed as a deeply flawed character, combining violence and gentleness, hatred and love, a sense of duty and a tendency to recklessness. The film combines breathtaking long shots of Monument Valley with close-ups that focus on the fury and unpredictability of the human heart. Visitors to Monument Valley are now regularly shown by Navajo guides the locations made famous by the film, including the dune fields near the sand springs, the North Window, Totem Pole, Ford Point, and the Mitten Buttes.

Other John Ford films look at the mythic West in strikingly different ways. The best example is Ford's Oscar-winning production of *The Grapes of Wrath* (Best Director, Best Supporting Actress, 1940), which featured thirty-five-year-old Henry Fonda as Tom Joad. In its compassionate portrayal of displaced farmers, the film also revealed Ford's populist sympathies for the betrayed and outcast. Having grown up poor in a working-class immigrant family, Ford reflexively sided with the underdog, whether the homeless Indians in *Cheyenne Autumn* (1954), the beleaguered Mormons in *Wagonmaster* (1950), or the migrant Oklahomans in *The Grapes of Wrath*. At his best, Ford has been called one of the finest creative minds to be associated with film in the twentieth century. To this day, no one has been awarded more Oscars than John Ford (six). At his worst, he has been labeled a sentimental purveyor of simplistic myths. His was often a nostalgic vision that replaced difficult facts with easy adaptations.

Of John Wayne, the same two statements have also been made. Wayne, in fact, became virtually synonymous with the film legend he created—at times, becoming almost a one-dimensional caricature. In later life, John Wayne the man and John Wayne the myth became indistinguishable. Both Ford and Wayne, though, would probably consider the mere fact that they are still remembered a compliment, and all discussion, even the minor grousing, a distinct form of praise. Criticism of them tends to be chrono-centric—to impose the values and tastes of the present unfairly on the past. Together these two celebrated mythmakers forever changed the Western scene, and to this day loom over lesser talents as the buttes and mesas of Monument Valley tower over the valley features. Their joint artistic legacy is inextricably bound with the landscapes they loved, and is as much a permanent part of the West as the real events of history that so fascinated and inspired them. Though they had very human flaws, one cannot imagine a mythic American West without John Ford and John Wayne.

Together these two celebrated mythmakers forever changed the Western scene, and to this day loom over lesser talents as the buttes and mesas of Monument Valley tower over the valley features.

TELEVISION WESTERNS
The Big Sky on the Small Screen

SINCE THE 1940s television has been the dominant form of media in the country. In the corner of every living room, from remote cabins to country-club estates, the television sits like a familiar member of the household, a resident wise man, a welcome comic presence, a raconteur extraordinaire, a trusted messenger that can report news from anywhere around the world (or universe) at anytime. Televisions come in all sizes, from miniature sets that can be placed on a kitchen counter to hefty behemoths that measure four feet across and can give even the sturdiest moving man a herniated disc. From birth to death, televisions are, for better or for worse, a more or less constant presence in virtually every American life. They baby-sit us when we are children, entertain us through adulthood, and assuage the suffering of the twilight years. They have transported us to the far side of the moon, taken us down to the wreckage of the Titanic at the bottom of the ocean, and brought us painfully close to the savagery of distant wars. Only a hundred years ago such amazing devices were the stuff of an H. G. Wells science fiction novel. Today it is difficult to imagine a world without them.

Central to the television, since the beginning of the media, has been the Western. At first the televised shows were little more than shortened versions of the formulaic Westerns seen on the big screen—self-contained episodes that would carry over from week to week, with the same characters and setting. By the 1950s, Westerns were among the most popular of television shows. Some of the early favorites were *The Gene Autry Show*, which ran on ABC from 1950 through 1955; *Death Valley Days*, which NBC showed with Ronald Reagan as host in the mid- to late-1950s; *The Lone Ranger* (ABC, 1948–1961), with Clayton Moore; *Hopalong Cassidy* (1948–1952), with big-screen actor William Boyd; and *The Roy Rogers Show*, which NBC and then CBS featured from 1951 through 1964.

Of these early Westerns, *The Roy Rogers Show* was probably the most influential, featuring as it did the beloved singer/actor Roy Rogers, who was well known to audiences from his big screen appearances in such pictures as *Tumbling Tumbleweeds*, with Gene Autry, in 1935, and *King of the Cowboys* in 1943. Always nearby were his faithful golden palomino Trigger (later stuffed and put in his museum), his witless sidekick Gabby Hayes, and his affable wife Dale Evans. Rogers was a major cultural presence and representative for the West during the 1940s and 1950s, and served as a general goodwill ambassador for the region in a number of roles—as a singing member of the original Sons of the Pioneers, as a cowboy-actor (eventually replacing Gene Autry in popularity), and later as a shrewd businessman, involved in rodeos, horse-breeding, and a national chain of lucrative restaurants. When he died in 1995 his personal fortune was estimated to be in excess of a hundred million dollars.

During the late 1950s and 1960s a number of Western television programs rose to prominence, most notably *Bonanza* (NBC, 1959–1973), which starred Lorne Greene and Michael Landon and aired right after dinner every Sunday night. Other important television Westerns of the period included *The Rifleman* (ABC, 1958–1962), with Chuck Connors; *Rawhide* (CBS, 1958–1966), with Clint Eastwood; *The Wild, Wild West* (CBS, 1965–1969), with Robert Conrad; *The Big Valley* (ABC, 1965–1969), with Lee Majors and Linda Evans; and *The High Chaparral* (NBC, 1967–1971), with Leif Erickson. Of these, *Rawhide* was particularly important because it gave audiences their first look at a gifted actor who would later become a dominant force in Western film (see Clint Eastwood essay in film section).

Hollywood interest in the television Western diminished in the 1970s and 1980s (which saw the rise of the situation comedy as an art form), although audiences remained faithful to the quality shows still presented. Michael Landon's *Little House on the Prairie* (NBC, 1974–1983) was based on the historical book series by Laura Ingalls Wilder that chronicled pioneer days on the western grasslands. The series was shot on location at Malibu Creek State Park near the actor/director's home. The show, with its simple Christian moralizing, was enormously successful (much to the chagrin of skeptical studio heads), and has entered a permanent second life in cable syndication. *Dallas*, which ran from 1977 through 1991, looked at the West and all of its familiar myths of wealth and abundance through the prism of a large, rambunctious oil-drilling family, the Ewings. Oil baron J. R. Ewing, played superbly by Larry Hagman, was a lovable villain in keeping with one of the oldest Western archetypes.

A case could be made that television Westerns were historically more influential, from a

Barkley family members Lee Majors (Heath), Peter Breck (Nick), Richard Long (Jarrad), Barbara Stanwyck (Victoria), and Linda Evans (Audra) from the hit TV-series THE BIG VALLEY, *(ABC, 1965–1969). Courtesy Photofest.*

mythmaking standpoint, than big-screen films. Most importantly, television Westerns were more easily and more frequently seen by national audiences than films. *Dallas*, for example, ran every Wednesday or Thursday night for fourteen years. Similarly, *The Roy Rogers Show* was seen every week for thirteen years. *Gunsmoke* ran for twenty years and Bonzana for fourteen. This gave audiences more of an opportunity to become exposed to Western mythology than if they viewed a ninety- or even a one-hundred-twenty-minute film such as *High Noon* or *Butch Cassidy and the Sundance Kid*. Even today, at the dawn of the twenty-first century, several outstanding Westerns can be seen each week on network and cable television, including *Walker, Texas Ranger* (CBS), *The Magnificent Seven* (TNN), and *The Call of the Wild* (Animal Planet channel). Many of the vintage programs—from *The Lone Ranger* to *The Real McCoys* (which starred three-time Oscar winner Walter Brennan)—are featured daily in cable syndication. Although the popularity of the mainstream Western has declined somewhat as the country has become more urbanized, there will always be a great romance between the small screen and the old frontier. It was in the Western landscapes that the mythic spirit of the country was found and forged, and television Westerns will always provide Americans with a visual recollection of their legendary past.

MARILYN MONROE
Innocence Betrayed

Marilyn Monroe's role as Roslyn Taber in THE MISFITS *(UA, 1961) was created for her by her third husband Arthur Miller. Courtesy Photofest.*

THE CAREER OF MARILYN Monroe as a Western mythmaker can be examined in a number of ways. We have, for example, the legendary dramatic performer, whose myriad roles created a popular image of beauty, warmth, humor, intelligence, and vulnerability. Over time Monroe came to embody all that is evoked by the word feminine. Surrounding the actress we have the major Western films themselves, including *River of No Return* (with Robert Mitchum, 1955), *Bus Stop* (with Don Murray, 1956), and most importantly, *The Misfits* (with Clark Gable, Montgomery Clift, and Eli Wallach, 1961). Together these Western films presented the actress as something more than just another dance-hall girl, or another lost soul on a cross-country bus, or another recently divorced woman in downtown Reno. Monroe was consciously portrayed, especially in *The Misfits*, as a metaphor for the Western landscape itself. Her voice was often allowed to rise up and become that of nature itself, with words and actions that spoke directly to the male world of brutality and violence.

The actress was born Norma Jean Baker in Los Angeles in 1926. Her mother worked as a negative cutter at RKO and her father has always been rumored to be a studio executive. Beset by mental illness, Monroe's mother, Gladys Pearl Baker, was institutionalized throughout the 1930s. As a result, her daughter's younger years were spent in various foster homes and orphanages, each worse than the last, in terms of abuse and neglect. Monroe married a factory worker at the age of sixteen. One year later she attempted to kill herself for the first time. Eventually she found a job as a paint sprayer at a defense factory. While there, she was photographed for a pinup calendar. The picture made her nationally famous and soon brought her to the attention of Hollywood moguls. Then divorced, Monroe was signed by 20th Century-Fox and provided with an array of acting, singing, and dancing lessons. There followed several years of anonymous toil in minor films, an essential though difficult transitional period during which the young woman developed her acting skills and made many friends among the influential leaders of Hollywood. By the early 1950s she had emerged as one of the major new stars on the West Coast. The rest of her career would see continued success, as well as a persistent and often public battle with mental illness.

The film of most interest in any consideration of Marilyn Monroe as a Western mythmaker is *The Misfits*. It was her third husband, the Pulitzer-prize winning writer Arthur Miller, who created this film specifically for his wife. (The couple divorced one week before the film came out.) The existential story focuses on four people who live in somewhat ghost-like fashion at the margins of a gambling town: Reno, Nevada. Their lives are unstable in every fundamental way,

and they struggle against grim odds to survive. At the center of the group is Marilyn Monroe, who plays a recently divorced woman. She has a radiant darkness about her, as well as a penchant for over-drinking. In love with her are three men. Eli Wallach plays a mechanic and part-time pilot who is still grieving over his dead wife. Montgomery Clift portrays a down-and-out rodeo cowboy looking for either a big sister or a surrogate mother. Clark Gable is cast as an over-the-hill rangeman who has been shattered by various tragic events (most notably the loss of his children in a divorce), but who is not yet ready to surrender to despair or cynicism (as is clearly the case with both the Montgomery Clift and Eli Wallach characters). Thelma Ritter is included as a comic foil to Monroe's angst.

Clark Gable as Gay Langland and Marilyn Monroe as Roslyn Taber in John Huston's THE MISFITS *(UA, 1961). Courtesy Photofest.*

In the early scenes of the film we follow Ritter and Monroe as the latter's divorce becomes final. The two—opposites in every way—wander aimlessly through town, looking to celebrate and winding up, in defeat, drinking alone at a table in Harrah's gambling casino. Gable's hound dog, Tom Dooley, walks over and befriends Monroe, and soon Gable and Wallach join them. From there the story moves rapidly away from the city and out to Wallach's home in the country. For the rest of the film the Great Basin Desert—miles and miles of sagebrush and prickly pear cactus—plays an important role in the narrative, eventually becoming a silent but pivotal character. "Do you have a home?" Marilyn Monroe asks Clark Gable in a telling scene. "Sure," he replies, pointing to the desert, "Right here." Similarly, the action focuses on these three misfit cowboys, each living in a failed, brutal world mostly of his own creation, and the woman who attempts—successfully in at least one case—to civilize them. Her voice is the gentle voice of nature itself.

"What makes you so sad?" asks Clark Gable of Marilyn Monroe at one point. "You're the saddest girl I've ever met." Part of Monroe's sadness, as the film develops out in the desert, comes from her observations of the men in their pathetic, Ahab-like quest to capture a herd of wild horses that will be sold for dog food. After using Wallach's airplane to drive the mustangs out onto a salt flat, Gable and Clift run the horses down with a truck, lasso them from the flatbed, and then tie them up. The key scene in the film occurs at this point, as Monroe, suffering a necessary but excruciating breakdown,

Marilyn Monroe was consciously portrayed, especially in THE MISFITS, *as a metaphor for the Western landscape itself.*

screams at the men: "Killers! Murderers! Liars! You're only happy when you see something die! Why don't you just kill yourselves? You and your God's Country! Your freedom! I hate you! You're three ... dear ... sweet ... dead ... men!"

Wallach comments under his breath that Monroe is "crazy," but both Clift and Gable are deeply touched by her words. Her soliloquy has given voice to the spirit of nature in the West itself—an abused, misunderstood, and unloved realm. As a result of her honest, uncensored outburst, two of the three cowboys (Wallach is unmoved) see the degeneracy of their ways. As in all great dramas, the central characters have all changed. Monroe has entered a new, wiser phase of her life. Gable has hit rock bottom and has no where to go but up. Clift realizes that his gentleness is not yet gone. The horses are released, and Gable and Monroe drive off into some sort of a strange future together, the Nevada night sky above spangled with bright stars.

Within eighteen months after this film's release, Clark Gable, Montgomery Clift, and Marilyn Monroe were dead. At Monroe's funeral, the actor Lee Strasberg summed up her life and career as follows: "Marilyn Monroe was a legend. In her own lifetime she created a myth of what a poor girl from a deprived background could attain." In films like *The Misfits* she also helped to create a mythic vision of the New West—a place where men caught horses not to ride but to sell to dog food factories and where gambling casinos preyed heartlessly upon people's addictions, and yet still a place where the human soul was capable of regeneration and love.

CLINT EASTWOOD
The Pursuit of Justice

SINCE THE BEGINNING, the west has been perceived, and portrayed, as a wild region outside the boundaries of civil society, an unsettled territory largely beyond the pale of official courts and conventional tribunals. As John Wayne observed in *Chisum* (1970): "There's no law west of the Pecos, no God west of the Rio Grande." Films have often been used by Western mythmakers, in this context, to explore the nature of good and evil, the boundaries of justice and injustice, and the cycles of revenge and violence. Many of these law-and-order pictures have focused on the decades after the Civil War, a time when the Western territories had yet to achieve statehood. It was in this forty- or fifty-year period, before the familiar comforts and quiet boredom of civilization arrived, that the West was the fabled domain of outlaws and vigilantes, cattle thieves and desperadoes, con men and bank robbers, Texas rangers and territorial marshals, frontier sheriffs and hanging judges. The landscape was awash in all manner of criminals—many who had fled West to escape the law—and these individuals engaged in more or less constant battle with the ever-vigilant (but often ineffective) forces of justice. It was during these years that the only law was often found at the end of a revolver or a rifle, and more than one destructive crime spree ended quietly on the far side of the farthest hill.

Early Western films tended to deal with this period in flat and one-dimensional ways, with comic-book-like characters that were more superficial caricatures than believable human beings. One thinks of the many popular Gene Autry films, which emphasized the necessity of virtue in a monochromatic world of good and bad, or the early shoot-'em up movies of

> There's no law west of the Pecos, no God west of the Rio Grande.
>
> —*John Wayne*
> CHISUM *(1970)*

Clint Eastwood directs and portrays retired gunslinger William Munny on one last job in UNFORGIVEN *(Warner Bros., 1992). Courtesy Photofest.*

John Wayne, which were as unimaginative as they were sentimental. Gradually, as the law-and-order Western matured, a new moral ambiguity and heightened aesthetic sensibility was introduced to the form. This artistic—one might even say, Shakespearean—gravity was first seen in the later frontier films of John Ford, especially *My Darling Clementine* (1946) and *The Man Who Shot Liberty Valance* (1962). It was left to the actor/director Clint Eastwood, though, to truly master this important Western film genre.

Clint Eastwood was born in Los Angeles in the spring of 1930, just as the Great Depression brought uncertainty and poverty to the country. His early years were spent with his single-parent father, who worked as a mechanic at gas stations along the West Coast. After graduating from high school, Eastwood worked in Los Angeles at various dead-end jobs and studied acting by night. By the late 1950s he had somehow risen from the ranks of mediocrity (with minor roles in such forgettable B-grade films as *Lady Godiva* [1955] and *The First Traveling Saleslady* [1956]) and won a part as Rowdy Yates in the TV Western series *Rawhide*. He subsequently secured leading roles in three "spaghetti Westerns" by Italian director Sergio Leone (*A Fistful of Dollars* [1967], *For a Few Dollars More* [1967], and *The Good, the Bad, and the Ugly* [1967]). From there, Eastwood emerged as one of the most gifted actor/directors in Hollywood, with one successful film after another: *Paint Your Wagon* (1969), *Two Mules for Sister Sara* (1969), *Joe Kidd* (1972), *High Plains Drifter* (1972), *The Outlaw Josie Wales* (1976), *Pale Rider* (1985). As critics and

scholars were solemnly proclaiming the Western a dead genre, Eastwood was laughing all the way to the bank with his successful creations. Believable characters, solid stories, and effective use of the landscape were all utilized by Eastwood, brilliantly at times, to create serious art in this often-maligned and misunderstood genre.

Clint Eastwood's mythical vision of the West, both as an actor and as a director, achieved its most complete realization in his 1992 film *Unforgiven*, which won Oscars for Best Picture, Best Director, and Best Supporting Actor (Gene Hackman). The film tells a simple revenge story, as a group of frontier prostitutes in Big Whiskey, Wyoming, seek justice against a pair of local cowboys who have grievously injured one of them, mutilating the woman's face with a knife because she made a joke about his manhood. Combining their savings, the women post a thousand-dollar reward for the man or men who will kill the two offenders. Word spreads across the territory and soon reaches the obscure cabin of William Munny, played by Clint Eastwood. Two years earlier (in 1878), Munny had lost his wife, Claudia, who had rescued him from a notorious life as a murderer and thief. Alone now with their two children, the former outlaw is struggling to make ends meet on a failing pig farm. He decides to make a try for the bounty and enlists the aid of an old friend and former gunslinger, played by Morgan Freeman. The two then set out for the sagebrush wilderness of Wyoming (the film was shot on location in Alberta), accompanied by an unstable young misfit who calls himself the Scofield Kid.

...he emerged as one of the most gifted actor/directors in Hollywood, with one successful film after another...

The town of Big Whiskey is run by a local bully who is also the sheriff—Little Bill, played by Gene Hackman. The sheriff is distraught when he learns the prostitutes have put up the bounty (they wouldn't have if he had done his job), because he understands all manner of hired guns will soon drift into town. The first to arrive is the legendary English Bob, played by Richard Harris. The sheriff publicly beats up English Bob and throws him in jail for possessing a firearm. English Bob is accompanied by his biographer, W. W. Beauchamp, who has also composed a number of ten-cent novels. Beauchamp soon develops a parasitic relationship with the sheriff and begins taking notes for the sheriff's biography. By including this character, Eastwood is making an important statement about the mythologizing of the West. One can see, in the stories that the sheriff tells Beauchamp, and Beauchamp's eagerness to exaggerate and embellish them, how easily myths are built upon ordinary facts.

Part of the reason *Unforgiven* succeeded as a Western before modern audiences is that Eastwood portrayed William Munny as such an ambiguous, complex character: Munny is a man who repeatedly falls off his horse, who develops a bad chill in the rain and becomes feverish, and who is constantly plagued by self-doubt, fear, and misgivings. In the end the offending cowboys are both killed—one shot while working cattle on the range and the other executed while using an outhouse. Shortly after, the sheriff captures Ned, the Morgan Freeman character,

and tortures him to death. In retaliation, Munny rides into town, confronts the sheriff and kills him and his three deputies, as well as the owner of the bordello (for having allowed Ned's body to be publicly displayed outside his front door). As he rides out of town in the rain Munny shouts defiantly to anyone who can hear: "You better bury Ned right and not cut up or otherwise harm no whores, or I'll come back and kill every one of you sons of bitches."

In an unexpected and paradoxical way, the outlaw in *Unforgiven* has become the civilizing force, bringing justice to the frontier community when the corrupt sheriff was incapable of rendering it himself. In a note at the end of the film, we learn that outlaw William Munny, too, has been changed by this violent experience—he later moves his two young children to San Francisco, where, we are told, he prospers in dry goods. In the modern world, personal justice is often difficult to find. Eastwood's films offer viewers a chance to achieve a vicarious victory over their enemies, as they watch their beloved hero—however sinned against and humiliated—triumph against his enemies. "Revenge," according to the old proverb writer Jim Harrison is so fond of quoting, "is a dish best served up cold." Eastwood, at this writing, is the preeminent Western actor/director of the age. As a cinematic mythmaker, he has few equals—one thinks only of John Ford and John Wayne. If *Unforgiven* is to be Eastwood's final western, it will secure his reputation as one of the most visionary and successful mythmakers in the history of the American West.

You better bury Ned right and not cut up or otherwise harm no whores, or I'll come back and kill every one of you sons of bitches.

—*Clint Eastwood*
UNFORGIVEN *(1992)*

ROBERT REDFORD
Heroes and Anti-Heroes

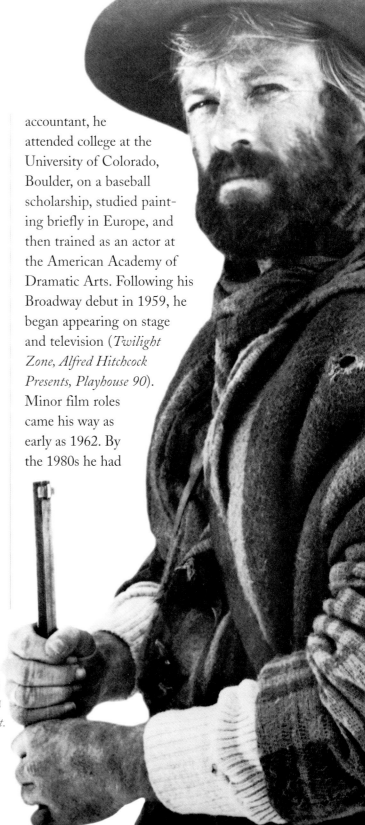

THE WRITING CAREER OF NORMAN MACLEAN and the moviemaking career of Robert Redford converged in the creation of the 1990 film *A River Runs Through It*. The picture, like the novella, tells a story set in the Far West in the years during and after World War I. This was a time when something of the old mythos still lingered about the landscape and in the lives of the people, but when such developments as electricity and automobiles were intruding on what remained of the frontier. There were still people around who could catch a trout as thick as your arm in a river close to town; or play cards with miners and bar girls all night and then go to church in the morning; or commit a murder to settle a bad debt and quietly cover it up. That Redford—whose life has been devoted to exploring the old and new myths of the West—was attracted to this slim, 104-page story is not surprising. That he made such a successful film from that book is a tribute to his genius as a cinematic storyteller and as a Western mythmaker.

When Redford came to this film in 1990 he was fifty-three years old and a respected member of the film community. After growing up in Santa Monica, California, the son of an accountant, he attended college at the University of Colorado, Boulder, on a baseball scholarship, studied painting briefly in Europe, and then trained as an actor at the American Academy of Dramatic Arts. Following his Broadway debut in 1959, he began appearing on stage and television (*Twilight Zone, Alfred Hitchcock Presents, Playhouse 90*). Minor film roles came his way as early as 1962. By the 1980s he had

Robert Redford as mountain man Jeremiah Johnson in Sydney Pollack's JEREMIAH JOHNSON *(Warner Bros., 1972). Courtesy Photofest.*

achieved international celebrity status as one of the finest Western actors of his generation, in films as diverse as *Downhill Racer* (1969), *Butch Cassidy and the Sundance Kid* (1969), *Jeremiah Johnson* (1972), and *The Electric Horseman* (1979). He was also widely respected as a director of unusual skill for his Academy award–winning *Ordinary People* in 1980. Additionally, Redford's annual Sundance Film Festival in Utah provided an important venue for alternative filmmakers around the country and the world.

Norman Maclean led a very different sort of life—as uneventful and private as Redford's has been action-filled and public. Born in 1902, Maclean's childhood and youth were spent in Missoula, Montana, where he was one of two sons of a minister. In 1924 he received a degree in English from Dartmouth College. Sixteen years later, at the age of thirty-eight, he was awarded a Ph.D. in English from the University of Chicago. Maclean taught there until his retirement in 1973, living the quiet, owlish, cloistered life of an English professor. It was only in retirement, when he was in his early seventies, that he set out to write down some stories from his youth in Montana. That book—*A River Runs Through It and Other Stories* (1976)—was nominated for a Pulitzer Prize and has gone on to sell over a half-million copies. It is now regarded as one of the classic works of literature from the twentieth-century West. Maclean died in 1990, shortly before filming of his book began.

There are always difficulties in bringing a novel to the screen. In the case of *A River Runs Through It*, which is actually a novella, the challenges were formidable. Redford has summed up the situation he faced as a director as follows: "The story is slight and relies heavily on Norman's voice as narrator. It is a maddeningly elusive piece, dancing away from the reader like the boxer Norman had once been, coming in fast to whack you between the eyes with the beauty of its language, or in the solar plexus with the depth of its emotion." In fact, more than half of the story consists of descriptive passages, including some fascinating but cinematically useless digressions into the art and science of fly-fishing. At the core of the story is a family living in Missoula: a stern Presbyterian minister, his emotionally withdrawn wife, and two young brothers on the verge of leaving late adolescence and entering manhood. Redford decided that the relationship between the two brothers—one of whom is destined for success and the other for early death—would be at the core of the film.

What is most compelling about this film, in terms of Western mythology, is its detailed exploration of an archetypal Western family. From the beginning, the mythic family has been the basic building block of the American West. Its relationship to the region has been as that of the carbon molecule to the diamond. In this sense, the Maclean family of Missoula, Montana (the novella is an adaptation of real events in Norman Maclean's youth), is a metaphor for all families in the West. We peer closely into the lives of the four Macleans, and in so doing we look, more broadly, into human society across the landscape of the region. In the fragment is seen all of the pathos and travail, all of the happiness and good fortune, all of the flaws and perfection, of the whole. Behind the story, behind the people, is the magnificent scenery of western Montana—aspen-covered mountains, soaring snow-covered peaks, and quiet rivers that move in deep channels among the cottonwoods and alders.

The film ends, as the novella does, with a movingly beautiful evocation of the past, and of all the happy myths—lost youth, unmarred innocence, hopeful dreams—that we associate with our personal and regional past: "Eventually, all things merge into one, and a river runs through it. The river was cut by the world's great flood and runs over rocks from the basement of time. On some of the rocks are timeless raindrops. Under the rocks are the words. And some of the words are theirs. I am haunted by waters."

Eventually, all things merge into one, and a river runs through it. The river was cut by the world's great flood and runs over rocks from the basement of time.

—*Norman Maclean*
A RIVER RUNS THROUGH IT (*1990*)

Craig Sheffer (Norman Maclean), Brad Pitt (Paul Maclean), and Tom Skerritt (Reverand Maclean) in Robert Redford's A RIVER RUNS THROUGH IT *(Columbia, 1992). Courtesy Photofest.*

KEVIN COSTNER
Requiem for the Past

IN HIS INTRODUCTION to the screenplay for *Dances With Wolves*, Kevin Costner wrote about his relationship with Michael Blake, the novelist upon whose story the film is based. What most attracted him to the script, Costner observed, was that Blake had "created a story that embraced a culture that has traditionally been misrepresented, both historically and cinematically." Blake himself observed that it was Dee Brown's influential history of the Native American in the American West, *Bury My Heart at Wounded Knee*, that inspired him to write his novel—to tell, for once, a story of the Old Frontier from a non-Euroamerican point of view. Both Blake and Costner were committed to creating a film that not only had compelling characters and an action-filled story line, but that also achieved some measure of fidelity to the time, place, and people it portrayed. Costner writes, "[*Dances With Wolves*] wasn't made to manipulate [the audience's] feelings, to reinvent the past, or to set the historical record straight. It's a ... look at a terrible time in our history, when expansion in the name of progress brought us very little and, in fact, cost us deeply."

Costner (who both directed and starred in the film) wanted to show audiences the real Old West, as opposed to the mythic West.

Kevin Costner both directed and starred in DANCES WITH WOLVES *(Orion, 1990). Courtesy Photofest.*

[Dances With Wolves] *wasn't made to manipulate [the audience's] feelings, to reinvent the past, or to set the historical record straight. It's a ... look at a terrible time in our history, when expansion in the name of progress brought us very little and, in fact, cost us deeply.*

—Kevin Costner

The truth is that the frontier West was a complex landscape, and that for every Iliad-like event such as the Battle of the Little Bighorn, there were a hundred more stories involving common people in everyday events that were inherently just as fascinating.

Instead of the heroic exploits of Custer and Crazy Horse, the film explores the lives of ordinary people: a sensitive young Army veteran from the Civil War suffering from post-traumatic stress syndrome, a visionary Indian leader who realizes he needs a trusted friend among the whites, an emotionally scarred woman who had been captured by the Pawnee as a child and who has been since cared for by the Sioux. From start to finish, the prairie landscape of the Dakotas is featured as a strong presence, almost a major unspoken character, in the story. (Some of the scenes were shot against the magnificent backdrop of the Badlands.) *Dances With Wolves* is one of the few Westerns ever made that is authentic in terms of setting (it was filmed on public, private, and Sioux land around the Black Hills), language (the Lakota dialect is often spoken, with English subtitles added), and dress (among others, paintings by Karl Bodmer and George Catlin were studied for accuracy). One can believe this is the Dakota Territory in 1863, when the buffalo still roamed at will over the prairie and the Sioux had yet to experience the post–Civil War migration across their historic homeland.

The film begins on a Civil War battlefield, a scene shot in South Dakota using orange paint so that the summer cottonwoods would evoke an eastern autumn. A young Union lieutenant, John J. Dunbar, has learned that his injured foot is to be amputated. When the doctors are not looking he slips out of the hospital tent, mounts a horse, and gallops toward the Confederate line, clearly intending that the enemy soldiers end his life for him. Instead, his actions rally the Union troops, who overrun the rebel position. The three-star general in command then intercedes and insists that Dunbar's foot be saved. As a further gift, he offers Dunbar a posting anywhere he chooses. Dunbar asks to be billeted on the Western frontier, and that he be permitted to take his cherished buckskin horse, Cisco.

The narrative then moves to the far Dakotas, where Dunbar finds himself stationed at "Fort Sedgewick," a ten-by-eight sod house with a six-foot ceiling in the middle of nowhere. Elated at his isolation, Dunbar writes in his journal: "The country is everything I dreamed it would be. There can be no place like this on earth." He has escaped the crowded East, with its allegorical war, and has found a lovely Western sanctuary, the isolation of which evokes both the Eden of the past and some utopian landscape of the future. Over the course of the summer, Dunbar settles into a quiet Robinson Crusoe existence, befriending a wolf (which he names Two Socks) and learning about life on the grasslands. Eventually he meets a Sioux medicine man of the Ten Bears band named Kicking Bird (played by Graham Greene).

The rest of the film focuses upon the complex relationships that grow between Dunbar and the Ten Bears band. Although he is at first an object of disgust and ridicule, Dunbar over time wins the acceptance, respect, and eventually love of the Sioux. He lets them know when the buffalo migration begins, and they later save his life when he is recaptured by federal troops. He falls in love with the woman Stands With A Fist (played superbly by Mary McDonnell) and becomes a member of the Ten Bears band, who give him a Lakota name that means Dances With Wolves. He helps to defend the Sioux village when a band of marauding Pawnee mounts an attack. In the end, Dunbar realizes he must leave the Sioux because his presence will draw increasing attention to them. Before he departs, his friend Kicking Bird says to him: "I was just thinking that of all the trails in this life, there is one that matters more than all the others. It is the trail of a true human being. I think you are on this trail, and it is good to see."

Dances With Wolves went on to win seven Oscars, including awards for Best Picture and Best Director. No Western film has ever been so acclaimed by the Academy of Motion Pictures. The enduring popularity of the film attests to the fascination the world has with this period of Western American history, especially if cultural stereotypes, one-dimensional characters, and empty myths are dispensed with. The truth is that the frontier West was a complex landscape, and that for every Iliad-like event such as the Battle of the Little Bighorn, there were a hundred more stories involving common people in everyday events that were inherently just as fascinating. *Dances With Wolves* celebrates that "other" mythic West, the quieter, more expansive landscape that is often overlooked as people—artists, writers, filmmakers—rush to immortalize the epic monuments.

Mark Twain's ROUGHING IT *was one of the first serious literary treatments of the West. Courtesy Photofest.*

THE LIGHT OF THE WESTERN STARS

The Western Writer as Fabulist

WALLACE STEGNER ONCE DESCRIBED THE AMERICAN WEST as "the geography of hope." He wrote: "We simply need that wild country available to us, even if we never do more than drive to its edge and look in." Since the beginning, the mythic West has been seen, much as Stegner suggests, as the landscape of hope and regeneration, challenge and adventure, inspiration and understanding. For centuries now there have been writers who have tried to sort out the region for themselves and their readers, to consciously advance certain myths, as Zane Grey did in his romantic Southwestern novels, or to methodically debunk certain other myths, as Captain Bourke tried to do in his dusty journal of life along the border with the famous (or infamous) General Crook. Some of the myths have been lies masquerading as truths. The myth of how great it was on the Old Frontier would fall into that category (Geronimo's autobiography, or Jason Betzinez's memoir of life with Geronimo, provide corrective reminders). Other myths have been truths based on lies—that, for example, Major Reno really did make an effort to save General Custer's command (when the truth was that, not being insane, he only wanted to save the lives of his men).

Some Western writers have become legends themselves. One thinks of Everett Ruess, friend of Edward Weston, Maynard Dixon, and Dorothea Lange. Ruess disappeared from the face of the earth one day on the lower Escalante in southern Utah, an area later explored by Edward Abbey, John Nichols, and other literary disciples. Or of Ernest Hemingway, who took complete leave of his senses one dark morning in Sun Valley, Idaho. Or of Theodore Roosevelt, who told some sort of a fairy tale about beating up a bully in a saloon in the Dakota Territory for so long he actually believed it was true. Or of the enduring Margaret Murie, still residing, as these lines are written, at the age of ninety-eight

Custer's book MY LIFE ON THE PRAIRIES *helped to shape eastern views of the West. Photo by Klaus Kranz.*

in her antique cabin in Moose, Wyoming. Or of the colorful journalist Hunter S. Thompson, living in Aspen, Colorado, as much a self-made Western legend as his former songwriting neighbor John Denver.

As mythmakers, the writers of the American West fall naturally into the three cultural periods that describe the history of virtually any frontier on Earth, from the European annexation of wild Africa, to the Russian advance into the hinterlands of Siberia, to the British appropriation of the Australian subcontinent. In the precolonial era we have the first official government surveys. Although striving to be empiricists—to factually note and catalogue without analysis—these earlier writers were still human beings, and the myth-making urge can not be completely suppressed. Thus we have Lewis and Clark excitedly describing the Upper Missouri country in a language of abundance

that evokes the Book of Genesis—i.e., the American West as a fertile Eden waiting to be re-entered. Lewis observes that the "beaver are very abundant" and that "the bald eagles are more abundant here than I ever observed them in any part of the country." We read of "great quantities of game: buffalo, elk, and antelopes feeding in every direction" and that Lewis and Clark "kill whatever we wish." The "country is, as yesterday, beautiful in the extreme." Although accurate reportage, these journals are also first-rate mythmaking, the sort of discourse that went on to incite a generation of young men to paddle up the Missouri and become another sort of myth: mountain men.

The colonial era in the American West, more commonly known as the age of Manifest Destiny, was a noisy, chaotic, and ultimately violent period in which one culture, the Euroamericans, seized a vast territory from another culture, the Native Americans. During this time, many of the great myths of the West were born, and lovingly nurtured, by several generations of writers. Chief among them was Theodore Roosevelt, a twenty-five-year-old New Yorker, who came out to the Dakota Territories in 1883, purchased a cattle ranch on the Little Missouri River with his

The works of Zane Grey and Luke Short were popularized in comic books for decades in the twentieth century. Photo by Klaus Kranz.

inheritance, and then endeavored to live out his dream of being a frontier cowboy. Along the way he wrote several books, all of which exalted the heroic cowboy myth that Frederic Remington and Charles Russell were, at the same time, busily painting into history. Roosevelt's word pictures would perform a similar mythic function:

For over an hour we [cowboys] steadily rode around the herd, saying nothing, with our greatcoats buttoned, for the air was chill toward morning on the northern plains, even in the summer. Then faint streaks of gray appeared in the east. A coyote came sneaking over the butte nearby and halted to sing. The dawn brightened rapidly; the little skylarks of the plains began to sing, soaring far overhead, while it was still much too dark to see them. Their song is not powerful, but it is so clear and fresh and long-continued that it always appeals to one very strongly; especially because it is most often heard in the rose-tinted air of the glorious mornings, while the listener sits in the saddle, looking across the endless sweep of the prairies.

A romantic image of a mythic age, to be sure, but also one that is bittersweet when all the other historical facts—the unconscionable

massacre of the buffalo herds, the wholesale loss of the open range, the tragic demise of the Plains Indians—are taken into consideration.

In the modern age (the postcolonial period to historians) the American West has been revisited and reinterpreted by several generations of writers. One group has looked backward into the myths of the past. Among these were Nebraskan Mari Sandoz, who wrote two powerful novels—*Crazy Horse* and *Cheyenne Autumn*—about the Plains Indians, and Montanan A. B. Guthrie, who wrote two classic novels—*The Big Sky* and *The Way West*—about the mountain men and the Oregon Trail homesteaders, respectively. A second group of writers has turned their attention to the present, attempting to create a new mythic West. John Nichol's satiric *Milagro Beanfield War,* for example, tells the story of a conflict between indigenous Hispanic people and Anglo developers in northern New Mexico,

A romantic image of a mythic age, to be sure, but also one that is bittersweet when all other historical facts are taken into consideration.

and lampoons all the damage that unbridled human greed can inflict upon a landscape. Edward Abbey's *The Monkey Wrench Gang* presents readers with a mythic group of ecoterrorists determined to return Major Powell's Glen Canyon to its wild and pristine past (before the dam). Larry McMurtry probes the collision of traditional Western values and modern Western values in his novel about a Texas ranching family, *Horseman, Pass By.* Other novels by McMurtry similarly explore the rich territory of the present as a natural landscape of legend and fable.

The epigraph for this section is from Jim Harrison's *Legends of the Fall,* which relates—in great mythic Western tradition—the story of a Montana ranching family that never existed in a place that really does exist, the lovely Rocky Mountain Front. A father and three sons make

their way through the early twentieth century, and the reader follows intently, for the Ludlows are poised on the cusp of the last bit of the wild frontier, as the modern world, with all of its impatience and superficiality, is being born. By the end of the novella, the old has been exchanged for the new, but the Western landscape, and the tough souls who live upon it, still endure. Contemporary writers like Nichols, Abbey, McMurtry, and Harrison, as much as the first pioneering writers, understand that people need the refuge of the imagination, the sanctuary of stories, and the comfort of myths. To use a country metaphor, the myths these Western writers provide are like the wad of cheese the veterinarian puts around the antibiotic pill, to make it easier for the hound to absorb the bitter medicine that is the truth.

LEWIS AND CLARK
Paradise Found

THANK GOD FOR NAPOLEON. Were it not for his inept governance, the United States never would have had the opportunity to buy an area larger than England, Scotland, Ireland, France, Spain, and Portugal combined for the total sum of fifteen million dollars. In the age of Thomas Jefferson that vast region—the windswept, buffalo-filled heart of the American West— was about as well known as the surface of some moon circling Neptune is today. Of the Missouri country there were vague and often inaccurate maps, drunken anecdotes from sun-darkened *coureur du bois*, dusty wolf skulls and exotic Indian

artifacts, and all manner of earnest speculation, but for the most part the immense prairie and mountain region drained by the Missouri River, the Platte River, and the Arkansas River was *terra incognita.*

Into this wilderness President Thomas Jefferson dispatched the Neil Armstrong and Buzz Aldrin of their time—Captains William Clark and Meriwether Lewis. Their two-year mission of discovery was to proceed up the Missouri River, cross the Rocky Mountains, somehow reach the Pacific Ocean, and then retrace the route. What they returned with from the back of that vast and often dangerous beyond—detailed maps, daily accounts, accurate drawings, catalogued specimens, fresh impressions—would forever change the world. Paradise had been found, and it could be entered about one hundred miles upriver from the century-old French colony of St. Louis. What followed was the short-lived age of the trappers and mountain men (Jim Bridger, Kit Carson, and company). Thereafter would come the railroads, then the buffalo hunters and the cattlemen, and finally the homesteading farmers who would, in time, raise enough crops to feed the entire nation. The American West was, based on the expedition journals, Eden, Utopia, Arcady, Elysium, and Atlantis all wrapped up in one—a mythic land of plenty where the sweet grass grew stirrup deep and the views went on forever.

In looking back over the distance of nearly two hundred years, what most stands out in the journals of Lewis and Clark are the moving portraits of pristine landscapes and the almost unbelievable descriptions of natural abundance. Truly, Clark and Lewis present the reader with a lively vision, or perhaps more accurately, a literary version, of the Promised Land. On Monday, June 3, 1805, for example, Captain Meriwether Lewis recorded the following observation in what is today eastern Montana:

Between the time of my A.M. and meridian [observations] Capt. C. & myself stroled out to the top of the hights in the forks of these rivers from whence we had an extensive and most inchanting view; the country in every derection around us was one vast plain in which innumerable herds of Buffalow were seen attended by their shepperds the wolves; the solatary antelope which now had their young were distributed over it's face; some herds of Elk were also seen; the verdure perfectly cloathed the ground, the weather was pleasant and fair;

Harvard historian Bernard DeVoto's edition of THE JOURNALS OF LEWIS AND CLARK *reignited interest in the fabled mission of discovery. Photo by Klaus Kranz.*

to the South we saw a range of lofty mountains...behind these Mountains and at a great distance, a second and more lofty range of mountains appeared to stretch across the country in the same direction with the others...this last range was perfectly covered with snow.

A person would today have to journey to the remotest regions of northern Alaska—the Brooks Range and adjacent Arctic Coastal Plain—to find anything resembling the contents of this word picture (garbled as it is by Lewis's phonetic spelling).

Anyone interested in the American West as a mythic region should begin their studies with a reading of the Lewis and Clark journals.

Everything is there—the Pawnee and Sioux, Arikara and Mandan, the untiring Sacajawea, the salt-of-the-earth Charbonneau, the determined Lewis, the ebullient Clark, the mysteries of the Yellowstone region, the fights with grizzly bears (Lewis at one point saving himself only by swimming out into the Missouri River), the toothaches and dysentery, the first view of the Pacific Ocean, the long journey back to what they called, for lack of a better word, civilization. When one considers all that followed— the violence and devastation that accompanied the myth of Manifest Destiny—one is tempted to recall the line from Mark Twain: "It was wonderful to find America, but it would have been more wonderful to miss it."

WASHINGTON IRVING AND FRANCIS PARKMAN
The Birth of the Literary West

FOR HALF A CENTURY after the expedition of Lewis and Clark, a myriad of quasi-serious explorers, unabashed adventurers, would-be fur trappers, trophy hunters, idle curiosity-seekers, wide-eyed city dudes, proto-ethnographers, restless artists, and ambitious writers journeyed out to the American West to have a look around and report back to their friends and readers in the East on what they had seen and experienced. Quite often, these chronicles took the form of nonfiction (with some measure of fiction), a genre that scholars now generally categorize as the western adventure narrative. In these works we can see many of the later myths of the American West begin to take on a recognizable shape and form: that Native Americans led a life free of all the formalities and inhibitions of civilization; that the Western landscape offered a vision of how the world was once, and how it should be again; and that the destiny of the nation lay in the political control and productive economic use of the West. That these central myths often conflict is only to express the paradox at the heart of the West—that Euroamericans were destroying the very thing they professed to love.

At the distance of nearly two centuries, two writers from this historic period stand out: Washington Irving, who visited what is today Oklahoma in 1832, and Francis Parkman, who traveled along the Oregon Trail in 1846. Both men were well educated and, by the standards of then or now, professional writers of considerable skill. Both produced myth-making books, which were widely read by serious readers back East—in other words, books that shaped public discourse and emerging views on the American West. (Parkman's book was favorably reviewed by none other than Herman Melville.) Neither were averse to exaggerating what they did and saw, as opposed to standing critically apart from events (as Helen Hunt Jackson would with respect to Native Americans in her later book *A Century of Dishonor*, or as Mark Twain would in his myth-debunking narrative *Roughing It*). And both men, finally, were quite obviously in love with the West and its nascent myths.

Washington Irving came to the subject of the frontier by a circuitous route. Released by his London publisher of long-standing in 1832, Irving dejectedly decided to return to that sleepy backwater of world culture, the United States. He was forty-nine and had not a clue as to his future. While on the voyage back to the New World he befriended two Europeans who were intent on exploring the Western frontier. Irving agreed to go along:

The offer was too tempting to be resisted: I should have an opportunity of seeing the remnants of those great Indian tribes that are now about to disappear as independent nations, or to be amalgamated under some new form of government. I should see those fine countries of the 'far west,' while still in a state of pristine wilderness, and behold herds of buffaloes scouring their native prairies, before they are driven beyond the reach of a civilized tourist.

The rest, as they say, is history. The journey was a success both personally and professionally, as the subsequent book—*A Tour on the Prairies* (1835)—revived Irving's stale writing career. What most stands out in Irving's book are the lyric descriptions of the wilderness, as he consciously worked within the myth of the West as a natural Eden:

The broad sandy shore where we had landed was intersected by innumerable tracks of elk, deer, bears, raccoons, turkeys, and water-fowl. The river scenery at this place was beautifully diversified, presenting long shining reaches, bordered by willows and cottonwood trees, and rich bottoms, with lofty forests among which towered enormous plane trees. The foliage had a yellow autumnal tint, which gave to the sunny landscape the

Washington Irving as seen in a daguerreotype said to be taken by Mathew Brady. Courtesy Photofest.

golden tone of one of the landscapes of Claude Lorraine [a noted French artist of the time].

Elsewhere Irving offered one of the first literary descriptions of the wide open spaces:

After a toilsome march of some distance through a country cut up by ravines and brooks, and entangled by thickets, we emerged upon a grand prairie. Here one of the characteristic scenes of the Far West broke upon us: an immense extent of grassy [and] rolling country with here and there a clump of trees, dimly seen in the distance like a ship at sea, the landscape deriving sublimity from its vastness and simplicity.

Francis Parkman's THE OREGON TRAIL *and Washington Irving's* A TOUR ON THE PRAIRIES *captured the authors' love for the West and its myths. Photo by Klaus Kranz.*

In passages like this, one can see how much the author of "The Legend of Sleepy Hollow" had been transformed by the landscape of the American West. If the collective mind of a country can be compared to the mind of an individual person, one can detect here a new perspective emerging—as well as a new mythology—as the nation struggled to incorporate an unfamiliar geographic and spiritual territory into its consciousness.

Francis Parkman was half Irving's age—twenty-three—when he journeyed out from Boston to experience the Oregon Trail. A graduate of Harvard Law School, a direct descendent of the esteemed Puritan minister John Cotton, and the son of a prominent Unitarian minister, Parkman was as well prepared as anyone of his time to provide a lucid account of the Western frontier. In fact, his book *The Oregon Trail* (1849) remains one of the most accurate written impressions we have of this exciting, rapidly changing period in Western history. Parkman was fascinated by the wilderness and, as an historian, saw it as the key to understanding both America and the West. Yet even as he celebrated its beauty and freedom, he saw its demise:

Great changes are at hand in that region. With the stream of emigration to Oregon and California, the buffalo will dwindle away, and the large wandering communities who depend on them for support must be broken and scattered. The Indians will soon be corrupted by the example of the whites, abased by whisky and overawed by military posts; so that within a few years the traveler may pass in tolerable security through their country. Its danger and its charm will have disappeared together.

This same observation would be echoed later in the ranching narratives of Theodore Roosevelt, the wilderness essays of John Muir, and the Monument Valley films of John Ford.

What most stands out in Parkman's lively narrative are the careful, almost photographically detailed word pictures, as in this picture of heavy furniture—symbolic of the European/East Coast–based civilization—left beside the Oregon Trail:

[I saw] the shattered wrecks of ancient claw-footed tables, well waxed and rubbed, or massive bureaus of carved oak. These, some of them no doubt the relics of ancestral prosperity in the colonial time, must have encountered strange vicissitudes. Brought, perhaps, originally, from England; then, with the declining fortunes of their owners, borne across the Alleghenies to the wilderness of Ohio or Kentucky; then to Illinois or Missouri, and now at last fondly stowed away in the family wagon for the interminable journey to Oregon. But the stern privations of the way are little anticipated. The cherished relic is soon flung out to scorch and crack upon the hot prairie.

What these pilgrims also left behind—as these images starkly convey—was any notion of the past. The frontier was the metaphoric and mythic landscape of the future, and all the baggage of the past had to be left behind. One had to travel light and fast, or else be bound to the Earth and all of the perils that shadowed the slow-footed.

Both Irving and Parkman were self-conscious Adamic mythmakers. They, like the Adam of old, had been inside the gates of Eden, had known the natural gardens of plenty, and had returned to tell their readers that paradise did exist, or rather, *had* existed, but was now a thing of the past, fading as quickly as a wild rose picked before the eyes. The explorer's frontier had become the trapper's frontier had become the Oregon emigrant's frontier—each succeeding the other with a new agenda and a new mythology. In the words of their contemporary, Walt Whitman:

> All the past we leave
> behind, We debouch upon a newer, mightier
> world, varied world,
> Fresh and strong the world we seize, world
> of labor and the march
> Pioneers! o pioneers!

Both Francis Parkman and Washington Irving reported hunting for elk, buffalo, and deer during their western trips.

Parkman was fascinated by the wilderness and, as an historian, saw it as the key to understanding both America and the West. Yet even as he celebrated its beauty and freedom, he saw its demise.

JOHN BOURKE, O.O. HOWARD, COCHISE, AND GERONIMO: *How it Was*

AMONG THOSE WHO FOUGHT in the Indian Wars, which ranged from minor skirmishes along the early Santa Fe Trail in the 1820s through the debacle at Wounded Knee in 1890, there are literally hundreds of accounts. Unfortunately, the vast majority of these chronicles are written in English by former U.S. officers, in keeping with the old axiom that history is written by the victors. These include books written by some of the West's most infamous figures—as with Lieutenant Colonel George Custer's *My Life on the Plains* (1874)—as well as those

composed by some of its rare humanitarians—as in General O. O. Howard's 1907 *My Life and Experiences Among Our Hostile Indians*. (Howard brokered Cochise's peace agreement with postman Tom Jeffords, a story later told in the 1950 movie *Broken Arrow*, with Jimmy Stewart as Jeffords.) In the former category, the vision of the West is nostalgic and elegiac, and the sentimental and often-exaggerated descriptions are aimed primarily at idealizing the actions of the author. In the latter, there is a genuine effort at truth-telling, at self-criticism, and at a sympathetic and knowledgeable portrait of the plight of the Native Americans.

Geronimo's life story is one of the great myths of the West. Born by his own account in the year 1829 (the exact date is probably incorrect) in southwestern New Mexico, he later became a medicine man, married, and fathered several children. His original name was Goyathlay, meaning "One Who Yawns." While still a young man, his family was massacred at Janos in northern Mexico, an event that proved life-changing. From that point forward, Geronimo was a determined and skillful enemy of the Mexicans, and later, the Americans. His subsequent exploits as a leader of the general

Apache resistance (roughly from 1861 through 1886) have been recounted in dozens of popular biographies and histories, as well as in several films (the most recent, *Geronimo: An American Legend*, starred Gene Hackman and Robert Duvall, was filmed near Moab, Utah, and was released in 1993).

The name Geronimo, probably an adaptation of "St. Jerome," was given to him after a particularly violent battle with the Mexicans. (When my father parachuted into battle during the Second World War he and the other airborne troops often shouted "Geronimo!" as they exited the plane—a tradition that continues in some airborne units today.) During his later years, Geronimo moved in and out of Southwestern reservations, finally surrendering at Skeleton Canyon in the southern Arizona Territory in 1886. Thereafter he was held at government bases in Florida and Oklahoma, although he was permitted to travel to various expositions and public events (pageants, parades, fairs). In one of the more curious events in U.S. history, Geronimo appeared as a guest in Theodore Roosevelt's inauguration parade. He died of pneumonia after riding his horse in a rainstorm on the Oklahoma reservation in 1909.

Unlike most Western Native American leaders, for whom we have no personal records, Geronimo provided posterity with his own version of his life. In *Geronimo, His Own Story,* which was dictated in 1905 to a transcriber, we learn about a far different Geronimo and Apache than are represented in history. Of his childhood in the 1830s Geronimo recounts:

In that country which lies around the headwaters of the Gila River I was reared. This range was our fatherland; among these mountains our wigwams were hidden; the scattered valleys contained our fields; the boundless prairies, stretching away on every side, were our pastures; the rocky caverns were our burying places. I was the fourth in

a family of eight children—four boys and four girls.... As a babe I rolled on the dirt floor of my father's teepee, hung in my tsoch at my mother's back, or suspended from the bough of a tree. I was warmed by the sun, rocked by the winds, and sheltered by the trees as other Indian babes. When [I was] a child my mother taught me the legends of our people; taught me of the sun and sky, the moon and stars, the clouds and

Geronimo was born in the canyon country of southwestern New Mexico. Courtesy John Murray.

storms. She also taught me to kneel and pray to Usen for strength, health, wisdom, and protection. We never prayed against any person, but if we had aught against any individual we ourselves took vengeance. We were taught that Usen does not care for the petty quarrels of men.... With my brothers and sisters I played about my father's home. Sometimes we played at hide-and-seek among the rocks and pines ... while our parents worked in the field.... When we were old enough to be of real service we went to the fields with our parents; not to play, but to toil. When the crops were to be planted we broke the ground with wooden hoes. We planted the corn in straight rows, the beans among the corn, and the melons and pumpkins in irregular order over the field. We cultivated these crops as there was need.

The picture that Geronimo paints of the Apache as a peace-loving people in their homeland is dramatically different from that perpetuated in the popular mythology. The Chiricahua Apache were—and we see this consistently throughout his myth-debunking account—like all normal people, most interested in nurturing their families and protecting their homeland. Of that landscape I have some personal experience—one of the first books I ever wrote was a

Jason Betzinez's I FOUGHT WITH GERONIMO *provides an alternative history to the military accounts of U. S. officers. Photo by Klaus Kranz.*

hiking guide to the Gila Wilderness in southwestern New Mexico, the area where Geronimo grew up. I have often camped at the confluence of the West Fork and the Middle Fork of the Gila River. Anyone who has spent any time in this beautiful canyon country—the vast ponderosa forests filled with elk, mule deer, black bear, and wild turkeys; the numerous hot springs along the rivers; the deep barrancas—understands why the Apache fought so tenaciously to repel the alien fur trappers, gold prospectors, copper miners, cattlemen, and settlers. It is evident in Geronimo's memoir (even with its occasional inaccuracies and embellishments) that the Apache were simply doing what all human beings have the right to do—defend their lives and their homeland.

Another reliable Apache source on the Indian Wars in the Southwest is Jason Betzinez's memoir *I Fought With Geronimo*. A cousin and lifelong associate of Geronimo, Betzinez served with Geronimo in the Apache resistance, was present during Geronimo's surrender in 1886, and later was held with him as a prisoner of war in Florida and Oklahoma. He also attended the Carlisle Indian School in Pennsylvania. When his memoir was published in 1959, the veteran warrior was nearly a century old and lived on a farm in Oklahoma with his family. Betzinez spoke bluntly of the white man's biased way of recording history:

> To the Indian it is a curious thing that white people accept as fact only that which is written on paper, whereas events retold by word of mouth, even if of greater importance, are disparaged as being mere folklore. For example, I have read that a slaughter of Apaches at Santa Rita del Cobre in 1837 and another at Janos twenty years later were notable occurrences in the history of my people. Actually these were only two of a series of treacherous attacks made upon us by whites or Mexicans. We have little remembrance of what happened at Santa Rita, and the affair at Janos is noted mainly because my cousin Geronimo's family was killed there, thus setting his hand against the Mexicans forever. So far as we are concerned the ghastly butchery of our families at Ramos and the terrific revenge raid which followed constitute the greatest and bloodiest conflict in which Apaches were ever involved. You will, nevertheless, search the libraries in vain for some mention of it. I believe I am here telling the story in public for the first time.

Of Geronimo the man (as opposed to the myth), Betzinez wrote:

> Though Geronimo was a great wartime leader, after he surrendered he lived at peace and never thereafter caused trouble. Much has been written about him, a great deal of it being exaggerated or completely false... He was [often] visited and interviewed by numerous white journalists, some of whom were far from accurate in writing up what he told them about his life. If they couldn't get enough fire and bloodshed out of his account, they used their lively imaginations. For example, one day I acted as interpreter for a writer who asked to see Geronimo's coat made of ninety-nine human scalps. On hearing his question Geronimo was speechless. He had no such coat. It never was his custom to scalp his fallen enemy. He didn't know what to say to this man. Finally he just turned and walked away.

One of the more accurate military accounts of the Apache Wars is provided by John Gregory Bourke, who served as a captain with General Crook in the Arizona Territory in the 1870s and 1880s. Bourke had some skill as an ethnologist (he later became president of the American

It is evident in Geronimo's memoir (even with its occasional inaccuracies and embellishments) that the Apache were simply doing what all human beings have the right to do—defend their lives and their homeland.

The simple factual story of the struggles of Geronimo and Cochise is, in the end, a legacy that is more powerful than any myth. With some lives there in no need for myth.

Folklore Society) and, trusted by the Indians, was often used as a liaison between the military and the Apache. His two books—*On the Border With Crook* (1891) and *An Apache Campaign in the Sierra Madre* (1883)—actively counter some of the popular mythology with regards to the Old Frontier. As a middle-level federal officer, Bourke was in a unique position to understand the overall situation of the Apache, which included corrupt Indian agents, hysterical local miners and ranchers, inept territorial officials, witless mayors and city councils, and ethically challenged journalists. Although he participated in many great events, much of his period of service was marked by—and this will be familiar to anyone who has ever served in uniform— monotony, boredom, and tedium, pretty much in that order. Bourke was not one to add to the sensational mythologizing of the West. He tried, rather, to introduce a measure of realism and sympathy to his subject. When the Apache sur-rendered to General Crook he recorded—no doubt surprising some readers of his time—that "It brought tears to the eyes of the stoutest vet-erans to witness this line of unfortunates [which included women and children], reminding us of our mothers, wives, sisters, and daughters. All possible kindness and attention were shown them."

Similarly, the memoir of General O. O. Howard, who later founded Howard University for African-Americans in Washington, D.C., is distinctive in its devotion to truth-telling and to a simple measure of humanity with respect to the Indians. Howard, who had lost an arm in the Civil War, was dispatched by President Grant to Arizona in 1872 to negotiate a final truce with Cochise, the last hereditary chief of the Chiricahua Apache. (Geronimo was a former medicine man turned warrior, but was not a chief.) The meeting took place at Cochise's Stronghold in the Dragoon Mountains (now part of the Coronado National Forest) near Willcox, Arizona. Although Howard had been instructed to persuade Cochise to move his tribe to a reservation, he had to abandon that proposal and give in to Cochise's wishes—that the reservation actually be his homeland.

Although we have no transcript of their talks, one does exist of an earlier meeting between Cochise and General Granger near Fort Craig, New Mexico. If true, it attests to the power, eloquence, and persuasiveness of Cochise as a public speaker:

I have come with my hands open to you to live in peace with you. I speak straight and do not wish to deceive or be deceived. I want a good, strong, and lasting peace. When God made the world he gave one part to the white man and another to the Apache. Why was that? Why did they come together? Now that I am to speak, the sun, the moon, the earth, the air, the waters, the birds and beasts, even the children unborn shall rejoice at my words. The white people have looked for me long. I am here!... When I was young I walked all over this country, east and west, and saw no other people than the Apaches. After many summers I walked again and

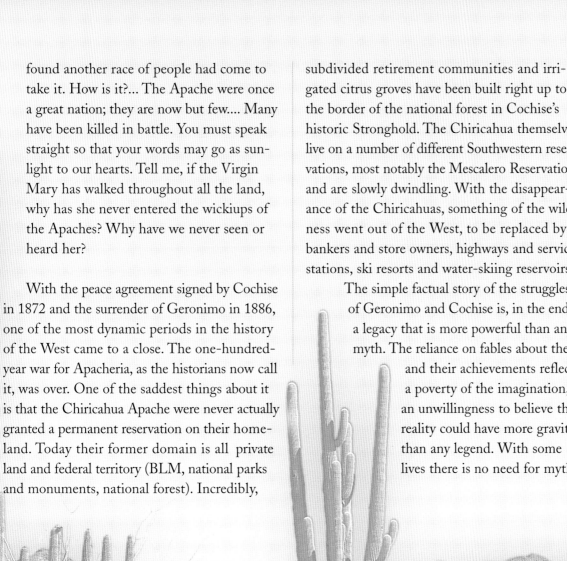

found another race of people had come to take it. How is it?... The Apache were once a great nation; they are now but few.... Many have been killed in battle. You must speak straight so that your words may go as sunlight to our hearts. Tell me, if the Virgin Mary has walked throughout all the land, why has she never entered the wickiups of the Apaches? Why have we never seen or heard her?

With the peace agreement signed by Cochise in 1872 and the surrender of Geronimo in 1886, one of the most dynamic periods in the history of the West came to a close. The one-hundred-year war for Apacheria, as the historians now call it, was over. One of the saddest things about it is that the Chiricahua Apache were never actually granted a permanent reservation on their homeland. Today their former domain is all private land and federal territory (BLM, national parks and monuments, national forest). Incredibly,

subdivided retirement communities and irrigated citrus groves have been built right up to the border of the national forest in Cochise's historic Stronghold. The Chiricahua themselves live on a number of different Southwestern reservations, most notably the Mescalero Reservation, and are slowly dwindling. With the disappearance of the Chiricahuas, something of the wildness went out of the West, to be replaced by bankers and store owners, highways and service stations, ski resorts and water-skiing reservoirs. The simple factual story of the struggles of Geronimo and Cochise is, in the end, a legacy that is more powerful than any myth. The reliance on fables about them and their achievements reflects a poverty of the imagination, an unwillingness to believe that reality could have more gravitas than any legend. With some lives there is no need for myth.

Apacheria ranged from Tucson and Tubac on the west to the Rio Grande on the east, from the Gila River country to the north, deep into Mexico on the south. Courtesy John Murray.

MARK TWAIN
The Comic West

WE JUMPED INTO THE STAGE, the driver cracked his whip, and we bowled away and left "the States" behind us. It was a superb summer morning, and all the landscape was brilliant with sunshine. There was a freshness and breeziness, too, and an exhilarating sense of emancipation from all sorts of cares and responsibilities, that almost made us feel that the years we had spent in the close hot city, toiling and slaving, had been wasted and thrown away. We were spinning along through Kansas, and in the course of an hour and a half we were fairly abroad on the great plains.

So writes Mark Twain at the start of his celebrated Western travel narrative, *Roughing It.* After two desultory weeks in the Confederate Army of 1861, the irrepressible young character then known to the world as Samuel Clemens had bought a stage ticket and lit out for the distant territory of Nevada, there to join his brother, recently appointed secretary to the provisional Governor.

Along the way, the future author of *Tom Sawyer* and *Huckleberry Finn* would lampoon everything from the frontier society of Nevada ("for a time the lawyer, the editor, the banker, the chief desperado, the chief gambler, and the saloonkeeper occupied the same level in society, and it was the highest") to the Mormon Bible ("it is 'smouched' from the Old Testament and no credit given"), from San Francisco before the fire ("It has only snowed twice in San Francisco in nineteen years, and then it only remained on the ground long enough to astonish the children") to Mono Lake ("the dead sea of California"), from sagebrush ("imagine a live oak tree reduced to a little shrub two feet high") to coyotes ("A living breathing allegory of *Want*. He is always poor, out of luck, and friendless"). Nothing was sacred to him and nothing would escape his barbed wit. Most especially, Twain would laugh at himself. Suffice it to say, the West would never be the same, nor would it ever see his like again.

Mark Twain was the first author of any literary weight to laugh heartily at the American

Mark Twain brought a fresh Lincolnesque perspective to the Literary West. Courtesy Photofest.

West and all of its pretentious myths. Although other professional American writers had preceded him—most notably, Washington Irving—Twain was the first of his guild to view the landscape and the people with some sorely needed skepticism. The whole concept of Manifest Destiny seemed to him ruthlessly absurd. The idea of searching for silver and gold was, to his way of thinking, a cruel joke perpetrated on the gullible by greedy merchants and corrupt mayors. The very notion of taking the land of Native Americans offended his sense of humanity and fairness, although he also provided a critical perspective on the whole mythology of the Native American. He brought to the subject of the American West a fresh Lincolnesque perspective that involved measuring everything—from mountains to men to myths—with a little common sense. Seen in this way, not much of the West held up to what it purported to be, whether it was the "legendary" outlaw Slade the Terrible or the inflated frontier rhetoric of Horace Greeley.

A classic example of Twain's technique is his description of the Utah desert, often romanticized as a place of spiritual inspiration and contemplative discipline:

> Imagine a vast, waveless ocean stricken dead and turned to ashes; imagine this solemn waste tufted with ash-dusted sagebushes; imagine the lifeless silence and solitude that belong to such a place; imagine a coach, creeping like a bug through the midst of this shoreless level, and sending up

tumbled volumes of dust as if it were a bug that went by steam; imagine this aching monotony of toiling and plowing kept up hour after hour, and the shore still as far away as ever, apparently; imagine team, driver, coach and passengers so deeply coated with ashes that they are all one colorless color; imagine ash drifts roosting above mustaches and eyebrows like snow accumulations on boughs and bushes. This is the reality of it.

This is cutting-edge realism, during the Victorian Age, as it would not be seen in American literature for another fifty years. The humorous passage is also, consciously, a successful attempt to demolish a popular myth about the natural beauty of the region.

Gold miners have sought their mythic fortunes in nearly every western mountain range. Courtesy John Murray Collection.

Mark Twain was an Everyman who spoke with penetrating insight and disarming practicality. He was a writer who believed in the power of democracy and the wisdom of the middle class (pretty much in that order), and he was also a man who loved the open spaces and freedom of the American West. It was Twain who first gave the American West a serious literary identity, even when he was laughing about it. He was the first major author who saw the West not from the viewpoint of the hurried, self-involved tourist, but who actually came out and stayed for a few years. He was among the earliest to describe the frontier not in fundamentally idyllic terms, but who painted it more accurately as an often unpleasant place where people who could not exist anywhere else went to escape the law. He was particularly skilled at recording the unique idioms and speech patterns of the West—the informal vernacular language that has come to be identified with the place. Above all, he brought the story-telling powers of a novelist and the reporting skills of a journalist to the task of writing about the West, and in the process created an indispensable source book to the Old Frontier.

THEODORE ROOSEVELT
Last Light Breaking

THEODORE ROOSEVELT presents one of the most fascinating biographical studies in the history of the mythic American West. He was born an invalid and suffered from serious ailments all his life, and yet he projected an image of vitality and invincibility. He has been called a chauvinist and yet as a senior at Harvard he wrote his thesis on the equality of

American President Theodore Roosevelt in front of Bridal Veil Falls at Yosemite National Park. Courtesy Photofest.

men and women. He was a product of capitalism and a scion of a two-hundred-year-old plutocratic family, and yet he fought for the rights of the worker and warned that large corporations were inherently corruptive of American democracy. He was an aggressive, even belligerent warrior and president, and yet he was the first president to receive the Nobel Prize for peace. He was an outspoken champion of traditional masculine virtues, and yet he loved birdwatching and would romp like a child for hours on the White House lawn. He was fluent in four languages, wrote dozens of books, and could comfortably discourse with kings and popes, and yet he was perfectly at ease living the hardscrabble life of a cowboy on his Dakota ranch. He killed hundreds of animals as a sport hunter in the Far West, and yet he created the national wildlife refuge system, the national monument system, and the forest service, and set aside 151 million acres as national forests and/or parks, including the Grand Canyon.

The Roosevelt legend has come to occupy a unique place in the cultural history of the country. Here is a man who holds his dying wife in his arms as his new born baby cries in the next room, and who afterwards turns not to the bottle but to hard work in the Dakota Territory as a natural curative, a man whose heart is so weak at Harvard that a doctor tells him to lead a quiet life at home among his books, and yet who eventually leads the charge up San Juan Hill. While the Roosevelt story gathers its strength from its similarity to the Christian theme that unmerited suffering is redemptive, there is another strain in the American experience that it represents equally well. Roosevelt was, paradoxically, a preeminent example of the rugged individualism and self-reliance that Americans, with their long history of frontier struggle, have always cherished. No political personality has ever better expressed the American popular temperament, the resonant bass tone of the middle class, than Roosevelt: self-confidence, hard work, generosity, good humor, and optimism, as well as a Romanesque sense of destiny, a Calvinistic fear of moral weakness, and an Aristotelian view of the human condition.

Theodore Roosevelt first saw the American West in the summer of 1883. He was in love with the great romance of the cowboy, of the big-game hunter and of the wide open spaces that accompanied the heyday of the short-lived cattle ranching culture. His later sojourn on the last of the Old Frontier was partly restorative—to grieve over the death of his wife and mother (both occurring on the same day)—but it was also something more. It was a pathway into the future, both for him personally and, insofar as he would one day emerge as a national political leader, for the country as well. Working daily from his cattle ranch on the Little Missouri River, Roosevelt experienced a country like none he had known before—a realm where, just a few short years earlier, the buffalo had still roamed freely and the Indians had still hunted them as they had for thousands of years. Most of all, Roosevelt loved the beauty and solitude of the northern prairies and, especially, of the badlands:

> I grow very fond of this place, and it certainly has a desolate, grim beauty of its own, that has a curious fascination for me. The brassy, scantily wooded bottoms through which the winding river flows are bounded by bare, jagged buttes; their fantastic shapes and sharp, steep edges throw the most curious shadows, under the cloudless, glaring sky; and at evening I love to sit out in front of the hut and see their hard, gray outlines gradually grow soft and purple as the flaming sunset by degrees softens and dies away; while my days I spend generally alone, riding through the lonely rolling prairie and broken lands.

Not surprisingly, his classic book of essays on the Old Frontier, *Ranch Life and the Hunting*

The Roosevelt legend has come to occupy a unique place in the cultural history of the country.

Trail (1888), would be illustrated by his fellow Western mythmaker Frederic Remington (who later would paint the historic canvas of Colonel Roosevelt leading the charge up San Juan Hill in Cuba).

Always in his books there is that underlying tone of melancholy so characteristic of Roosevelt (and Lincoln). He writes of "lonely plains" and deserts of "iron desolation," the "forlorn empty hills" and the "sadness of endless marshes... where death broods in the dark and silent depths." These words—lonely, desolation, empty, sadness, death—appear again and again throughout his literary works. The overall sense in his writing is of a brooding man who genuinely loves the beauty of nature, but who has not yet learned that it is not necessary to kill something—to possess it—in order to enjoy it. In this we might say that Roosevelt was representative of his age, an era which had begun to preserve nature from the ravages of industrial civilization, but which was still intensely resource-exploitive (as when the same Theodore Roosevelt who gave national monument status to the Grand Canyon also

Theodore Roosevelt's favorite big game animal was the bull moose. He eventually named his political party "The Bull Moose" party. Courtesy John Murray.

authorized the damming of Hetch Hetchy Valley in Yosemite National Park).

To the bitter ironies, subtle ambiguities, and stark tragedies of the dying frontier, Roosevelt seemed strangely immune. If ever the Western myth of Manifest Destiny had its unquestioning champion, it was Theodore Roosevelt:

> Like all Americans, I like big things: big prairies, big forests and mountains, big wheat fields, railroads, and herds of cattle too, big factories, steamboats, and everything else.... Here we are not ruled over by others, as is the case in Europe; here we rule ourselves.

Roosevelt, however, was painfully aware that the West he had known was dying before his eyes:

> The life that we lead will shortly pass away from the plains as completely as the red and white hunters who have vanished from before our herds. The free, open-air life of the ranchman, the pleasantest and healthiest life in America, is from its very nature ephemeral. The broad and boundless prairies have already been bounded and will soon be made narrow. It is scarcely a figure of speech to say that the tide of white settlement during the last few years has risen over the West like a flood; and the cattlemen are but the spray from the crest of the wave, thrown far in advance, but soon to be overtaken. As the settlers throng into the lands and seize the good ground, especially that

near the streams, the great fenceless ranches, where the cattle and their mounted herdsmen wandered unchecked over hundreds of thousands of acres, will be broken up and divided into corn land, or else into small grazing farms where a few hundred head of stock are closely watched and taken care of.

As Roosevelt predicted, the Old Frontier he had lovingly embraced as a young man of twenty-five in 1883 would shortly perish from the Earth. By the time of his life's end in 1919, only a few of the Old Frontier mythmakers survived—most notably, Charles Russell and Thomas Moran—and they would not endure much longer. The world they had known, though, would live on in countless memoirs, novels, films, paintings, and folk songs. We see, in the end, that Theodore Roosevelt, the consummate Western mythmaker, embodied both the best of the Old Frontier—its passion for nature, its love of adventure, its comradery—and the worst—its obsession with power and control, its patronizing view of the natives and its tendency toward excess (including violence). The steady, determined image of the "cowboy president" will remain up there for thousand of years on Mount Rushmore, along with the images of Lincoln, Jefferson, and Washington, a historical assessment that seems about right. "Life is a great adventure," Roosevelt once observed, as if to summarize the big-spirited age in which he lived, "and the worst of all fears is the fear of living."

JOHN MUIR
Nature's West

IN HIS SEVENTY-SIX-YEAR LIFE California naturalist John Muir wrote a dozen books and hundreds of newspaper and magazine articles. All of his works, including his letters and extensive journals, remain in print today, and by all accounts still sell briskly. The organization he founded in 1892—the Sierra Club—remains one of the most prominent voices for nature, with over half a million members nationwide. The organization comprises a powerful lobbying force in Congress and in the fifty state legislatures. Its legal division specializes in lawsuits against those who would harm the environment (and the people who live in it). The Club is Muir's chief political legacy, and has been instrumental in preserving the integrity of the natural landscape, both in the American West (especially Alaska) and elsewhere. In California there is a half-million acre wilderness area in the High Sierras

John Muir and John Burroughs were the two leading nature writers of their time. Courtesy of the Fred Harvey Collection, Cline Library, Northern Arizona University.

named for Muir, as well as a five-hundred-acre national monument protecting a rare grove of redwood trees just north of San Francisco. The John Muir trail, which runs through some of the most beautiful country in the Sierra Nevadas, further honors the man and the legend. John Muir found a kind of eternal life in his love of nature. Not only did he actively promote the myth of nature, he actually became a myth himself: the lost man who wandered into a valley the Indians called Yosemite, had an epiphany, and found a Moses-like destiny as a devoted prophet of that which saved him.

Behind every myth are facts. Here are a few about Muir. Like most Westerners, Muir was born elsewhere. In his case, elsewhere meant Dunbar, Scotland, as Muir spent his first eleven years in the cold dreary fishing port on the North Sea. In 1849 he immigrated with his family to Wisconsin, which is a nice place if one doesn't mind the permaclouds, Canadian winters, and provinciality. Finally, even the mild-mannered Muir could not take the boredom of the place anymore. At twenty-nine, he lit out for the territories, a long rambling walkabout that led him through the American South, Cuba, Panama, and ultimately to Yosemite Valley in the High Sierras. Here, in the Range of Light, a glacial paradise where the sun shines three hundred days a year, Muir found *la vita nuova*. Of his first view of the range he wrote: "The sky was perfectly delicious, sweet enough for the breath of angels. I do not believe that Adam and Eve ever tasted better in their balmiest nook."

As can be inferred from this observation,

The John Muir trail, which runs through some of the most beautiful country in the Sierra Nevadas, further honors the man and the legend.

Muir had discovered his personal version of Eden. For the rest of his life he worked tirelessly to save the Western wilderness from the advances (or regressions) of industrial civilization. Although he did not have the Harvard degrees of Henry David Thoreau and Ralph Waldo Emerson (those other great proselytizers of transcendental nature in the nineteenth century) or the East-coast connections of John Burroughs (his chief competitor for the unofficial title of national "nature laureate"), Muir had something more important—a quiet but unshakable belief that words must be wed to action. It is difficult to imagine the circumspect Emerson or the owlish Burroughs using blunt language like this:

These temple destroyers, devotees of raging commercialism, seem to have a perfect contempt for Nature, and instead of lifting their eyes to the God of the Mountains, lift them to the Almighty Dollar.

Muir took nature-loving out of the airless parlor rooms and polite lecture halls and made it something to fight for in the federal courthouses and state capitol committee rooms. As a result of his firm but rational militancy, Muir was instrumental in forming Yosemite National Park, Sequoia National Park, and General Grant National Park. Although he lost the battle to defeat Hetch Hetchy Dam, his heroic David-and-Goliath effort inspired later dam-fighters, such as David Brower, to greater success with ill-conceived Western dam projects (such as those planned in the 1950s for Dinosaur National Monument and Grand Canyon National Park).

Muir was a late bloomer as authors go. Like Norman Maclean (author of *A River Runs Through It*), Muir did not publish his first book until he was a senior citizen. Muir's *The Mountains of California* (1894) did not appear until the white-bearded naturalist was fifty-six. Although other Californians—most notably, Clarence King and Clarence Dutton—were known for their nature writing, Muir was the first to move beyond mere description to a more inclusive eloquence, a prose that addressed the spiritual qualities of the land as well as its superficial grandeur. His words, though more than a century old, still ring true: "... thousands of tired, nerve-shaken, over-civilized people are beginning to find out that going to the mountains is going home; that wildness is a necessity; and that mountains, parks. and reservations are useful not only as fountains of timber and irrigating rivers, but as fountains of life."

Without John Muir, the American West would have a very different appearance today. A deeply religious man, Muir actively promoted the myth of the wilderness as a natural Eden, as a place of healing and inspiration. He saw, rightly, that if we were to survive as a people— to keep our democracy intact—we would have to maintain a strong balance between civilization and wild nature, the latter of which he understood, with Thoreau, to be the ultimate repository of political freedom. What Muir argued for, too, was the spiritual reclamation of the West, the restoration of a loving relation-

ship with the landscape. In the end, his innocence and enthusiasm were infectious, and a whole green army formed around this friendly Pied Piper. Like all great leaders, he gave people faith and hope. Although his mortal body was laid to rest nearly a century ago, John Muir, the eternal mythmaker, is still very much alive.

WILLA CATHER AND MARI SANDOZ
O Pioneers!

BOTH MARI SANDOZ (born 1896) and Willa Cather (born 1874) grew up in rural Nebraska— Mari Sandoz along the Niobrara River and Willa Cather along the Republican River—during the transitional period when the Old Frontier had faded into history and the modern world was just being born. Despite this similarity of time and place, their literary approaches to the mythology of the West could not have been more different. Mari Sandoz turned her genius more to recapturing the mythic frontier in novels like *Crazy Horse,* which traced the legendary life of the mystical Sioux war chief Crazy Horse, and *Cheyenne Autumn,* which related the biblical-like exodus of a displaced band of Cheyenne Indians. Willa Cather, on the other hand, focused more on creating fictional interpretations of the new West. In novels like *Death Comes for the Archbishop* and *The*

Mari Sandoz and Willa Cather forever changed the way people looked at the West. Photo by Klaus Kranz.

Professor's House she explored the landscapes, as well as the men and the women, of the twentieth-century West. She is particularly noted for her strong heroines. Her novels examine the legends of the present through the lens of the old.

Both women were highly successful from a commercial standpoint: Mari Sandoz's novel *Cheyenne Autumn* was the basis for John Ford's final film in Monument Valley. (The 1964 film starred Richard Widmark, Edward G. Robinson, Carroll Baker, and Jimmy Stewart.) Willa Cather's 1923 novel *One of Ours* was awarded the Pulitzer Prize for fiction. Their pioneering work has since inspired generations of Western women writers, ranging from Katherine Ann Porter (*The Collected Stories*, winner of the Pulitzer Prize for fiction in 1966) to Jane Smiley (*A Thousand Acres*, subsequently made into a 1997 film starring Jason Robards). Most importantly, in terms of the writing guild, is that their works established a lofty standard of literary excellence based on meticulous research and complete fidelity to character and place. Sandoz in particular is known for her encyclopedic knowledge of the prairie region and for the accuracy and realism of her historical novels.

Mari Sandoz devoted several years to the research and writing of her masterful epic about the life of Crazy Horse, one of the great mythic figures in the Indian Wars (1855–1876) of the northern plains. Crazy Horse was born in the Black Hills in 1842, learned to hunt buffalo at an early age, attended the Great Council of Teton Lakotas in the summer of 1857, fought in numerous battles from 1865 to 1872, was a war chief at the Battle of the Little Bighorn on June 25, 1876, and was betrayed and killed on September 5, 1877. Sandoz spent two winters in the Department of Interior archives in Washington (reading all the files of the Indian Bureau for the trans-Missouri region from 1840 to 1880), made research visits to historical repositories in Nebraska, Colorado, Wyoming, and the Library of Congress, and traveled three thousand miles through Sioux country with her friend Eleanor Hinman in 1930. She also interviewed associates and relatives of Crazy Horse who were then still living: Red Feather, Little Killer, Short Bull, and He Dog, one of Crazy Horse's closest friends.

As a result of her exhaustive preparation, the finished novel paid fitting tribute to one of the West's greatest defenders, Crazy Horse. Even from the opening lines, the reader knows that he or she is in the presence of an expert narrator:

The drowsy heat of middle August lay heavy as a furred robe on the upper country of the Shell River, the North Platte of the white man. Almost every noon the thunders built themselves a dark cloud to ride the far crown of Laramie Peak. But down along the river no rain came to lay the dust of the emigrant road, and no cloud shaded the gleaming adobe walls and bastions of Fort Laramie, the soldier town that was only a little island of whites in a great sea of Indian country two thousand miles wide.

Most importantly... is that their works established a lofty standard of literary excellence based on meticulous research and complete fidelity to character and place.

By the end of the novel, Crazy Horse has attained heroic stature as a leader of unusual courage and vision. Despite the paucity of historical information about him, Sandoz succeeded in creating an authentic biography that went beyond the myth to the man who really lived, who led the horse charge against the blue coats that hot and terrible afternoon on Last Stand Hill, and whose image is now being carved into a rock outcropping in South Dakota (to counterpoise those four found nearby at Mount Rushmore).

Willa Cather based several of her novels on the small town of Red Cloud in southern Nebraska where she grew-up. These novels include *My Ántonia* and *The Song of the Lark*. Like William Faulkner, she found inspiration from the landscape and the living people around her. Quite often her novels involve the early immigrants who settled on the wild prairies after the Homestead Act in 1862. In these novels the land frequently becomes an active character in the narrative—a brooding, mythic presence resembling the all-knowing, omnipresent choruses of ancient Greek tragedy. In blizzards and tornadoes, droughts and floods, the forces of mother earth quietly but firmly make themselves known. Later novels, most notably *The Professor's House* and *Death Comes for the Archbishop*, moved restlessly out of the prairie region to the Southwest. The former relates the discovery of cliff-dweller ruins in Arizona and contains some of Cather's finest writing, as in this passage describing Monument Valley with wonderful eloquence and precision:

From the flat red sea of sand rose great rock mesas, generally Gothic in outline, resembling vast cathedrals. They were not crowded together in disorder, but placed in wide spaces, long vistas between. This plain might once have been an enormous city, all the smaller quarters destroyed by time, only the public buildings left.... This mesa plain had an appearance of great antiquity, and of incompleteness; as if, with all the materials for world-making assembled, the Creator had desisted, gone away and left everything on the point of being brought together, on the eve of being arranged into mountain, plain, plateau. The country was still waiting to be made into a landscape.

These two women, so similar and yet so different, each brought a unique experience and vision to the West and to the myths that sustain the region. Their manifold accomplishments are all the more remarkable when one considers that when they were born women could not vote in the United States (outside that solitary bastion of civilization, Wyoming) and were scarcely represented in colleges and universities,

Willa Cather wrote movingly of life in Nebraska and elsewhere in the West. Courtesy Library of Congress (LC-USZ62-42538).

both in the West and elsewhere. With inexhaustible energy and extraordinary talent, Mari Sandoz and Willa Cather brought their skills to bear upon the mythologies of the West and told stories as they had never been told before. What they have left posterity is a permanent record of the West during that time when it ceased to be a frontier and began to be something else entirely.

MARY AUSTIN
Days In the Field

THE MOJAVE DESERT and its environs comprise one of the most beautiful countries on Earth. It ranges from the sage-covered Great Basin Desert on the north to the frontier of the Colorado Desert on the south, from the sun-baked foothills of the Sierra Nevada Range on the west to the sprawling suburbs of Las Vegas on the east. It includes great woodlands of Joshua Trees, lost oases with native California fan palms, the Alabama Hills below Mount Whitney (a favorite photographic hunting ground of Ansel Adams), the Kelso Dunes, the Old Dad Mountains, secret bat-filled caverns, the desolate salt flats where atomic bombs were tested, and the vast splendor and stark grandeur of Death Valley. Here are canyons with crystallized marble over a billion years old, tiny pupfish that live in some of the saltiest water on Earth, and desert turtles that endure over a century. This vast, wild province was the creative realm of Mary Austin, a pioneering naturalist, writer, and feminist of the American West.

Mary Austin was born in 1868 and lived until 1934—in other words, through the height of Manifest Destiny and well into the modern era of the early twentieth century. She graduated from Blackburn College in Illinois in 1888 and then moved west with her family to farm the San Joaquin Valley in California. For a time she lived as a farmer's wife, first in the central valley near Bakersfield and later in the Owens Valley near Mount Whitney. At thirty-one, the restless young woman sold her first piece of prose to Bret Harte's *Overland Monthly* and, ready for a change, divorced her husband and moved to Carmel (then a nascent artist colony similar to Taos, New Mexico). Over the course of the next thirty-five years Austin would live in California, New York, and finally, Santa Fe, writing along the way some twenty books,

Mary Austin was fascinated by "The Land of Little Rain," otherwise known as The Mojave Desert. Courtesy John Murray.

including nine works of fiction and eleven books of nonfiction.

While John Muir was hard at work exploring and documenting the beauty of the Sierra Nevada Range, and Charles Russell was busily chronicling the dying frontier in eastern Montana, Austin staked out the Mojave Desert as her chief source of inspiration. In so doing, she became one of the first Western writers to advance what would later become (in literature, art, music, and popular culture) one of its most popular myths—that the desert is a source of contemplative solitude and spiritual insight. Today, Austin is chiefly known for her collection of Mojave Desert essays *The Land of Little Rain,* which was published in 1903. In this book she writes about both the landscape of the desert and the people—Indians, prospectors, wagon drivers—who live upon it.

One senses throughout the book that the land, and the people, are but a metaphor for an interior landscape in the author's spirit—a spare, disciplined world where bounties are infrequent and stoicism is the reigning philosophy. In this respect, she was representative of her age and her region, for the desert was a particularly inhospitable place before interstate highways, automobiles, and resort towns. Throughout the book, though, there is the overriding sense of the desert as a realm of physical sanctuary, mystical vision, and even quiet romance:

For all the toll the desert takes of a man it gives compensations, deep breaths, deep sleep, and the communion of the stars. It comes upon one with new force in the pauses of the night that the Chaldeans were a desert-bred people. It is hard to escape the sense of mastery as the stars move in the wide clear heavens to rising and settings unobscured. They look large and near and palpitant; as if they moved on some stately service not needful to declare. Wheeling to their stations in the sky, they make the poor world-fret of no account. Of no account you who lie out there watching, nor the lean coyote that stands off in the scrub from you and howls and howls.

Mary Austin paved the way for all those writers who followed—from John Van Dyke to Joseph Wood Krutch, from Wallace Stegner to Edward Abbey, from Ann Zwinger to Susan Zwinger—in defining the deserts of the American Southwest as a

Mary Austin's THE LAND OF LITTLE RAIN *is one of the classics of western literature. Photo by Klaus Kranz.*

mythic region possessing an abundance of philo-sophical lessons for those willing to stop and watch. Hers was a quiet world of observation and reflection: "There is always a little wind on the mesa, a sliding current of cooler air going down the face of the mountain of its own momentum, but not to disturb the silence of great spaces." Or, "The origin of mountain streams is like the origin of tears, patent to the understanding but mysterious to the sense." When one considers the busy, self-absorbed his-torical era in which Mary Austin lived, such observations are far ahead of their time. In hear-kening back to one of the oldest myths of her Christian-based culture—the desert is a realm of purity vision—she gave her age, and ours, a new and powerful understanding of the deserts.

ZANE GREY
Pulp Fiction

Before there was Louis L'Amour, there was Zane Grey, actively cultivating the romantic myth of the frontier. Courtesy Photofest.

THE NOVELIST ZANE GREY was born in 1872, four summers before the Battle of the Little Bighorn, in the peaceful Midwestern community of Zanesville, Ohio. Twenty-four years later he gradu-ated from the University of Pennsylvania with a degree in, of all things, dentistry. Like many working professionals before and since (John Grisham comes to mind), Zane Grey the dentist secretly entertained hopes of becoming Zane Grey the novelist. He also had an unrequited love affair with the American West. His dilem-ma was the age-old existential one: Monthly bills needed to be paid. Fortunately, Grey had a wife—Lina Elise Roth Grey—who fervently believed in her husband's writing ability. Using most of her life savings, she financed Grey's first trip out to Arizona Territory in 1907. It was Zane Grey's good fortune to have a partner who was as valuable an influence on his creative life as was Charles Russell's wife to the painter's career. In both cases, it is unlikely that either Western mythmaker would have been as com-mercially successful without the unflagging encouragement and astute business guidance of their devoted spouses.

The result of Grey's Arizona trip was a popular novel entitled *The Heritage of the Desert* (1910). This novel would be followed by over two dozen more, each portraying the then-contemporary American West as a realm of natural beauty, widespread regional change, passionate romance, and frequent personal danger. Grey held up a mirror to the tumultuous landscape of the postfrontier West and showed the real people—schoolteachers, Navajo sheepherders, cowboys, miners, merchants—who were trying to build a new future for the region. Quite often the novels involved coming-of-age stories and "code heroes"—individuals, both male and female, who lived in accordance with a rigid internal system of ethics. Grey's novels would go on to become hugely successful and allow the author to pursue an affluent life-style that involved big-game hunting and sport fishing all around the world. Grey was the West's second author to garner great wealth from his literary craft and his skillful mythologizing of the region. (The first was drifter-turned-storyteller Jack London.)

Zane Grey's novels would also go on to be frequently adapted into films, most notably with *The Vanishing American, Riders of the Purple Sage, The Light of the Western Stars, Western Union,* and *Code of the West. The Vanishing American*, filmed by director George B. Seitz in 1925, was the first movie to be shot on location in beautiful Monument Valley (later the fabled domain of John Ford and John Wayne). The film was quite faithful to Grey's then-controversial story, which involved a tragic love affair between an educated Navajo, Nophaie (played by Richard Dix), and an Anglo school teacher (played by Lois Wilson). Many of Grey's other novels were adapted into films at the Old Paramount Ranch in the Santa Monica Mountains of southern California and the Old Pariah film site, located about thirty miles west of Page, Arizona. (The Old West town is now maintained as a historic filming location by the Bureau of Land Management.)

Grey, the consummate Western mythmaker, had an enormous influence on his times, through his paperback novels, his film adaptations, and his prodigious magazine serializations. His characters and stories helped to shape how the rest of the country viewed the emerging modern West. It was, for Grey, a region populated by strong men and determined women who, together, were bringing "civilization" to a post-Edenic landscape. The West after the first pioneering generations was, to Grey, a fallen world, with clever outlaws and unscrupulous Indian agents, corrupt mayors and bullying ranchers, all in a kind of biblical war with the good souls who would one day prevail. By the time of Grey's death in 1939, the transitional age between the Old Frontier and the modern West was gone, as much a thing of history as the era of the trappers or the age of the railroad. Although there were other practitioners of the early Western novel who possessed more literary craft—most notably Stephen Crane *(The Blue Hotel),* Owen Wister *(The Virginian),* and Walter Van Tilburg Clark *(The Ox-Bow Incident)*—none had as much success as Zane Grey did in changing mass public perceptions of the West.

Grey, the consummate Western mythmaker, had an enormous influence on his times, through his paperback novels, his film adaptations, and his prodigious magazine serializations.

JOHN STEINBECK
The Realistic Southwest

JOHN STEINBECK IS THE ONLY WRITER of the American West to have been awarded the Nobel Prize in Literature. His was a view of the world, and a literary style, in keeping with the realism that dominated the arts in the 1930s and 1940s, a realism that can be seen elsewhere in the work of Ansel Adams, Edward Weston, Dorothea Lange, Grant Wood, John Ford, and Woody Guthrie. John Steinbeck painted the human condition with exacting detail, whether it was a retarded man who could not comprehend homicide *(Of Mice and Men),* a tragically flawed family *(East of Eden),* a couple who are destroyed by good fortune *(The Pearl),* or a struggling group of displaced farmers *(The Grapes of Wrath).* He held up a mirror to the landscapes and the people of the American West and, quite simply, did it better than anyone before or since. He was to the American West what Charles Dickens was to Victorian England or Anton Chekhov was to Romanov Russia. His works have come to be synonymous with both a place and a time. What most concerned Steinbeck as a mythmaker was the dark side of the happy myth, the unpleasant part that had been glossed over by other writers such as Mark Twain, Bret Harte, Owen Wister, or Jack London. He knew that for every story of easy success there is one of utter failure, that every earthly landscape—even the featureless prairie—must have its shadows, and that for every world there is an anti-world.

John Steinbeck was born on February 27,

1902, during the first year of Theodore Roosevelt's first term, in the farming community of Salinas, California. The Salinas Valley was, and still is, an idyllic landscape, set broadly between the Gabilan Mountains to the east and Monterey Bay to the west. Steinbeck later wrote of "light gay mountains full of sun and loveliness and a kind of invitation, so that you wanted to climb into their warm foothills almost as you want to climb into the lap of a beloved mother." His family owned a summer cottage on Monterey Bay, which was then as it now, a thriving bohemia of artists, writers, and photographers. These two areas—the Salinas Valley and Monterey Bay—would deeply imprint themselves upon Steinbeck's imagination, and appear in many of his later stories and novels. Steinbeck went to Stanford University, which he attended off and on for five years (ultimately leaving, like many creative types, without a degree). There followed a time of drifting and indecision.

In 1930—the first year of the Great Depression—Steinbeck married Carol Henning and moved to Pacific Grove, where the young couple lived in the family cottage with few resources other than true love and a beautiful setting for true love. It was during this period that Steinbeck also met Ed Ricketts, a marine biologist who operated from Pacific Grove and would later exert a powerful personal and creative influence on Steinbeck (heading the scientific voyage that led to Steinbeck's nature nonfiction work, *The Sea of Cortez*). During the 1930s Steinbeck industriously wrote a series of mediocre novels *(To a God Unknown, The Pastures of Heaven, Tortilla Flat).* It was not until his two social-protest novels—*In Dubious Battle* and *The Grapes of Wrath*—that the middle-aged author finally achieved a mature vision and craft.

The Grapes of Wrath is, arguably, the finest novel ever written about the American West, if not the American experience. Steinbeck paints a stark portrait of the injustices at the core of the American dream, of the brutal price the poor pay for the bright success of the wealthy. The novel is also a story of the revenge of nature— her literal wrath—on those who have abused her, as well as the indestructibility of the human spirit. The setting is the "nuclear winter" of the Oklahoma Dust Bowl:

> The dawn came, but no day. In the gray sky a red sun appeared, a dim red circle that gave a little light, like dusk; and as that day advanced, the dusk slipped back toward darkness, and the wind cried and whimpered over the fallen corn. Men and women huddled in their houses, and they tied handkerchiefs over their noses when they went out, and wore goggles to protect their eyes.

From this point on, the story only gets worse, as a family experiences one indignity after another in their long hopeful journey to the Arcady of California, where they find only disappointment and tragedy.

In granting John Steinbeck the Nobel prize in 1962, the Swedish Academy summed up his immortal achievement as follows:

> Steinbeck has no mind to be an unoffending comforter and entertainer. Instead, the topics he chose were serious and denunciatory, for instance the bitter strikes on California's fruit and cotton plantations.... [Over the years] his literary power steadily gained impetus. The little masterpiece *Of Mice and Men* was followed by those incomparable short stories which he collected together in the volume *The Long Valley*. The way had now been paved for his greatest work, the epic chronicle *The Grapes of Wrath*.

Like his fellow Nobel Laureates William Faulkner and Ernest Hemingway, John Steinbeck was a writer who believed in the power and truth of myth. He knew the American West as few did; having been born and raised in the region makes him especially unique in this respect. He understood that the tales of the dispossessed are as necessary as the stories of the happily content. He saw, finally, that future generations must have a proper accounting of the past— of the myths, to be sure, and of all the shadows that surround the myths.

John Steinbeck is the only western writer to have been awarded the Nobel Prize for Literature. Courtesy Photofest.

A. B. GUTHRIE AND WALLACE STEGNER
West of the Hundredth Meridian

TWO WESTERN MYTHMAKERS loomed large in the third quarter of the twentieth century: A. B. Guthrie and Wallace Stegner. Both were born and raised in the Far West, which makes them unique among so many others who immigrated to the region from the East. Both were consummate writers of prose, and both were awarded the Pulitzer Prize, the nation's highest literary award. The first achieved his greatest success primarily through his works of the imagination, and the latter exerted more of an influence with his nonfiction. Guthrie chose journalism as an initial career, and Stegner chose college teaching. Through their many fine books and deeds (for both were politically active), they helped to shape the way American civilization viewed the West during a critical period in its development, when the transition was being made from the age of dirt roads and quiet little towns that shut down at sunset to the era of interstate highways and cities that stayed up all night.

Wallace Stegner was born on February 18, 1909, on Lake Mills, Iowa. After a childhood on the Upper Plains, he studied at the University of Utah and eventually earned a doctoral degree in English from the University of Iowa (with a dissertation devoted to the Western explorer/writer Clarence Dutton). From 1940 through 1971 Stegner served as an English professor at Stanford University, where he also taught in the creative writing program. (Such writers as Larry McMurtry and Edward Abbey participated in the program.) Although Stegner's novels were widely respected and received several awards, it was his nonfiction— such books

A. B. Guthrie and Wallace Stegner were two of the West's most loving and devoted chroniclers. Photo by Klaus Kranz.

as *Beyond the Hundredth Meridian, The Sound of Mountain Water*, and *Where the Bluebird Sings to the Lemonade Springs*—that exerted an influence on perceptions of the West a region of legend and myth.

Stegner saw the West, and wrote about the West, primarily in terms of its landscape:

The western landscape is of the wildest variety and contains every sort of topography and landform, even most of those familiar from farther east. Bits of East and Middle West are buried here and there in the West, but no physical part of the true West is buried in the East. The West is short-grass plains, alpine mountains, geyser basins, plateaus and mesas and canyons and cliffs, salinas and sinks, sagebrush and Joshua tree and saguaro deserts.... There is nothing in the east like the granite horns of Grand Teton or Teewinot, nothing like the volcanic neck of Devil's Tower, nothing like the travertine terraces of Mammoth Hot Springs.

Stegner saw the West as a region defined by its aridity, a descriptive term that may also serve as a useful metaphor, as when he observed that "we may love a place and still be dangerous to it." His West was the Edenic West of old, but it was also a West that came with a modern warning label—handle with care.

A. B. Guthrie was born on January 13, 1901, one of nine children (only three of whom survived to adulthood). He grew up in one of the sweetest towns in the West, Choteau, Montana, located an hour east of Charlie Russell's old home in Great Falls and an hour west of the magnificent Rocky Mountain Front

Wallace Stegner often wrote of his love for the Colorado Plateau, including Bryce Canyon National Park in Utah. Courtesy John Murray.

Country. The Choteau region is the realm of the Blackfeet Indians. A drive up nearby U.S. 89 passes several historical pull-outs, including the spot where Meriwether Lewis killed a young Blackfoot man who was attempting to steal one of Lewis's horses. This magnificent, and historic, landscape permanently imprinted itself upon the lively imagination of young Guthrie. After twenty years of working as a reporter for a Midwestern paper, Guthrie went to Harvard University under a Niemann Fellowship and studied in Widener Library under the venerated Western historian Bernard DeVoto, who won a Pulitzer prize for one of his Western histories. It was during this time that Guthrie wrote his finest work: *The Big Sky*.

The novel tells the story of three men and their lives in the Upper Missouri country from 1830 through 1843, at the height of the mountain man period. The chief character is a young man named Boone Caudill, a dark figure who mixes the mythic qualities of the historic frontier legend, Daniel Boone, with the atavistic nature of Joseph Conrad's half-wild protagonist Kurtz in the novella *Heart of Darkness*. By the end of the novel, all is changed. The age of the trappers is over, beaver having gone out of fashion, and the Far West is being settled by dusty pilgrims on the Oregon Trail. One of the three original characters is dead, another has settled back into civilization, and the last has disappeared into the wilderness. They say that some novels are remembered just as clearly as a first kiss. Passages like this from *The Big Sky* resonate that way for me:

> Already autumn was coming to the Upper Missouri, the short northern autumn that was here and gone like a bird flying. Flecked in the green of the cottonwood

trees, telltale leaves hung yellow, giving limply to the breeze. The blood-red berries of the *graisse de boeuf* sparkled along the silver limbs. It was often chilly in the morning, warming as the sun got up and lay on the land in a golden glow, and cooling again as it finished its shortened arch and fell in flames among the hills.

In such lyric lines Guthrie captures all the grandeur and beauty of the mythic Montana country he knew so well.

Although Guthrie's later novel *The Way West* would win the Pulitzer prize, *The Big Sky* was the finest in what turned out be a trilogy. (Both would later be made into movies, with actor Kirk Douglas starring in both films.) Guthrie would subsequently earn an Oscar nomination for the screenplay he wrote for the classic Western film *Shane* (1953), which starred Alan Ladd as a wandering gunfighter who comes to the aid of a young ranching couple, played by Jean Arthur and Van Heflin. The film was shot on location at the Turner Ranch just below the Teton Range near Jackson, Wyoming. (The film would also win an Oscar for best cinematography.)

Both Wallace Stegner and A. B. Guthrie helped people in their age—a time of manifold change for the West—better love and understand the West as a cultural region and as a natural landscape. They understood the responsibility the Western writer has to not merely be a passive observer of his or her times, but to actively participate in events. Stegner was a powerful voice for conservation issues in California and the Southwest, and Guthrie—even at the age of ninety—was doing battle with oil and gas companies along the Rocky Mountain Front in northwestern Montana, whose activities conflict with critical grizzly bear habitat.

It was my singular good fortune to speak with Guthrie in the year before his death. I was living in Alaska at this time, and the conversation was over the phone. At ninety he was still sharp as a pine needle and was able to regale me with colorful stories of the Old West and of Hollywood. A few years after his death I visited his home while staying at the nearby Nature Conservancy's Pine Butte Grizzly Bear Preserve. While there I saw buffalo jumps (cliffs over which the horse-less ancestors of the Blackfeet drove bison), ancient teepee rings, fragmented dinosaur bones, chipping grounds and, best of all, Ear Mountain (which figures so prominently in *The Big Sky*). The place where Guthrie lived was a wonderland, an inspiring landscape that resonates with historical associations of the mythic West, from the age of the fur trappers to the present time.

While Guthrie looked into the past for inspiration, Stegner searched for answers in the present. Even in prehistoric times, though, Stegner found signs. He wrote that "Every western city hell-bent for expansion might ponder the history of Mesa Verde." Both men had a long historical sense of the region, and understood that its myths could save it or destroy it.

Both Wallace Stegner and A. B. Guthrie helped people in their age—a time of great change for the West—better love and understand the West as a cultural region and as a natural landscape.

EDWARD ABBEY
Mother Nature's Son

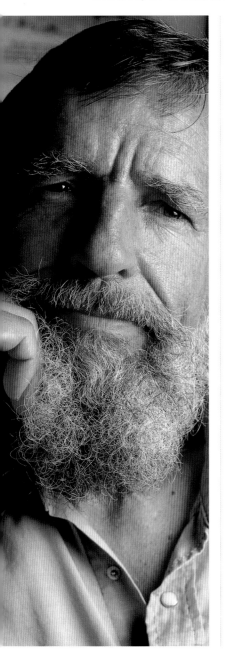

IN MARCH 1988, one year to the month before he died, sixty-one-year-old nature writer/environmental activist Edward Abbey gave a reading at the Trinity United Methodist Church in Denver. The church, a massive century-old structure, occupies nearly an entire city block in the downtown area. It sits directly across the street from the historic Brown Palace Hotel, where President Theodore Roosevelt stayed before his 1905 hunting trip and painter Thomas Moran lived for a time during his later years. When filled to capacity, the Trinity United Methodist Church seats fourteen hundred people in its serried wooden pews. That day, the church was filled to overflowing, with people sitting in the aisles and standing in the rear beneath the stained glass windows.

Abbey was there ostensibly as part of a Western tour to promote his latest, and what would be his last major novel, *The Fool's Progress.* Instead of reading from the novel, though, he read an introduction he had written for a recent edition of his first work of nature nonfiction, *Desert Solitaire* (1968). In the audience that day, along with my father, I remember thinking: How many contemporary American writers could fill a venue this large to overflowing? How many could attract a paying crowd of

Edward Abbey was a tireless defender of the western wilderness. Courtesy Jack Dykinga.

even a tenth of that magnitude? Afterwards my father and I went downstairs to the reception area to see if Abbey could autograph our copies of *Desert Solitaire.* It was impossible to even shake his hand—the thronging crowd of admirers was gathered six deep around the gentle desert giant.

That was as close as I ever got to the most influential Western mythmaker, in terms of wild nature, since John Muir. Like Muir, Abbey believed that words were useless unless they were married to action. His life was dedicated to the proposition that one person can, and should, make a difference. Like Muir, he was a foe of all those who would diminish the landscapes and the people of the West. And, like Muir, he possessed a deeply spiritual nature akin to that of the biblical figure Jeremiah. Abbey lambasted the degradation of the wilderness—from the Glen Canyon Dam to livestock grazing on public lands—and used language just as militant (and, in a way, Jeffersonian) as Muir's in nature's defense:

> If the wilderness is our true home, and if it is threatened with invasion, pillage, and destruction—as it certainly is—then we have the right to defend that home, as we would our private quarters by whatever means are necessary ... not to defend that which we love would be dishonorable (from the essay "Eco-Defense").

Still later, his subversive ecological novel, *The Monkey Wrench Gang,* gave birth to the Earth First! movement of offensive (as opposed to defensive) environmental activism.

Edward Abbey's beginnings were as mundane and unlikely as those of John Muir's. Abbey was born in the coal hills of Appalachia near Indiana, Pennsylvania, in 1927. His first visit to the West occurred in the summer of 1944, when he hitchhiked out to see the deserts and canyon-lands of northern Arizona. Like so many others before and after, he fell hopelessly in love. After a brief stint in the Army, Abbey enrolled at the University of New Mexico, eventually earning a bachelor of arts degree (1952) and a master of arts degree in Philosophy (1956). There followed a transitional period of roughly a decade in which he traveled and worked widely in the West. He also wrote three novels *(Jonathon Troy, The Brave Cowboy,* and *Fire on the Mountain).*

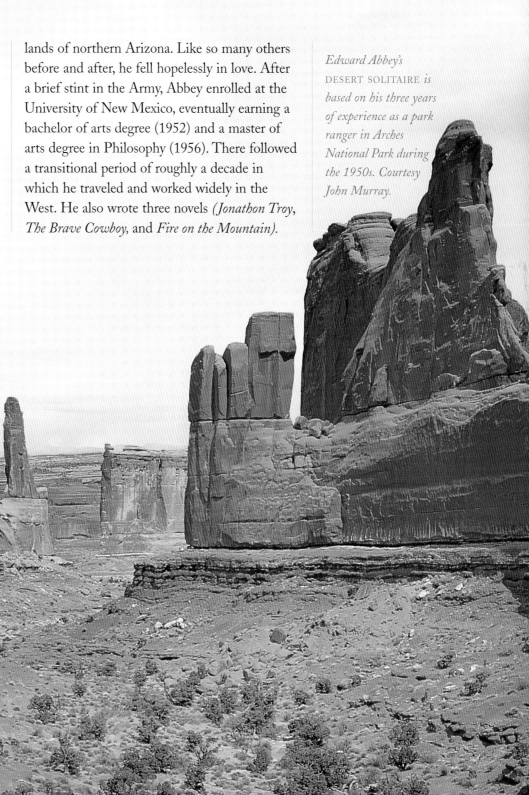

Edward Abbey's DESERT SOLITAIRE *is based on his three years of experience as a park ranger in Arches National Park during the 1950s. Courtesy John Murray.*

The Brave Cowboy was made into the acclaimed film *Lonely Are the Brave* (1962), which starred Oscar-winning actor Kirk Douglas as Jack Burns, the last of the open-range cowboys.

Most importantly, it was during this period that Abbey was employed three summers as a seasonal ranger in Arches National Monument (now a national park). These experiences he would later craft into his Walden-esque master-piece *Desert Solitaire*, a sort of extended love poem to the slickrock country of southeastern Utah. The format of the book is one of the oldest in Western literature—the naturalist's calendar. The essays and nonfiction stories take the reader from April through October in the painted desert. Throughout the book, Abbey the master mythmaker deliberately portrays the area—especially in essays like "Havasu" and "Rocks"—as a modern version of Eden, replete with symbolic snakes, spiritual temptations, prelapsarian beauty, and monumental peace and solitude:

> A weird, lovely, fantastic object out of nature like Delicate Arch has the curious ability to remind us—like rock and sunlight and wind and wilderness—that out there is a different world, older and greater by far than ours, a world which surrounds and sustains the little world of men as sea and sky surround and sustain a ship.

After initially failing to sell robustly, the book was re-released and shortly became a classic of the American West. Over the years the book has sold nearly a million copies—Abbey would joke that he never had to work a day of his life after its re-release.

A year after seeing Edward Abbey at the church in Denver I received a phone call early one morning from my mother. I was living in northern Alaska at the time, working as an English professor at the state university in Fairbanks. My mother reported that she had just read in the newspaper that Abbey had died after a short illness. Two weeks later I received a note from the author's widow, Clarke. She wrote that the last thing her husband had read before passing away was a review I had written in *The Bloomsbury Review* of his novel *The Fool's Progress*. It had heartened him because all the other reviews had been so harsh. Abbey was, to be sure, a controversial figure—as was John Muir—but time has a way of sorting out the truth about people and the age in which they live. Posterity will be kind to Abbey the writer and activist, as they have been to Muir. Both men saw the American West as a place to be young and free and whole again, as a mythic Eden waiting to be reclaimed. Both men offered, to a world often lost in greed and hubris, a clear and steady vision of faith and hope. In keeping with the spirit of that philosophy, Abbey chose as an epigraph for his final collection of essays *(One Life at a Time, Please)* a quotation of optimism and reconciliation attributed to Saint Francis of Assisi: "O Lord, make me an instrument of thy peace. Where there is hatred, let me sow love; where there is darkness, light; and where there is sadness, joy."

LARRY MCMURTRY
Yesterday and Today

TRADITIONAL MYTHS have portrayed the West as a region of hope and regeneration, as the landscape of the future, and also as a realm in which to reclaim the best part of the past, namely, our freedom. Over his long and productive career, Texas-born novelist Larry McMurtry has worked in very compelling ways with this regional mythology, often writing about people and places from his own times, but always from a mythic perspective. While McMurtry is a realist, he is also a fabulist—a legend-maker—whether telling the story of three high school friends in a mythical rural backwater *(The Last Picture Show)* or dissecting a modern cattle ranching family on the sun-baked steppes of north Texas *(Horseman, Pass By)*. His heroes, like Gus in *Lonesome Dove* or Sam the Lion in *The Last Picture Show,* tend to be ordinary people struggling heroically within the confines of conventional lives—trying to be as large as possible given a restricted destiny, to uphold personal dignity in the face of tragedy and death, and always to make the correct decision when faced with difficult ethical choices. The American West has rarely had such a devoted chronicler or such a loving mythmaker.

Larry McMurtry was born in 1936 in Wichita Falls, Texas. The descendant of North Texas cattle ranchers, McMurtry later earned an undergraduate English degree from North Texas State University in Denton, Texas, and a master's degree in English from Rice University in Houston. He also studied creative writing under the acclaimed writer Wallace Stegner for one year at Stanford University. With the publication of *Horseman, Pass By* in 1961, McMurtry emerged as the most promising novelist of his generation. What has followed that brilliant first work has been one of the most successful careers in Western American literature. One successful novel has followed another, culminating in the Pulitzer Prize for *Lonesome Dove* in 1986. Over half a dozen of his novels have been made into films, including the Oscar-winning *Hud* (from *Horseman, Pass By*) and *The Last Picture Show.*

The author's signature work—the one book that best shows his methodology and mythology—is his first novel, *Horseman, Pass By.* (The title comes from a William Butler Yeats poem—"Cast a cold eye on life, on death/Horseman, pass by.") The story takes place in the fictional town of Thalia in Archer County, Texas, where McMurtry himself was born and raised. The story focuses on the triangle-like relationship between three central characters, all related to one another: Homer Bannon, an over-the-hill rancher who keeps a

Larry McMurtry, like John Steinbeck, writes realistic novels of unusual originality and power. Courtesy Simon & Schuster.

pair of longhorns around to remind himself of the mythical good old days; Lonnie Bannon, the happy-go-lucky grandson of Homer; and Hud, Homer's rebellious, amoral, narcissistic son. When the cattle herd contracts hoof-and-mouth disease, a conflict arises between Homer and Hud, with Homer wanting to destroy the herd to protect surrounding livestock, and Hud arguing that the herd should be quickly sold off to unsuspecting buyers. Homer prevails, but later succumbs to a heart attack. Hud then inherits the ranch, planning to drill for oil. Lonnie departs, unable to accept Hud's vision of the future.

McMurtry once observed that "the place where all my stories start is the heart faced suddenly with the loss of its country, its customary and legendary range." His novels present often-bleak pictures of rural towns in collapse and country people in despair—in other words, the real modern West. He is an anti-mythmaker in the sense that he challenges all of the bright legends about the West being an agrarian para-dise, where the Earth is ever-bountiful and the people are forever content. At his best he captures the beauty and grandeur both of the region and of its people:

When I knew Granddad was in bed I went back to the windmill and stopped the blades, so I could climb up and sit on the platform beneath the big fin. Around me, across the dark prairie, the lights were clear. The oil derricks were lit with strings of yellow bulbs, like Christmas trees. The lights were still on in the kitchens of the pumper's cabins.... Twelve miles away, to the north, the red and green and yellow lights of Thalia shimmered against the dark. I sat above it all, in the cool breezy air the rig motors purr and the heavy trucks growl up the hill. Above the chattering of the ignorant Rhode Island Reds I heard two whippoorwills, the ghostly birds I never saw, calling across the flats below the ridge.

Above the chattering of the ignorant Rhode Island Reds I heard two whippoorwills, the ghostly birds I never saw, calling across the flats below the ridge.

Larry McMurtry's Texas is a big wild country in which the landscape is as important as the people living there. Courtesy John Murray.

Willie Nelson, working out of the long outlaw tradition, has become one of the most influential mythmakers in contemporary music. Courtesy Photofest.

MUSIC, SWEET MUSIC

Popular Song in the Service of Myth

As I walked out in the streets of Laredo,

As I walked out in Laredo one day,

I spied a poor cowboy wrapped up in white linen,

Wrapped up in white linen as cold as the clay.

—STREETS OF LAREDO
(anonymous source, 1880s Texas)

MANY OF THE MYTHS OF THE AMERICAN WEST have been nurtured by popular music, and with good reason: Music has a power over the human soul unlike that of any other art form. Play a few minor chords on a twelve-string guitar, and you can instantly create a melancholy mood, even in an audience that fills a stadium. Pluck out a major chord sequence on a banjo and even the centenarians of a nursing home will unconsciously begin tapping their feet to the cheerful beat. Joy, nostalgia, hope, love, pride—all can be summoned by the magic of music. One thinks of Ritchie Valens expressing all the passion of youth in his lively rendering of the traditional Mexican folksong "La Bamba," or Don Henley and the Eagles evoking the harmonic tranquillity of the California high desert in "Peaceful, Easy Feeling," or Glen Campbell extolling the anonymous workers of the rural West in "Wichita Lineman."

The myths of Western music are the enduring ones of the region: the beauty of the natural landscape, the freedom of the open road and the vast public domain, and the hope for a better life in a new country. Some of the other myths found in Western music are especially unique to the region, as in the clash of Southwestern cultures at the heart of Marty Robbins' 1959 country-western song "El Paso," which describes a tragic love affair between a young Texas cowboy and a beautiful Mexican señorita. Similarly, Brian Wilson wrote songs in the early 1960s about a mythical region like no other on the continent—the sun-washed surfing beaches of southern California. More recently, the Seattle "Grunge" bands of the 1990s, such as Pearl Jam and Nirvana, gave voice to the moody angst common to residents of the gloomy Pacific Northwest. Whatever their individual style, each of these musicians was working, often consciously, within the geographic boundaries of a particular mythical system.

The music of the American West is many things. It is a circle of Navajo elders beating deerskin drums and chanting around a cedar fire in a dirt-floored hogan along the San Juan River. It is the humming of a migrant worker picking fruit in a peach orchard outside Bakersfield. It is a country-western group from Austin playing at a beach bar in Miami and a garage band working out a new rock song in the back streets of Phoenix. It is a bluegrass festival in Telluride and a square dance in Clovis. It is Gene Autry yodeling "Back in the Saddle Again" and Jim Morrison belting out "L.A. Woman." It is a wrangler leading a herd of horses up to the night pasture, whistling a tune inspired by the song of a hermit thrush, and it is a young mother in a trailer at the end of a country road, singing a lullaby to her baby, a melody that just came to her in the night.

It is, just as much as these, the music of nature herself: the impassioned bugling of the elk in the Tetons, the uplifting call of the meadowlark in western Nebraska, the busy cackle of the sandhill cranes over the Rio Grande Valley, the sopranic yipping of the coyote in the Superstition Mountains, the mournful howl of the wolf along the Yellowstone River. It is the delicate rustle of the breeze in the quaking aspen leaves and the mellifluous sound of a waterfall at the bottom of a slickrock canyon, the discordant way the waves

Songwriters as diverse as Glen Campbell (left) and Gene Autry (right) have used popular music to advance the myths of the west. Courtesy Photofest.

crash along the rocky coast of Point Conception and the immaculate silence of a midnight snowfall on a prairie meadow. It is all the sounds of humanity and the wilderness that give rhythm and melody and life and movement to the West.

One hundred years, two hundred years from now, much of what we know in this world will be changed, and most of what we see will be forgotten, but one thing is certain—the songs and lyrics of the West will endure, just as surely as the English folk song "Greensleeves" can still move the heart half a millennium after it was composed by some unknown troubadour strumming a mandolin. The myths expressed by the songs of the West are at one with the landscapes that inspired them—the big skies, the free-ranging herds and the wild animals that follow them, the steady winds that blow forever from someplace far away. Rarely has a musical legacy been so closely married to the fables and legends, history and culture, mountains and valleys of a single geographic province.

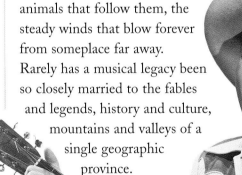

BALLADS AND LAMENTS
The Romance of the Cowboy

BEFORE THERE WAS BOB WILLS and His Texas Playboys, before there was Buddy Holly and the Crickets, before there was John Denver and Willie Nelson and Selena and all the others, there were the original Western music-makers: the cowboys. These sunburned, blue-jeaned, bowlegged minstrels of the open range spent whole days in the saddle, riding herd on longhorns or Herefords or whatever other sturdy breed the owners chose to graze. They were permanent bachelors, most of them, happily eschewing the responsibilities of family and the settled life for the natural beauty and simple camaraderie of the unstaked plains. They had missing teeth and grizzled beards and bad hat

At night, after a long day on the range, cowboys would gather around the cook's fire at the line camp. From such simple moments, and often in the presence of a guitar, fiddle, or harmonica, many of the cowboy songs known now around the world were born. Courtesy Alan Manley.

hair for their entire lives, and most were proud of it. At night they would gather round the campfires with their six-stringed guitars and rusty harmonicas and out-of-tune fiddles, and make spontaneous music inspired by those three ancient muses—the wheeling stars, the gentle breezes, and whatever fermented liquid could be found in a bottle.

Their myth, the legend of the cowboy, is one of the most powerful in the West. It is, at its core, a dream of independence from human society, of rugged self-reliance and intimate closeness with nature. The songs of the cowboys, which were based on this myth, in some cases echoed old English ballads and Colonial sea shanties. More often than not, though, they were native tunes, born naturally of the prairies and mountains. Whatever their origins, they were almost always intended to be sung slowly, as if the relaxed pace of the cattle country could be felt in their very rhythms. They were, to use a metaphor, meant to be rendered not at a gallop or a trot, but at a steady walk, the sort of humble ground-eating pace that got a wrangler thirty hard miles in a day without laming his horse. Running through the songs were the essentials of the cowboy life—the tedium of the cattle trail, the good wrangler who dies young, the beloved cutting horse, the barroom fights in town, the pursuit of thieves and rustlers, the true love lost long ago.

The first collection of cowboy songs appeared in 1910. Assembled by a pioneering musicologist named John Lomax, the book gathered together such well known (at the time) Western songs as "The Buffalo Skinners," which wistfully recalled the lost age of the buffalo hunt:

> Oh, its now we've crossed Peace River, boys,
> and homeward we are bound,
> No more in that hell-fired country shall
> ever we be found,
> Go home to our wives and sweethearts, tell
> others not to go,
> For God's forsaken the buffalo range and
> the damned old buffalo.

All of the sadness of that bygone era—of those who witnessed the final destruction of the prairie and the death of the buffalo herds that symbolized the frontier—were captured in the stanzas of the song.

Another favorite of the period was "The Old Chisholm Trail," which recollected the years directly after the demise of the buffalo herds, when the first longhorn cattle herds were pushed north from Texas and Oklahoma up into the central and northern plains. Some musical scholars have called "The Old Chisholm Trail" the single best folksong of the American West. Certainly no other song has ever better expressed the paradox that was the mythic American cowboy—a person both gentle and cruel, violent and peaceful, small-minded and big of heart, friendly and solitary, utterly homeless and fiercely loyal to place. The opening stanzas of the song, as well as the chorus born of the gleeful song of the coyote, are known to virtually every school-age child who has ever taken a music class:

All of the sadness of that bygone era—of those who witnessed the final destruction of the prairie and the death of the buffalo herds that symbolized the frontier—were captured in the stanzas of the song.

Oh, come along, boys and listen to my tale,
I'll tell you 'bout my troubles on the old
    Chisholm Trail.
I rode up the trail on April twenty-third,
Oh, I rode up the trail with the Bar Ten herd.
    Come-a ti yi yippy, I, yippy I, yippy ay,
    Cum-a ti yi yippy yippy I, yippy ay,
    Cum-a ti yi yippy yippy ay.
Oh, I ride with my slicker and I ride all day,
And I packed along a harp for to pass the
    time away;
With my feet in the stirrups and my hand
    on the horn,
I'm the best darned cowboy that ever
    was born.
    Come-a ti yi …
She's cloudy in the west and she looks
    like rain,
And my danged old slicker's in the wagon
    again;
The gale starts a-blowing and the rain
    begins to fall,
And it looks, by God, like we're a-gonna
    lose 'em all.
    Come-a ti yi …

One of the most memorable cowboy tunes, "Git Along Little Dogies," is thought to have been written by an anonymous wrangler in Kansas in the 1880s. The opening stanza and refrain are as poignant as any twelve-bar blues ballad of the Mississippi Delta (as in the similar blues song entitled "I'm a Poor Boy, A Long Way from Home"):

Oh I ain't got no father, I ain't got no mother,
My friends they all left me when first I
    did roam.
I ain't got no sister, I ain't got no brother,
I'm a poor lonesome cowboy and a long ways
    from home.
    Whoopee! Ti-yi-o, git along, little dogies,
    Its your misfortune and none of my own,
    Whoopee! Ti-yi-o, git along, little dogies,
    For you know that Wyoming will be your
    new home.

While it is true that the cowboy had his independence, and no one would deny the value of personal freedom, it is also true—as the lines of this song suggest—that the price he paid for that absolute freedom was, at times, a terrible loneliness. That, if anything, was the dark side of the bright myth of the American cowboy.

From west Texas to northern Montana, the cowboy worked in some of the hardest country in the West. Courtesy John Murray

BOB WILLS AND HIS TEXAS PLAYBOYS
As Free as the Wind

BORN IN HALL COUNTY, TEXAS, on March 6, 1905, James Robert Wills learned early on that he didn't much care for physical labor, whether harvesting the first crop of alfalfa, breaking horses to ride, or moving cattle on the range. He saw emancipation from this life sentence of Sisyphean labor in the form of a four-stringed fiddle. With this small but powerful instrument, together with his charismatic presence, Wills found he could actually be paid to have fun on stage, travel all over the Southwest, and meet lots of beautiful women—the perfect solution to the age-old existential dilemma of how to work for a living without living to work. It was also Wills' good fortune to come of age at the perfect time to pursue his natural bent for music—the era of the cowboy folk song was winding down, the once-popular regional acts of the Roaring Twenties were becoming passé, and restless crowds everywhere in the Southwest were anxious for a new sound to accompany the contemporary age.

Texas in the early 1930s was a country reeling from a series of biblical catastrophes—the Dust Bowl (the human toll of which would be so well documented by John Steinbeck and Dorothea Lange), the ravages of a devastating boll weevil infestation, and an enormous wave of displaced migrants from the medieval tenant farms of the Deep South. Into this adumbrated landscape of travail and suffering Bob Wills stepped with a steady smile, a cheerful song,

and a quick hand on the fiddle. Before Wills there had been "country" music, with a musical and mythic base east of the Mississippi. After he arrived on the scene, there was "country-western" music, with a lyric center, and a geographic source of inspiration, west of the big muddy river. Wills was in this sense a free-wheeling maverick, a musical figure who drew his immediate sources from the relatively recent sounds of the West, while still retaining a bedrock fidelity to the time-honored values of country music.

By 1933, the twenty-seven-year-old Wills had gone through three bands in rapid succession—the Wills Fiddle Band, the Aladdin Laddies, and the Light Crust Doughboys. While modestly successful, Wills felt hamstrung by the familiar problems that beset many young musicians—unscrupulous managers, temperamental band members, and a lack of significant venues. Finally, in frustration with the static Texas scene, Bob Wills and his banjo-playing brother Johnnie Lee Wills moved north to Oklahoma and signed a contract with Brunswick records in 1935. The world of American music would never be the same. With his noon-time show on Tulsa's KVOO (bear in mind that radio was a relatively new

Bob Wills' raucous music and steady smile cheered listeners during the Great Depression. Courtesy Corbis Images.

form of media at this time), the twenty-nine-year-old Wills became an overnight phenomenon and the first musician folk-hero in American history. Simply put, no one had ever heard music such as he and his colorful Texas Playboys were making before.

Wills' unique gift to Western music was the creation of the large, multi-instrument country-western band. The sound that resulted was an unlikely but brilliantly successful mixture of Mexican mariachi, French Quarter jazz, southern bluegrass, urban swing, and traditional country. With the repeal of Prohibition in 1933, people—particularly denizens of the free-spirited Southwest—were eager to get out and dance again. Roadhouses sprang up overnight, and crowds drove for miles to listen to this musical rebel Bob Wills, with his custom-made cowboy boots, wide-brimmed cowboy hat, big-lapeled cotton suits, and broad, perpetually happy face. His bright raucous music—fiddles and steel guitar, clarinets and saxophones, drums and rhythm guitar—cheered folks up during a difficult time, and reminded them, even during the darkest moments of the Great Depression, that better days were just ahead on the trail.

Part of the attraction was also that Wills and his fourteen-piece ensemble were attempting things instrumentally no one had ever done before—such as putting drums and a horn section in a country dance band. What's more, the Playboys sang the southern blues with a country-and-western twang. Even today, almost seventy years later, the songs of the Playboys can be heard on the radio, tunes such as "Sitting on Top of the World" (later performed by the Rolling Stones, as well as by Bob Dylan), "Take Me Back to Tulsa," "Steel Guitar Rag," "San Antonio Rose," and "My Confession." Seen from the perspective of many decades, it is clear that Bob Wills and the Texas Playboys were to the 1930s what country star Shania Twain was to the 1990s—a powerfully original musical force that boldly took conservative mainstream country into a new direction.

In the end, it was Bob Wills' unique destiny to create the first modern Southwestern band and to invent a form of music, and a form of entertainment, that forever transformed the cultural landscape of the West. Wills built a musical bridge between the solitary cowboy-poet strumming his guitar beside a lonely desert campfire and the likes of Willie Nelson and Waylon Jennings playing a live Farm Aid concert to the entire planet via satellite hook-up. The core message of Bob Wills, like that of the legions who later imitated and emulated him, came directly from his rural cowboy roots—be happy, be productive, but, above all, be at a distance from all that which diminishes life and the human spirit. In giving voice to these beliefs, he embraced the oldest Western myth of all: freedom.

Part of the attraction was also that Wills and his fourteen-piece ensemble were attempting things instrumentally no one had ever done before.

WOODY GUTHRIE
The Dark Side of the Dream

IN *CRITIAS* PLATO DESCRIBED ATLANTIS as a mythical realm far to the west of Greece. Atlantis was, Plato wrote, "an island larger than Libya and Asia together" which vanquished Greece because of its superior technology and tactics and then was "engulfed by earthquakes" and destroyed. Atlantis was (or so the ancient Egyptian priests had told Plato's sources) a fabled paradise, a fairy tale of a place that was, as a cultural entity, even greater than Athens. This notion of a perfect realm residing in the far west, where the sun goes each night, has persisted in our civilization through the ages. From the beginning, the American West (anything west, as Wallace Stegner wrote, of the 100th meridian) was also seen as a sort of mythical utopia. It would fall upon folksinger Woody Guthrie to write songs that explored the dark side of the Arcadian or Utopian myth, exposing the plight of the common person and the injustices that accompany human greed. Guthrie brought to American folk songs the strong social consciousness that later would become so important to songwriters like Bob Dylan, Joan Baez, Tom Paxton, Phil Ochs, and others in the 1960s.

Woodrow Wilson Guthrie was born on July 14, 1912, in Okemah, Oklahoma. He grew up in rural poverty and entered young manhood just as the Great Depression began to ravage the country, especially the country of the poor. Guthrie saw firsthand the American experience from the very bottom, and it influenced forever the way he viewed the landscape and its people. Before graduating from high school, Guthrie had already experienced his share of adult hardship: He had watched his father's business fail; his sister had been killed in a coal oil stove explosion; and his mother had been committed to a state mental institution. One of the most formative events in his early life occurred in 1932, when he traveled to the wild mountains of southwestern Texas (now Big Bend National Park) in search of a mythical gold mine, a colorful story told in his

Like John Steinbeck, Woody Guthrie reminded us of the often cold reality behind the popular myth. Courtesy Photofest.

posthumously published travel narrative *Seeds of Man,* as well as in his autobiography *Bound for Glory.* It was during this trip that his lifelong romance began with the beauty of the wild American West. The trip also helped crystallize Guthrie's other central beliefs regarding the value of natural freedom and the need to help the exploited (for he had also witnessed the terrible poverty of the lower Rio Grande Valley).

Throughout the 1930s Guthrie traveled widely across the West, moving around with the other Dust Bowl refugees, working at various blue-collar jobs and performing the occasional musical gig. Wherever he was, Guthrie played guitar and wrote songs—sometimes at the phenomenal rate or one or two a day. These songs— "Grand Coulee Dam," "This Land is Your Land," "Union Maid," "Dusty Old Dust," "Goin' Down the Road," "Deportee," "Pastures of Plenty," "I Ain't Got No Home," "Why Oh Why," "God Blessed America," "Tom Joad"—have permanently helped to shape the way people perceive the West and its people. Eventually Guthrie found himself on the East Coast, where he joined creative forces with other folk artists, including Pete Seeger, and began recording and giving public concerts. During the late 1930s Guthrie and Seeger formed the Almanac Singers and played around the country, often appearing at union meetings. Many of their songs were subsequently recorded for the Library of Congress Archive of Folk Song as the *Dust Bowl Ballads.* The complete recordings fill twelve albums.

After service in the Merchant Marines and Army during World War II, Woody Guthrie returned to the United States and married his second wife, Marjorie, a dancer with the Martha Graham dance ensemble. (Their children included Arlo, a wll known folksinger of the late 1960s.) Throughout the 1950s Woody Guthrie often appeared with blues legends Huddy Ledbetter (Leadbelly) and Blind Sonny Terry, as well as with old folk friends such as Pete Seeger. By the early 1960s, Guthrie was already feeling the effects of Huntington's chorea, the hereditary degenerative muscular disease that would eventually kill him. Before the old mythmaker died at Greystone Park Hospital in New York he was visited by a guitar-playing teenager from northern Minnesota who introduced himself as Robert Zimmerman. The young man idolized Guthrie. Within a few years the world would know this young folksinger as Bob Dylan.

Guthrie's relevance as a Western mythmaker is that he created a body of work that questioned one of the most appealing of Western fables— that the American West is the universal land of plenty. Like John Steinbeck, who in *The Grapes of Wrath* held an unflattering mirror up to the West, Guthrie reminded us of the cold reality behind the myth. His was a compassionate soul, and his songs are collectively as much celebrations as lamentations, expressions of faith and hope as well as of dismay and disillusion. Guthrie would undoubtedly be happy that his songs are still sung in schoolrooms and union halls across America, though many in the former group are perhaps unaware of the deep irony and hidden subversiveness in many of the lyrics.

Guthrie's relevance as a Western mythmaker is that he created a body of work that questioned one of the most appealing of Western fables—that the American West is the universal land of plenty.

BUDDY HOLLY AND THE CRICKETS
The Power of Optimism

SINCE THE BEGINNING, the American West has been seen as a living repository of hope, as the figurative and literal territory of the future, and as a vibrant province that by its very nature—awash in light and cloudless skies—is filled with positive expectations. Thoreau said as much when he wrote in his essay "Walking" that "Eastward I go only by force, but westward I go free.... We go westward as into the future, with a spirit of enterprise and adventure." Horace Greeley expressed the same sentiment in his well known pronouncement: "Go west, young man!" It would be songwriter/singer Buddy Holly who would make a small but immortal body of music based on this regional myth of optimism. His lyrics and melodies have come to embody the good humor, untiring hope, and cheerful outlook of the American West. The collective influence of these mythic songs, even more so than with those of his regional predecessor Bob Wills, is still being felt.

During his brief but brilliant career Buddy Holly made a permanent contribution to American music and mythology.

Charles Hardin Holley, a.k.a. Buddy Holly, was a native son of west Texas, born and raised in Lubbock, a busy ranching town in the heart of the Bible Belt. It was both an unlikely and the ideal place for one of the first rock-and-roll stars to grow up. Lubbock, unofficial capital of the southern prairie, is laid out in a geometric grid pattern of numbered and lettered streets, with older homes built in quaint Victorian styles. The core of the city consists of solid red brick buildings that reflect the unimaginative architectural tastes of a bygone era. There are literally dozens of churches in the town. During the days of Buddy Holly, there were no bars or liquor stores within the city limits. This all-American, "Main Street" sort of community is also home to Texas Tech University, known nationally for its football team (which sometimes actually beats Nebraska). The mainstays of Lubbock's economy are irrigated cotton, feedlot cattle, and deep-drilled oil and gas. It is both a hard and an easy place to live. There are blizzards every winter and tornadoes every spring, but in between the weather is mild and the prairie sun often finds itself alone without a cloud.

The Buddy Holly story has been recounted by myriad biographers and told in at least one feature film, which starred actor Gary Busey as Buddy Holly. After showing unusual musical talent at an early age, Holly soon mastered the six-stringed guitar and, with his friends, regularly played songs around town that were typical for 1950s Texas—bluegrass, folk, and country-western. His roots were in the conventional music scene of the West, but his natural instincts, budding talent, and youthful restlessness soon pulled him in other directions. Holly's earliest recording, made in Wichita Falls in 1954 when he was eighteen, featured him and his buddy Bob Montgomery. The two, together with Sonny Curtis on fiddle, recorded two home-grown compositions: "Down the Line" (an Elvis-style rockabilly number) and "Soft Place in My Heart" (a heartbreak tune in the Hank Williams mode). From this modest start, Holly developed as a songwriter at phenomenal speed. Just two years later, in January 1956, the twenty-year-old Holly had somehow made his way to Nashville, where he recorded "Blue Days" and "Love Me," both songs ahead of their times. Just as Bob Wills had fused disparate musical forms in creating his own cutting-edge Southwestern style, so Holly was now trying to weld pure acoustic country (the Hank Williams line) and electric rhythm and blues (the Gene Vincent/Elvis Presley influence).

Although Holly had been signed briefly by a record company in Nashville, he was soon released from the contract, (one of the biggest mistakes in music history). Exiled back to Lubbock, the irrepressible Holly formed a band with drummer Jerry Allison, bassist Joe Mauldin, and rhythm guitarist Niki Sullivan. Remembering how much he loved the peaceful sound of crickets on a hot prairie night, Holly decided to name his group the Crickets. On February 25, 1957, the quartet went into the studio and recorded two songs—"That'll Be the Day" and "I'm Lookin' for Someone to Love." Released as a 45-rpm record a few months later by the New York–headquartered Coral-Brunswick recording company, the songs unexpectedly rocketed to the top of the national charts. They were rapidly followed by a succession of other now-familiar hits: "Not Fade Away," "Words of Love," "Every Day," "Oh Boy!," "Peggy Sue," "Maybe Baby," "Rave On," "Heartbeat," and "It's So Easy (To Fall In Love)." At no other time in the history of modern music has a single songwriter at such a young age created so many masterpieces in such a short span of time. The entire body of work—so small and yet filled with so much melodic and lyric brilliance—is imbued with the distinctive positive voice the world now associates synonymously with Buddy Holly.

The rest of the story is familiar to all lovers of rock and roll. A year later, Buddy Holly appeared on the Ed Sullivan television show. The fans adored him—the ridiculous black plastic glasses of an accountant, the innocent exuberance of a choir boy, the natural self-confidence of a lanky, tall Texan. Sullivan brought him back for a second time on his Sunday-night program, and Holly's career was poised on the cusp of what is now called superstardom. Six months later the recently married Holly went out on a Midwestern tour with Ritchie Valens, the Big Bopper, and the Belmonts. With him was a young electric bass player named Waylon Jennings. On February 3, 1959, Waylon and Buddy stood on a snowy airport

...Buddy Holly appeared on the Ed Sullivan television show. The fans adored him—the ridiculous black plastic glasses of an accountant, the innocent exuberance of a choir boy, the natural self-confidence of a lanky, tall Texan.

runway in Iowa and flipped a coin to see who would fly in the small plane and who would ride in the tour bus. Buddy was glad he won the toss. He had developed a bad cold on the poorly heated bus and needed to reach the next town so that he could do his laundry. Waylon joked that he hoped Buddy died in the plane. Buddy joked that he hoped Jennings died on the bus. Soon afterward, twenty-two-year-old Buddy Holly was dead. The plane had not been properly de-iced and crashed near Mason City, Iowa. Also on board were Ritchie Valens, the Big Bopper, and pilot Roger Peterson.

Throughout his short career, Buddy Holly never wavered from the bright outlook that had been part of his upbringing on the Texas prairie. Every song he made, even the sad ones, are filled with faith and trust, good cheer and optimism. Part of this is the nature of youth—the hope that one's generation will somehow transform the world with its raw energy and new ideas—but part of this also derived from the geographic and cultural landscape in which Buddy Holly was born and raised. He carried with him the same hopeful disposition that brought the first pioneers to the inhospitable plains of west Texas and that caused them to always see the promise of a wonderful future. Their entire belief system was based on the notion that people could forge a better life.

Had Holly lived, there is little doubt but that he would have been a major force in the international music scene of the 1960s. This much is certain: He gave the world the first rock-and-roll quartet (electric rhythm guitar, electric lead guitar, electric bass, and drums), an innovation that influenced such bands as the Beach Boys, the Beatles (whose very name was inspired by Holly's playful Crickets), the Rolling Stones, the Kinks, the Who, the Byrds, Cream, the Doors, the Jimi Hendrix Experience, and Led Zeppelin, to name just a few. His music, more importantly, made a permanent impression on an emerging generation of young songwriters, most notably Bob Dylan and John Lennon, both of whom would carry Buddy Holly's simple message of hope, compassion, and love into the turbulent 1960s.

PACIFIC COAST MUSIC
The Far West as Creative Wellspring

SINCE THE BEGINNING, the West has been considered the literal and figurative landscape of the future. Nowhere is this myth more evident than in the popular music of the West Coast. Over the last forty years the world has learned to look to the songwriters and bands of the Pacific West for the newest, cutting-edge musical sounds. The three chief centers of music-making on the West Coast are Los Angeles, San Francisco, and Seattle. While each city is part of the same Pacific shoreline, the musical traditions and respective mythical systems could not be more different. Together they have helped to shape the future of music around the planet.

Los Angeles
Endless Summer

Washed by the sun and warmed by the sea, the southern coast of California offers a vision, however simple and false, of endless summer, carefree days, and most especially, eternal youth. Human beings yearn for such easy myths because they simplify what is complex, render comprehensible what is inscrutable, and satisfy the natural longing for order in life. The myth of southern California is a happy, if shallow, fiction. It is the essence, in some respects, of the American dream. It leads people to believe—perhaps more easily in the presence of the calm, blue eternity of the Pacific—that they, too, will endure forever and enjoy perfect health, absolute

freedom, and constant prosperity along the way. Over the last century the appealing fable has transformed Los Angeles into one of the most densely populated (and polluted) cities on the planet. Even as this book was being written, another massive housing development east of L.A. was being considered by civic leaders as the metroplex continued to grow (some would say metastasize) without restraint into the surrounding deserts.

From the beginning of modern music—and this was true even in the days of Frank Sinatra, Dean Martin, and Sammy Davis, Jr.—performers have actively explored the myth of L.A. in their songs. They have written in loving terms of its virtues ("California Dreamin'" by the Mamas and the Papas) and they have spoken out more critically of its shortcomings (as in "James Dean" by the Eagles). Their ranks include such familiar names as Joni Mitchell and such unusual characters as Frank Zappa. Many of these artists have chosen to permanently live in the L.A. area, ranging from icons such as Bob Dylan (Malibu) and Bruce Springsteen (Beverly Hills), to lesser figures such as Julian Lennon (Hollywood Hills). As a result, Los Angeles has become the recording capital of the popular music industry (with Nashville as the recording capital of country-western music). For the past forty years the city has also consistently offered some of the best club venues in the world for musical acts.

The beautiful Pacific coast serves as a powerful inspiration for songwriters. Courtesy John Murray.

The songwriter most responsible for the modern musical legend of southern California is Brian Wilson. Born on June 20, 1942, in the seaside suburb of Hawthorne, California, Brian Wilson grew up in the era of long-playing vinyl records, hand-held transistor radios, and black-and-white televisions. His musical influences included Chuck Berry, Elvis Presley, Bill Haley and the Comets, Sam Cooke, Jerry Lee Lewis, Little Richard, the Ronettes, the Crystals, and, though less often recognized, the legendary Stratocaster-playing of surfer/guitarist Dick Dale (of the Del-Tones). From an early age, with his strong tenor/soprano voice, Wilson enjoyed singing traditional tunes for relatives and playing Top Forty hits on the family piano. He also performed as a vocalist in the local church choir and at high school functions. By the time he was eighteen Wilson had, in the lively spirit of the times, formed his own rock-and-roll band with brothers Dennis and Carl, first cousin Mike Love, and beach buddy Al Jardine.

Inspired by the timeless beauty of the southern California landscape, the bikini-clad young women of the summer beach, and the innocent *joie de vivre* of adolescence, Wilson soon began to write his own songs. Interestingly enough, it was surfer-brother Dennis Wilson who first suggested that Brian specifically concentrate on composing songs about the burgeoning surfing craze. (Contrary to popular mythology, Brian Wilson was afraid of the water and never surfed.) Although he was initially imitative of the pioneering rock hits of Chuck Berry ("Surfin' USA," for example, echoes Berry's "Sweet Little Sixteen") and the brilliant studio work of Phil Spector (with the Ronettes and the Crystals), Brian Wilson ultimately proved himself to be an original and powerful creative force.

Many songwriters labor for years before recognition. One thinks of Bruce Springsteen, who played obscure East Coast venues for the better part of a decade, or of John Lennon and

The music of the Beach Boys formed a cultural bridge between the conservative fifties and the liberal sixties. Photo by Klaus Kranz.

Paul McCartney, who worked a long line of smoky beer halls from Liverpool to Hamburg. Not so for Brian Wilson and the Beach Boys, who rocketed to the top of the charts with their first recorded song, "Surfin'." I can still remember, when I was nine, listening with my older brother Bill for hours to the first 33 1/3 rpm record released by the Beach Boys. No one had ever heard music like that before—a vocally diverse ensemble of young men harmonizing upon the beauty of nature and all that is imperishable in the human spirit. With Mike Love on lead vocals, Dennis Wilson on drums, Carl Wilson on lead guitar, Alan Jardine on rhythm guitar, and Brian Wilson on bass or keyboards, the Beach Boys made an impressive stage presence. The band combined the well-crafted singing style of Doo-Wop groups such as Danny and the Juniors ("At the Hop"), the Penguins ("Earth Angel"), the Everly Brothers ("Kathy's Clown"), and the Marcells ("Blue Moon") with the kinetic rhythms of pure West Coast rock.

With the unexpected success of their first album, the Beach Boys soon had all of the sudden wealth and fame that comes with the bright myth of eternal youth. (And it is important to remember that they were still boys—Carl Wilson, for example, was not yet old enough to carry a driver's license.) The Beach Boys literally took the nation, and later the world, by storm. Part of their success derived from the fact their songs were fresh and innovative from a melodic and thematic standpoint. Another aspect related to their unconventional stage presence, which was the living embodi-

ment of southern California informality. They performed in baggy Bermuda shorts, colorful Hawaiian shirts, and leather sandals. Not surprisingly, the Beach Boys' friendly upbeat music and relaxed demeanor ushered in a new era of casualness in the popular culture, a refreshing change after the culturally repressed 1950s, and helped to spawn a profitable series of beach movies starring former Disney Mouseketeer Annette Funicello and her on-screen beau Frankie Avalon, also a pop singer.

Rock-and-roll bands across the country watched helplessly as the Beach Boys became the premier performing act of the early 1960s. The combo appeared as often on national television as they did in large concert halls, including Dick Clark's *American Bandstand*, the *Andy Williams Show*, the *Jack Benny Show*, the *Bob Hope Show*, the *Red Skelton Show*, the *Ed Sullivan Show*, and, most coveted of all for southern Californians, Johnny Carson's L.A.-based *Tonight Show*. The message of the Wilson clan was as simple as it was appealing—be young at heart and be close to nature. Their environmentally based songs evoked, if unconsciously, the ancient Greek myth of Antaeus, a man who could only be killed if he was separated from the Earth. In Brian Wilson's sunny lyrics of first love, fast cars, and fun-filled beaches, which collectively evoked an unreal image of an ideal myth, millions of postwar baby boomers had found their resident minstrel and spiritual leader.

Looking back from the distance of nearly half a century, Wilson's songs can be seen as an

With the unexpected success of their first album, the Beach Boys soon had all of the sudden wealth and fame that comes with the bright myth of eternal youth.

expression of the old (dating back to Spanish Colonial days) southern Californian myth of eternal youth. The songs fall naturally into three categories. First, the bulk of Wilson's compositions are love songs, and romantic love, synonymous with youth, is an integral part of the eternal youth mythology. They include such now-familiar titles as "California Girls," "Wendy," and "Wouldn't It Be Nice."

A second category in the Wilson repertoire are surfing songs, ballads such as "Catch a Wave," "Surfin'," and "Surfin' USA." The last group can be loosely called Southern California life-style songs: "Good Vibrations," "Be True to Your School," "All Summer Long," and "This Car of Mine." A handful of compositions hint at a less pleasant side of the southern California myth—songs such as "I Just Wasn't Made For These Times," "Heroes and Villains," and the most introspective confessional of all, "In My Room."

Every myth has its dark side, and the myth of Brian Wilson and his endless summer is no different. Biographers have chronicled a turbulent middle class family life that resembles something from an Ingmar Bergman film. The relationship between father and son, the subject of a February 2000 made-for-television movie produced by ABC, was apparently conflict-ridden *in extremis*. We also know that Wilson at some point in his youth lost the hearing in one ear. Later, after the band had met with success, Wilson suffered several well-documented breakdowns and largely retired from public view, living as a near-recluse at his comfortable home in Malibu. Through the seventies and

eighties he appeared infrequently with the band. He lives today on a country estate with his third wife and their two children in, of all places, Illinois. Tragedy haunted the band in later years, as Dennis Wilson perished in 1983 (at the age of 39) in a drowning accident and Carl Wilson died unexpectedly in 1998 (at the age of 52) from lung cancer.

In the end, the Beach Boys will be remembered as much for having given definitive musical expression to the eternal youth myth of Southern California as for having been so innovative in their studio work. Brian Wilson's revolutionary thirteen-song album *Pet Sounds* (which was inspired by the Beatles' 1965 album *Rubber Soul*) was credited by Paul McCartney as having then served as the inspiration for the Beatles' finest album, *Sgt. Pepper's Lonely Hearts Club Band* (1967). That's not a bad legacy for a band that began in a Southern California suburban garage with borrowed instruments and was led by a shy, eccentric teenager, Brian Wilson, who had no formal music training. Such is the power of the luminous southern sea, and the warm southern sun, to stir the spirit and enrich the journey of life.

Even as the Beach Boys reached the peak of their success in the mid-1960s, the musical world, reflecting the cultural world, began to undergo a tremendous sea-change. Following the Cuban missile crisis in 1962, the assassination of President Kennedy in 1963, and the steady escalation of the Vietnam War by President Johnson after 1964, a new pessimism and world-weariness began to pervade the arts,

Following the Cuban missile crisis in 1962, the assassination of President Kennedy in 1963, and the steady escalation of the Vietnam War by President Johnson after 1964, a new pessimism and world-weariness began to pervade the arts, mirroring changes that were occuring in society at large.

mirroring changes that were occurring in society at large. This new point of view soon found expression in the music of West Coast rock bands, most noticeably in a new rock-and-roll group formed in 1965 by ex–UCLA film students Jim Morrison and Ray Manzarek and called the Doors (from Aldous Huxley's psychedelic book, *The Doors of Perception,* the title of which derived from William Blake's line, "If the doors of perception were cleansed, we would see everything as it is, infinite."). Morrison, the lead vocalist and chief songwriter, wrote hit songs such as "People Are Strange," "L.A. Woman," and "Twentieth Century Fox" that examined the dark side of the traditional L.A. myth of innocent youth and romantic love.

Morrison's controversial lifestyle, well documented in such biographies as *No One Gets Out of Here Alive* (Jerry Hopkins and Danny Sugerman, 1980), further embraced the dark side of the eternal youth myth. Morrison found himself arrested in March 1969 following a Florida rock-and-roll concert. The charges included committing a felony (lewd and lascivious behavior) and three misdemeanors (indecent exposure, open profanity, and public drunkenness) while performing on stage. In September 1970 a jury acquitted Morrison of the felony charge and of public drunkenness, but found him guilty of profanity and public exposure. The next month a judge sentenced Morrison (incredibly, in retrospect) to eight months of hard labor and twenty-eight months of probation for these two misdemeanors. He also gave the band leader a five-hundred-dollar

fine. The case was on appeal when Morrison's wife Pamela found the singer/poet dead in a Paris hotel bathtub on July 3, 1971, the victim of a heart attack. He was twenty-seven years old. Morrison's death occurred within eighteen months of the deaths of Janis Joplin and Jimi Hendrix and signaled the end of the bright period that had begun with the surfing ballads of Brian Wilson just ten short years earlier.

At this point the golden age of West Coast Rock was clearly over. What followed in the 1970s was, by comparison, a musical Silver Age. Two southern California bands stand out from that period, particularly with respect to the eternal youth myth: the Eagles and Fleetwood Mac. Both groups created songs that explored the central myth of their cultural province, but in very different ways. The Eagles were the brainchild of Texas-born Don Henley, who settled in L.A. in

Jim Morrison brought a new hard edge to the world of southern California music. Courtesy Photofest.

The Eagles were one of the most commercially successful rock bands of the seventies. Photo by Klaus Kranz.

1970 at the age of twenty-three. Playing steadily at west-L.A. night clubs, drummer Henley and his rock compadres, Glen Frey (guitar), Randy Meisner (bass, later replaced by Tim Schmit), and Bernie Leadon (guitar, later replaced by Joe Walsh), set out to create a California sound that would fill the void left by the demise of the Beach Boys and the Doors. In songs such as "New Kid in Town," "Tequila Sunrise," and "Life in the Fast Lane," Henley and Frey wrote eloquently of conflict, betrayal, and the pain of lost love. While musically acknowledging the influence of Brian Wilson and Jim Morrison, Henley and Fry also created a new sort of sound to express the L.A. eternal youth myth.

After the Eagles broke apart in 1981, the melancholy-voiced Don Henley pursued a successful solo career that expanded upon the work he had begun with the band. In songs such as "Dirty Laundry," "Johnny Can't Read," "Tender is the Night" (recorded by Jackson Browne), and especially, in *The End of the Innocence* (1989) album, Henley created a unique body of work that provided a compelling look at the myth of

Los Angeles in modern times. When listened to collectively, the songs of Henley project a sense of maturity and of the tragic that was only nascent in the songs of Brian Wilson and Jim Morrison. Henley held up a mirror to his times—the purpose of any artist—but he also attempted to lead people into a place that included greater understanding, compassion, and forgiveness (also the purpose of any artist).

Similarly, the chief songwriters of the L.A.-based Fleetwood Mac—Stevie Nicks and Lindsey Buckingham—attempted to re-examine the old myths of love and youth in a contemporary way. The band had actually formed in the late 1960s when Mick Fleetwood, who had left John Mayall's Bluesbreakers, decided to form a new band with John McVie, also a former member of the Bluesbreakers. Eventually they added other members, including singer Christine Perfect (later McVie), guitarist Lindsey Buckingham, and Buckingham's folksinging girlfriend, Stevie Nicks. The band was, and is, unique in that there were two very passionate romances at its core—one between John and Christine, and the other between Lindsey and Stevie. These intense love relationships provided the emotional energy that inspired the group to create the signature rock album of the 1970s: *Rumours.* The legendary songs on the best-selling album are constantly played on FM radio stations even today. Compositions such as "Go Your Own Way," "You Make Loving Fun," and "Rhiannon" look at the ancient themes of love and betrayal, freedom and responsibility, despair and hope in ways that remain ever-fresh, both melodically and lyrically. Although the band attempted to mine the same mother lode in a later album, *Tusk* (1979), the earlier *Rumours* remains their finest work and one of the most successful commentaries ever on the mythology of romantic love, and on the larger myth of the L.A. experience.

The eighties and nineties saw literally dozens of pop bands quickly rise and fall upon the musical landscape of the City of Angels. A constant stream of musicians recorded at L.A. studios or performed at venues in town, and many performers called it home, including such major voices as Warren Zevon and Tom Petty. One of the most dynamic albums to come from an L.A.-based band was *Tragic Kingdom*, released by No Doubt in 1995. The Grammy-

winning album, which went on to sell fifteen million copies and remain on the charts for over a year, featured the brilliant singing of Gwen Stefani, with the songs co-written by her brother. Lyrics to songs such as "Spiderwebs" and "Don't Speak," which explored the terrain of lost love and innocence, could trace their musical roots to the earliest songs of Brian Wilson, and resonated with the same melodic power. In *Tragic Kingdom*, No Doubt proved that L.A. bands could still produce works of excellence despite what might be called the burden of the past—the intimidating presence of the monumental body

Fleetwood Mac explored the myth of Southern California in new and compelling ways. Courtesy Photofest.

of work produced by such giants as Brian Wilson and Jim Morrison. The band's follow-up album, *Return to Saturn,* was an instant success in the spring of 2000, with more songs from the mythic world of youthful love lost and found.

In an essay entitled "Summer in Algiers," the French philosopher and 1960 Nobel laureate Albert Camus describes the southern Mediterranean coast in terms that would be familiar to inhabitants of southern California. Camus writes of "the sea, visible from every corner, a certain heaviness of the sunlight, the beauty of the people." The perpetually sunny coast is a place of "sensual riches" where people find "a beauty that matches their youth" and "life follows the curve of great passions." The shore is, he observes humorously, a place where "the notion of hell is nothing more than an amusing joke." It is, finally, a place that recalls "the simplicity of the Greeks."

In the last observation, Camus strikes at a truth that relates as much to the landscape of southern California as it does to that of the southern Mediterranean: the myth of eternal youth goes back to the birthplace of western civilization, Greece. It was the Greeks who first extolled the beauty and power of youth, and made that bright blue myth the basis for a timeless body of lyric poetry, dramatic poetry, song, painting, and sculpture. Like the people of Albert Camus' Algeria or Brian Wilson's California, the Greeks lived by the sea. They loved the sand and the sun and all that is evoked by nature's song and light. Perhaps no higher tribute can be paid to the music and people of

southern California than this: if the men and women who created our civilization twenty-five hundred years ago could be reconstituted, they would, in the cultural and geographic landscape of southern California, feel perfectly at home.

San Francisco
Somebody to Love

For over a century and a half, the Bay Area has been *the* creative center of the American West. From the days of Mark Twain and, later, Maynard Dixon to the era of Ansel Adams and Allen Ginsberg, San Francisco has served as the heart of a vibrant artistic milieu. During the mid-1960s, a group of rock-and-roll musicians based in San Francisco created a distinctive sound that changed popular music forever. This band of psychedelic gypsies included such now-venerated performers as Janis Joplin ("Piece of My Heart"), Grace Slick ("Somebody to Love"), and Jerry Garcia ("Truckin'"). Their music captured the essence of the San Francisco experience—the notion of a city, and of a resident artistic culture, that is forever questioning the status quo, and pushing thought and art beyond traditional boundaries and into the future.

The band that best expressed the restless, independent spirit of San Francisco was the Grateful Dead. The group formed around guitarist Jerry Garcia, a Buddha-like musical figure who was, from the mid-1960s until the time of his death in 1997, perpetually clad in brightly colored T-shirts, well-worn blue jeans, and leather sandals. Garcia, who was born in 1942,

The musical legacy of the Grateful Dead remains ever-popular, as does their simple philosophy, which is based on a deep sense of community and an abiding notion of the grand possibilities of life.

grew up in the Bay Area and formed a number of proto-Dead, folk-electric bands during his early twenties, including Mother McCree's Uptown Jug Champions and the Warlocks. By 1965 the group was known as the Grateful Dead, a phrase that was meant to evoke happy affirmation in the face of the bleak absurdity of life. By 1967 the band had become a regular act at the Fillmore Auditorium, which was managed by promoter Bill Graham, and were often known to give free concerts in Golden Gate Park. At that time the Haight-Ashbury area (referring to the neighborhood surrounding the intersection of two streets) was the center of the worldwide psychedelic movement.

Eventually the band was signed by Warner Brothers, and it put out several successful albums in the late 1960s and early 1970s, including *The Grateful Dead* (1967), *Anthem of the Sun* (1968), *Workingman's Dead* (1970), and *American Beauty* (1970). In songs such as "Uncle John's Band," "Ripple," "Box of Rain," and "Truckin'" (their only Top 40 hit), Garcia and company (Bob Weir, Ron "Pigpen" McKernan, Bill Kreutzmann, and Phil Lesh) introduced a creative new strain to popular music. To those who had the good fortune to see the band live, their forte was clearly, more than studio work, afternoon-long, outdoor, improvisational concerts.

The Dead, more than any other band that came of age in the 1960s, believed in constantly touring. By appearing at different venues across the country year after year, decade after decade, the band built an enormous national follow-

ing—a sort of Grateful Dead Nation. At the heart of this cult, or clan, was the enduring myth of San Francisco—that one should be free of all that tends to diminish the spirit of life and should constantly endeavor to find new adventure, new knowledge, and new (for lack of a better word) fun. This band of smarter-than-they-looked Hippies (most were wealthy businessmen) offered people hope and joy in the face of the cynicism and despair of the late 1960s and 1970s. Incredibly, the band continued to tour through the 1980s and 1990s (including a celebrated tour in 1987 with Bob Dylan), right up until the death of leader Jerry Garcia in 1997.

A Grateful Dead concert was an experience like no other— a mixture of social gathering and musical celebration. Courtesy Photofest.

The musical legacy of the Grateful Dead remains ever-popular, as does their simple philosophy, which is based on a deep sense of community and an abiding notion of the grand possibilities of life. Garcia and his merry band saw, as the poet John Donne phrased it, that "no man is an islande," and that if we join hands and walk together the pilgrimage of life is all that much sweeter. That belief, too, is at the heart of the San Francisco experience, for the eclectic town is the most culturally rich urban area in America, and is held together, as the Dead Nation is, by tolerance, faith, and good humor.

Seattle
Purple Haze

Mention Seattle and most people think rain—lots and lots of rain. Rain that begins in the early fall and doesn't end until late spring. Rain that falls hour after hour, day after day, week after week. Rain that causes moss to grow up the sides of houses. Rain that causes streams and rivers to flood and the sides of mountains to slide away. Rain that leaks through the sturdiest of roofs and permeates even the strongest of consciousnesses. In fact, parts of the Olympic peninsula west of Seattle receive more annual precipitation than many tropical rain forests along the equator. During the perpetually overcast, rainy winter months, seasonal affective

disorder, a depressive, melatonin-based result of light deprivation, becomes epidemic in the Seattle area. (The region has the highest rate of Prozac use in the United States.) This geographic situation has helped to create a human environment and an artistic culture that, like those found in Scandinavia, Russia, or Alaska, tends to be introspective, brooding, and melancholy. Whereas southern California embraces the mythology of light, northwestern Washington moves more toward myths that accrete around darkness and shadow.

Jimi Hendrix provided an electrifying performance at Woodstock. Courtesy Photofest.

The artist who has given best expression to the moody angst that is synonymous with Seattle is Jimi Hendrix, who spent eighteen of his twenty-eight years in the city. Hendrix was born at Seattle General Hospital on November 27, 1941. After the age of four, he was raised by his single father, Al Hendrix. It was Al who encouraged his young son's musical abilities, teaching him the four-stringed ukele and buying him his first acoustic six-string guitar when Hendrix was eleven. Soon Jimi began visiting the downtown blues clubs and picking up records by the blues masters: Muddy Waters, Robert Johnson, Howlin' Wolf. After high school he joined the 101st Airborne and served as a paratrooper in a rifle company for a year and a half at Fort Campbell, Kentucky. While in the Army, Hendrix played his Stratocaster electric guitar in the barracks whenever he had a free moment and always in his unique left-handed style.

After being discharged, Hendrix moved restlessly around the country for several years, playing backup for such acts as B. B. King, Sam Cooke, Ike and Tina Turner, the Isley Brothers, and Little Richard. His first song, for the Los Angeles–based Revis label, was an unimpressive lyric entitled "My Diary." By 1965 Hendrix had moved to Greenwich Village in New York City. While there, he began performing at local clubs, including Cafe A'Go Go and Cafe Wha?, and it was in these venues that he was first noticed by such well-established figures as Mick Jagger, Keith Richards, Bob Dylan, Miles Davis, and Brian "Chas" Chandler (of the Animals). Chandler befriended Hendrix and persuaded

him to move to London. Once there Hendrix formed, with bassist Noel Redding and drummer Mitch Mitchell, one of the most original bands of all time: the Jimi Hendrix Experience. His 1967 debut album—*Are You Experienced?*—caused a sensation in the British music world, featuring as it did his spectacular guitar-playing and stellar songwriting.

A few months later, on June 18, 1967, Hendrix returned to the West Coast to play, with Otis Redding, Janis Joplin, the Grateful Dead, the Who, and others, the Monterey Pop Festival. His presence there, together with the release of such now-classic albums as *Axis: Bold as Love* and *Electric Ladyland,* brought about a revolution on the American musical landscape. On August 18, 1969, he made a riveting appearance at the Woodstock concert in New York. Peter Townsend of the Who later recalled, "I don't think I've ever had as much enjoyment out of a live performance as I had out of watching Jimi [at Woodstock], because I felt so free just looking at him." Guitarist Neil Young went further and observed that "No one [among us guitarists] was even in the same building as Jimi Hendrix." Although Hendrix's songs ("Purple Haze," "Manic Depression," "Castles Made of Sand," "The Wind Cries Mary") consistently dealt with dark themes—mental illness, suicide, failed dreams, pain, loneliness—they did so in a way that was both transcendent and inspiring. His songs were heroic in that they represented his own personal victory over the demons that plagued him, and eventually, on September 18, 1970, took his life.

No one [among us guitarists] was even in the same building as Jimi Hendrix.

—Neil Young

Today Hendrix is buried in his native Seattle. There are currently plans to build a memorial pavilion near the grave site to celebrate his life and musical achievements. His influence on musicians of the Seattle area is still being felt, as was seen most recently during the 1990s as the Seattle Grunge bands—Nirvana, Pearl Jam, and Hole—revisited the same psychological province of despair and alienation first explored by Hendrix. In the end, it was Hendrix's legacy to give to rock and roll what Robert Johnson gave to the blues—a sense of unlimited possibilities for the musical form. Although Jimi Hendrix traveled widely across the world (and, according to his pop biographers, the universe), he never really left Seattle as a spiritual place on the map, and his music remains emblematic of the unique ambiance of the Northwest.

JOHN DENVER
Rocky Mountain High

THE TRADITION OF THE TROUBADOUR—the folk balladeer who sings passionately of nature and love—goes back to ancient Greek poet/ songwriters such as Pindar (the word music comes from the Greek *mousike*, meaning devotion to a muse). Later came the Renaissance, with such lyric poets as François Villon ("Where are the snows of yesteryear?") and Shakespeare, who composed mandolin and guitar–accompanied songs for his plays. Still later we have such figures as Robert Burns, the eighteenth-century Scottish poet who wrote such familiar songs as "Auld Lange Syne" (sung drunkenly around the world every New Year's Eve) and "Green Grow the Rushes." Before the twentieth century, the closest that American music had to such an inspirational poet/singer was Stephen Foster (1826–1864), who created such popular tunes as "My Old Kentucky Home" (still heard at the opening of the Kentucky Derby the first Saturday of every May), "Jeanie with the Light Brown Hair," "Hard Times," and "Oh! Susanna."

In modern times the songwriter from the American West who best represented this long troubadour tradition was John Denver. Born in Roswell, New Mexico, in 1943 to an Air Force pilot father, Denver (born Deutschendorf) traveled widely around the world as a child and teenager. Later he briefly attended Texas Tech in Lubbock (the home of Buddy Holly) before heading west to Los Angeles. Every successful career must have its lucky break and Denver's occurred in 1965, when he was invited to join the Chad Mitchell Trio, a folksinging group. Denver toured with them from 1965 through 1969. It was during this time that he began writing his own material, including a lonesome love ballad entitled "Leaving on a Jet Plane." The song was subsequently recorded by Peter, Paul, and Mary in 1969 and went on to become a national hit.

The biggest change in the young troubadour's life occurred the following year, when he married his girlfriend, Anne Martell, and

qua muse and healer animated the lives and writings of other Western artists, including John Muir, Georgia O'Keeffe, and John Ford. It would be Denver's destiny to give to that belief system a musical form.

What followed after Denver's 1971 gold album, *Poems, Prayers, and Promises,* was one of the most extraordinarily successful careers in modern music and pop culture. In the Far West of the 1970s, the musical presence of folk-pop singer and Rocky Mountain mythmaker John Denver was everywhere. First were the nature and love songs, heard constantly on AM and FM rock and country stations (to the point that even his most ardent fans began to weary of them). At the core of these songs was the old myth that the Rocky Mountains were a kind of Western paradise—a place where you could move and your life would instantly become whole, happy, and free. In addition to the songs were the numerous outdoor concerts, television entertainment shows, and various specials, including an annual Christmas show watched by up to thirty million viewers. In 1974 the governor of Colorado, Richard Lamm, set aside a week in June as "Welcome Back Home Again, John Denver" week and issued a declaration proclaiming the singer "Poet Laureate of Colorado." The crowning achievement was the 1977 Carl Reiner movie (with two sequels) *Oh God!* in which Denver, as an ordinary man searching for meaning, co-starred with comedian George Burns, who played a friendly, down-to-earth God.

Songwriter John Denver came out of the long troubador tradition that goes back to the Renaissance. Photo by Klaus Kranz.

moved permanently to Aspen, Colorado. The beauty of the southern Rocky Mountains (the world-famous Maroon Bells were just a short hike from his home) inspired him to his most accomplished period of songwriting. These songs include such now-beloved classics as "Rocky Mountain High," "Country Roads," "Sunshine on My Shoulder," and "Thank God I'm a Country Boy." Denver's songs embraced one of the oldest myths in the American West, that the purity and beauty of the high mountains can be a source of creative inspiration, spiritual solace, and emotional healing. In fact, the larger concept goes back even further, to the Bible, in such passages as "I will lift mine eyes to the mountains...." As is seen elsewhere in these pages, this same principle of wild nature

The irony of the life and career of John Denver is that his myth-building songs attracted more and more people to the place he loved and ultimately helped, through the resulting sprawl along the Front Range and I-70 corridor, to destroy it. What happened to southern California in the 1960s—unbridled development and environmental degradation—came to Colorado in the 1970s and 1980s, and John Denver was at the center of it all, singing attractive paeans to the beauty of the place. Still, it is difficult to find fault with a man who met each day with a smile and who worked so tirelessly on nature's behalf. Over time Denver came to symbolize the Colorado wilderness, the way John Muir or Ansel Adams had come to epitomize the California wilderness earlier in the century, and in later years he devoted much of his energy and resources to conservation projects both in Colorado and elsewhere. When he died near Carmel, California, in 1998, after accidentally crashing his single-engine plane into the Pacific at sunset, his best years as a creative artist were behind him, but his musical legacy and the myths he had perpetuated would live on.

WILLIE NELSON
The Outlaw Life

SINCE THE BEGINNING, the West has been a province defined in part by its infamous outlaws. Almost every town of note in the West, from Dodge City to Tombstone to Virginia City, has had its notorious desperadoes. These characters first arrived in the region by steamship and railroad, stagecoach and wagon, on horseback and on foot. Like wolves following a herd of bison, they shadowed the vast influx of miners, cattlemen, homesteaders, adventurers, merchants, and bankers across the plains and mountains. Living outside the law, they preyed upon the weak and solitary. Sometimes they formed short-lived gangs, but usually, like most outcasts, they were loners, preferring to operate solo or with one or two tested partners. Some of the West's strongest myths have formed around some of these characters. Their names still ring out over the ages—Sam Bass and Belle Starr of Texas, Billy the Kid of New Mexico and Arizona, Butch Cassidy and the Sundance Kid of Utah, Bonnie and Clyde Barrow of central Texas.

The Western musical figure who has most parlayed this outlaw mythology into a career is Willie Nelson. Together with his fellow Texans, Waylon Jennings (who had been on that last fateful tour with Buddy Holly) and Kris Kristofferson, Nelson led a successful revolution against traditional country-western music in the 1970s largely based on the outlaw persona of himself and his compadres. Nelson, who was born in Fort Worth in 1933, has over the last

The Western musical figure who has most parlayed this outlaw mythology into a career is Willie Nelson.

Willie Nelson has been the ultimate musical rebel. Photo by Klaus Kranz.

forty years proven himself to be one of the most enduring songwriters in country-western music. He made his first public appearance at the age of ten as a gospel singer at a revival picnic. As a teenager he met Bob Wills (leader of the Texas Playboys), who encouraged him to continue to develop his skills as a songwriter. He was immediately and forever changed. Several years after the meeting with Wills, Nelson joined the Ray Price Band as a bass player and composed what is now his signature song, "Night Life." Hit after hit followed in the early 1960s, including "Hello Walls" (recorded by Faron Young), "Crazy" (recorded by Patsy Cline), and "Pretty Paper" (recorded by Roy Orbison). Nelson's muse, however, left him stranded without any gold-selling songs for an extended period in

the late 1960s and early 1970s, and for a time he seriously contemplated retiring from music.

Disillusioned with the pure country line of Nashville, and all of the politically correct restrictions it imposed on songwriters, Nelson took a left turn in 1974 and began writing music for a younger and different generation of country-western fans. His physical appearance changed at this time as well, as he grew his red hair out and tied it in two long braids. The songs that followed—such as "Bloody Mary Morning" and "After the Fire is Gone"—blazed a new trail into the future of country-western. Subsequent albums—*Red-Headed Stranger, Wanted: The Outlaws, Waylon and Willie, Highwaymen*—further built upon the rebellious, anti-authoritarian persona that Nelson was consciously creating around himself and his cadre of musician-friends. Once again, Nelson found that he was writing songs that the public loved: "Good-Hearted Woman," "Remember Me," "Sweet Memories," and others.

Nelson also began to branch out creatively and worked in the film industry, playing the role of Robert Redford's "outlaw" manager in *The Electric Horseman* (1979). He constructed a film set on his ranch near Austin, Texas, and began making picaresque dramatic films such as *Honeysuckle Rose* (1980), *The Songwriter* (1984), and *Red-Headed Stranger* (1987). Misfortune struck in the 1990s, when the IRS announced a $16.7 million tax assessment against him, and his son subsequently committed suicide. Showing great resilience, Nelson rebounded from defeat as he had earlier in his career and, even as he dealt with these issues, continued to write songs and release albums (such as the brilliant 1993 album *Across the Borderline,* which included duets with Bob Dylan, Bonnie Raitt, and other longtime musical friends). In 1993 Willie Nelson was inducted into the Country Music Hall of Fame and proclaimed a "Living Texas Legend" by the governor of Texas.

Over the past forty years Nelson has created an immortal body of music, songs that transcend standard country-western to reach out to people of all musical tastes. Part of his success is related to his mythological outlaw persona—fans can vicariously live out the life of the outlaw through his songs. The image of Nelson as renegade has become as important as his musical chronicle of a fugitive life "on the borderline." Nelson has become known around the world for his high, warbling voice, his simple musical arrangements, his austere guitar playing, and his memorable songs about romantic love, the beauty of the land, and the freedom of the road. He has also become respected (revealing a Woody Guthrie influence) as a man with a social conscious, both for his annual Dripping Springs benefit concerts and his legendary Farm Aid concerts (to help distressed small farm owners). Even his critics—tenacious devotees of pure country—would concede that this gentle rebel has changed popular music in the American West forever.

SELENA
Down By the River

IN A PBS DOCUMENTARY that aired several years ago Bill Moyers postulated that a new country was developing along the borderlands between the United States and Mexico, sprawling two thousand miles from San Diego and Tijuana on the far west to Brownsville and the outlet of the Rio Grande on the east. As a cultural region, the mythical emerging entity shared characteristics of both the northern European–based society of the U.S. and the Spanish-based society of Mexico. Some thinkers have gone further, and predicted that the formation of such a separate political province is inevitable (though perhaps in the distant future), and that its birth will correct some of the injustices that occurred after the Mexican War concluded in 1848, when the Treaty of Guadalupe Hidalgo brought California, Arizona, New Mexico, Nevada, and much of Colorado into the national territory of the United States. This new region would be based as much on the world of Cervantes as that of Shakespeare. It would bring together Spanish and English, south and north, warmer lands and colder lands, and create a rich new cultural entity whose collective strengths would transcend those of either of its precursors.

During the 1990s a musical figure emerged along the border country of Texas and Mexico who seemed to represent the restless voice of all those who live in this transitional region, and who long for a better and more inclusive way of life. Her name was Selena Quintanilla-Perez,

As a cultural region, the mythical emerging entity shared characteristics of both the northern European-based society of the U.S. and the Spanish-based society of Mexico.

and she was born in 1972 in Corpus Christi, Texas. Her birthplace was in the heart of the low border country along the bright blue Gulf of Mexico. The long subtropical coast has a Spanish history that goes back to the sixteenth century, with the legendary walkabout of the shipwrecked explorer Cabeza de Vaca. South Texas is a region with more sunny days than cloudy, with summers cooled by the ocean breezes, and winters so mild that snow rarely falls. It is a place where northerners come to vacation, especially when the days are short, and it is also home to some of the best cattle-ranching country in Texas, including the legendary 1.2-million-acre King Ranch.

Selena was born into a lower middle class family in Corpus Christi, one struggling for assimilation with North American culture but still deeply bound to Mexico and, at a greater distance, to Spain. Although Spanish was forbidden in the public schools, it was spoken at home, and so when Selena sang songs at home with her father, sister, and brother, it was often in Spanish. As Selena came of age in the late 1980s and early 1990s, she found herself singing what had become known as Tejano music. (The word Tejano had been adopted by Mexican-Americans of the border country to describe their cultural community.) Tejano music traces its roots to the Tex-Mex *conjunto* music popular in the 1950s and 1960s, which employed multiple vocals, guitars, accordions, and harmonicas based around a jumpy, polka-style dance beat.

This new form of music, and the instant and enormous success it enjoyed, signaled both the arrival of a new generation and the birth of a new cultural perspective. Tejano was full of optimism and faith, joy and good humor. From a technical standpoint, it utilized the latest in instrumentation and in digital recording effects.

Selena's reputation has only grown after her death. Ccourtesy Photofest.

These were, after all, songwriters, singers, and musicians who had been raised on MTV and VH-1. The awkward *conjunto* polka-beat was replaced with smoother dance rhythms. Melodies and chord progressions became more modern and more inventive. Concerts employed the latest in lighting and special effects, including pyrotechnics. Like all new musical forms, Tejano also began to absorb other sounds, including country-western, rock, and even classical.

Just as Brian Wilson had ridden the brief but powerful wave of the surfing craze, so did Selena and her family band, Los Dinos (brother A. B. on bass, sister Suzette on drums, father Abraham as manager), embrace a historic movement—the rise of the border communities—and give musical expression to a unique explosion of cultural energy. After signing with Sony in 1989, Selena and her band had the capital backing to reach an even wider audience outside her region. Song after song, almost all in Spanish, began to reach out to people around the country. Her best known song—"Amor Prohibido"—contained much of what is now known as the unique "Selena Sound," with its

combination of Caribbean-based reggae rhythms, hip-hop motifs, and strong, sometimes soaring lead vocals.

Like Ritchie Valens and Buddy Holly, Selena's tragic fate was to become world famous only after her death. Her primary legacy remains as a mythmaker more than a musician, as a woman who came to embody a broad social struggle for justice and recognition. Her albums—*Ven Conmigo, Entre a Mi Mundo, Selena Live, Mis Mejores Canciones, Amor Prohibido, Las Reinas del Pueblo*, and the posthumous *Dreaming of You* (1995)— give evidence of a formidable talent that was just beginning to emerge. The 1997 *Selena* movie, starring actress/singer Jennifer Lopez as Selena, only heightened the sense of loss, as viewers remembered an extraordinary voice that was silenced all too soon. The struggle for justice in the borderland continues, though, and Selena's place as a heroine on that landscape seems certain to endure, so long as people seek the dream of a better life that her beautiful songs symbolize.

Her primary legacy remains as a mythmaker more than a musician, as a woman who came to embody a broad social struggle for justice and recognition.

By the time this photograph was taken both Sitting Bull and Buffalo Bill were living Western legends known around the world. Courtesy Denver Public Library, Western History Collection (B-921).

A COUNTRY OF THE MIND

The Province of the West
in Popular Culture

I AM STANDING BESIDE THE LAST RESTING PLACE OF BUFFALO BILL Cody. Situated atop a grassy ridge in the foothills above Denver, the site provides a commanding view of all four points of the compass. To the east, stretching away like a calm blue sea, is the old buffalo prairie, with its open grasslands of sagebrush and prickly pear cactus, antelope and coyote, yellow-throated meadowlarks and red-tailed hawks. Rising in the center of the flatlands is the capital city of Colorado, its crowded steel and concrete skyline radiant in the high altitude sun. Behind me, rising rank on rank to the snow-capped horizon, are the Rocky Mountains, with spire-topped spruce, quaking aspen, bighorn sheep, black bears, rushing glacial streams, and tranquil alpine lakes. Above it all is the immaculate Colorado sky, so deep a cobalt blue as to be almost purple. Here, on this windy bluff set midway between the prairie and the mountains, reposes a noted legend, a consummate mythmaker, a passionate romantic who helped build a bridge from the antique frontier to the atomic age.

Although not a writer or an artist, Buffalo Bill Cody was every bit as much a Western mythmaker as George Catlin or Georgia O'Keeffe, Gene Autry or John Wayne, Geronimo or John Steinbeck. Indeed, many of the most prominent Western mythmakers have been individuals, like Cody, who worked independently and creatively outside the arts to advance a particular fable or set of legends. This alternative band of myth builders have helped to shape public perceptions of the region in often powerful and innovative ways. In Cody's case, his approach involved a rail-borne traveling revue, which included, among others, his good friend, the Sioux leader Sitting Bull (veteran of the Battle of the Little Bighorn), as well as such noted performers as Annie Oakley.

In his Wild West Show, Buffalo Bill Cody took the frontier outside the region. His lively productions included dramatic presentations from the age of Manifest Destiny—holdups, gunfights, Indian raids, prairie hunts, and Custer's Last Stand, as well as shooting, roping, and riding demonstrations. In a somewhat comical instance of history following myth (instead of the reverse, as is normally the case), Theodore Roosevelt named his San Juan Hill Rough Riders for the same-named horsemen of Buffalo Bill Cody's show. Filmed by Thomas Edison in 1894, the shows of William F. Cody literally paved the way for Western movies, and all Western films—from the transparent moralizing of *Stagecoach* (1939) to the dark ambiguity of *Unforgiven* (1992)—ultimately trace their roots back to the dusty stage arenas of Buffalo Bill.

Others who have worked as mythmakers in the popular culture have chosen entirely different ways to present and polish the mythology of the West. Every time there is a Fourth of July rodeo, for example, whether in Alabama, Iowa, or Arizona, the myth of the frontier cowboy is perpetuated. Every time a family travels West to spend a week or two on a dude ranch, the mythical age of the cattle rancher is maintained. Every time a pair of cowboy boots are carried out of a store, someone is longing for the unrestricted freedom of the open range.

Annie "Little Sure Shot" Oakley was one of the primary attractions of Buffalo Bill's traveling review. Courtesy Denver Public Library, Western History Collection (B-941).

Similarly, commercial advertising—featuring products as diverse as automobiles and alcoholic beverages—actively nurtures a whole array of uniquely Western legends and fables (the SUV as reliable horse-drawn family wagon, the 4WD Jeep as fearless trail horse, Coors beer as the spring-fed essence of the Colorado high country). Magazines do their part, too, as witnessed most vividly in the spectacular images of such esteemed publications as *Arizona Highways* and *Big Sky Journal*. Artisans and jewelers are also quiet and often unacknowledged mythmakers: each time a silver bracelet, ring, or necklace featuring a Kokopelli image is worn, a thousand-year-old Anasazi myth is perpetuated.

Much has changed about the world since the days of Buffalo Bill Cody and Sitting Bull and Annie Oakley, but much has also remained the same. The fourteen-thousand-foot granite peaks are still there, as well as the prairie dog–filled grasslands. Dark-billed meadowlarks still sing the sun up every April. Umber-maned bull elks still bugle the full moon down every October. And people everywhere in the West, and elsewhere, still need to be periodically immersed in the comfort of myths—the security of knowing there is a place out there where heroes still live and breath, where fact and fiction are pleasantly blurred, and where all is not hard and cold and all too mortal.

FOLK LEGENDS
The Call of the Wild

IN A STORY entitled "Soldier's Home," Ernest Hemingway, who is buried in one of the most beautiful valleys in the Rocky Mountain West, wrote about the birth of a myth. He described a young man who had come home from war and, when pressed repeatedly for memorable stories (when he had only a few), began to make them up:

> His lies were quite unimportant lies and consisted in attributing to himself things other men had seen, done or heard of, and stating as facts certain apocryphal incidents familiar to all soldiers.... Krebs acquired the nausea in regard to experience that is the result of untruth or exaggeration, and when he occasionally met another man who had really been a soldier and they talked a few minutes in the dressing room at a dance he fell into the easy pose of the old soldier among other soldiers: that he had been badly, sickeningly frightened all the time. In this way he lost everything.

Folk legends are born in exactly the same way. The creator of the legend takes a passing event—a minor bank heist or trailside holdup, an incidental skirmish with a band of Indians, a chance encounter with a grizzly bear—and exaggerates, revises, and embellishes that moment until simple reality becomes full-blown myth. Why? The reason is as simple as human nature is complex:

People make exaggerations (which is what myths are) to conceal, to entertain or edify (sometimes with a little humor added), or to make themselves appear more important. Some myths concern trivial matters, as with the example of the chance encounter with the grizzly bear (although Jedediah Smith's meeting was not so inconsequential). Others are more substantial, as with the shoot-out at the OK Corral, which has, among other things, been the subject of several full-length feature films (including *Wyatt Earp* [1994], *Gunfight at the O.K. Corral* [1957], *My Darling Clementine* [1946], and *Frontier Marshall* [1939]).

The legend of the gunfight at the OK corral in Tombstone, Arizona, actually begins in Dodge City, Kansas, in 1875. A little-known lawman named Wyatt Earp, who had previously been fired from a job as a policeman in Wichita for taking part in a street brawl (making him a sort of great-grandfather to the Dirty Harry character later played by Clint Eastwood), was hired as assistant city marshal. An expert at five-card poker and deadly accurate with a revolver, Earp proved himself a capable enforcer of the law in this fast-growing, rough-sided cattle town along the central rail line. This was the height of the great cattle drives, when Texas longhorn herds were being brought up en masse onto the plains. (The buffalo had all been slaughtered during the five years following the Civil War.) With the cattle came all manner of men, many of

The creator of the legend takes a passing event—a minor bank heist or trailside holdup, an incidental skirmish with a band of Indians, a chance encounter with a grizzly bear—and exaggerates, revises, and embellishes that moment until simple reality becomes full-blown myth.

whom were as wild as the prairies on which they lived.

Earp left Dodge City four years later, having served his apprenticeship in hell. By 1881 he had somehow found his way to Tombstone, Arizona, a notorious gold-mining town just a few miles north of Old Mexico. While there he joined forces with his brothers, Virgil and Morgan, and an alcoholic dentist named John H. ("Doc") Holliday in an often-difficult attempt to maintain law and order. Over time a dispute arose with a band of cattle-rustling cowboys from nearby Sulphur Springs Valley. Various charges were made, tensions rose, and finally, one October afternoon, the marshal (Virgil) and his deputies (Morgan, Wyatt, and Doc) walked over to the town corral to confront the miscreants. As the deputies attempted to make an arrest, things quickly turned bloody. When it was all over, three of the cowboys had been killed and both Virgil and Morgan were wounded. The gunfight remains one of the enduring legends of the American West. Had things gone slightly differently—a routine arrest quickly made—the encounter would be just another long-forgotten afternoon in the low desert, but high drama and deadly violence transformed the armed confrontation into a near epic myth.

Other popular legends concern such historic characters as Wild Bill Hickock and Bat Masterson. Hickcock gained his fame as town marshal of Abilene, Kansas, during the early 1870s. He came to the job after a colorful career as a constable, a teamster on the Santa Fe Trail, a stagecoach driver, and a federal scout for that little-known frontier officer George Custer. Known for his flamboyant attire, Wild Bill most often wore a beaded buckskin suit, a dark cowboy hat, and high-heeled cowboy boots. He stood ramrod straight and well over six feet tall and wore his dark brown hair down to his shoulders. Unlike most marshals, who spent the day in their offices, Hickock could most often be found in gambling parlors, saloons, and bordellos. His moment of fame came in a shootout with a gambler named Phil Coe, during which he killed both Coe and a hidden assailant. Bat Masterson was another Kansas peace officer who became renowned for his deadly shooting in the streets of Dodge City. (President Theodore Roosevelt, aware of Masterson's reputation as a tough and capable enforcer, appointed him a Deputy United States Marshal in 1905.)

Other popular myths grew out of the Native American culture. Chief among those, toward the end of the Old Frontier, was the legend of the Ghost Dancers. This legend was born out of a time of great despair and cultural disintegration. The year was 1890, and the Indians of the northern plains—the Cheyenne and the Sioux—had been sent to reservations in South Dakota. Although the exact origins of the legend remain obscure (it was perhaps created among the Paiute in Nevada), the final content of the myth is well known: those who participated in a ritual dance, a Ghost Dance, could glimpse a better future and acquire special powers. Among the Sioux, the Ghost Dance legend was advanced by a mystic named Kicking Bear, who also stated that those who wore buckskin ghost shirts (adorned with special visionary symbols) would be impervious to attacker's bullets.

The U.S. government and army were both alarmed by the Ghost Dance movement, which, they feared, would lead to another general uprising in the northern plains. As more troops were sent into the area, the Indians, in turn, became equally concerned, fearing another bloody crackdown. Distrustful of the white man, many of the Indians fled for the Badlands east of the Black Hills. On December 14, 1890, the nationally respected Sioux leader Sitting Bull was killed when Indian police attempted to arrest him at the Pine Ridge Agency south of Standing Rock. This resulted in more fear and turmoil on the reservations. Shortly, a horrific incident occurred among the followers of Big Foot, a Sioux leader. On December 28, at a place called Wounded Knee Creek, cavalry troops under the command of Colonel James Forsyth killed several hundred largely unarmed men, women, and children traveling with Big Foot. Many of the dead wore the legendary ghost shirts.

There are enough historical legends in the American West to fill a thousand books or make a hundred films, ranging from those based on reality, such as Judge Roy Bean and Jesse James, to those derived purely from the imagination, like Pecos Bill and Sasquatch. These legends form the cultural basis for the enduring mother lodes that are continuously mined by mythmakers to produce contemporary versions of the legendary West. As an integral component of our national history and consciousness, these fables comprise part of what it is to be an American. To no small extent, these Western myths and legends are also a living tradition—one that continues to persist and to grow, protoplasmically absorbing today's mundane events and magically transforming them into tomorrow's hoary legends.

MORMONISM
Exodus to the West

TRYING TO UNDERSTAND the cultural landscape of Utah, and many other Mormon regions of the West (including parts of Idaho, Wyoming, California, Arizona, and Montana), without an appreciation for the underlying culture can be compared to visiting Saudi Arabia and having no knowledge of the Islamic religion. It is, at best, an incomplete experience. Since the 1840s, the Mormons have played an active and powerful role in the mythologizing of the American West, particularly in portraying the valley, mountain, and desert regions of Utah as a new-found Eden. Their collective myth has been a familiar one—that there is a utopian sanctuary in the Far West where the beehives overflow with honey, the apple branches hang low from

The Mormons are known around the world for their striking temples. Courtesy Denver Public Library, Western History Collection (GB-5650).

the weight of the fruit, and the valley fields provide an abundance of crops for a peace-loving people.

The story of Mormonism begins in 1820 with Joseph Smith, a restless young man who grew up near Manchester, New York, questioning many of Christianity's traditional tenants and occassionally delving into mysticism. Smith told people that he had had an encounter with an angel named Moroni. According to Smith, the angel showed him where he could find several golden plates containing information on two distinct groups of ancient inhabitants that populated the Western Hemisphere. The angel, again based on Smith's account, also provided special implements that could translate these plates from a form of Egyptian hieroglyphics into modern English. After publishing *The Book of Mormon* in 1830 (the book is named for a prophet in the book), Smith and his band of followers found themselves subjected to increasing levels of hostility in New York, Ohio, Missouri, and later Illinois, both for their ideological zealotry and for their controversial practice of polygamy (not to mention Smith's claim that he was a prophet of God). In 1844 Joseph Smith and his brother Hyrum were killed by an angry mob at the jail in Carthage, Illinois, after they had been arrested in connection with the destruction of a printing press that had published material critical of Mormonism (charges also included arson, treason, and polygamy).

Following this, a man named Brigham Young became the second leader of the Church of Jesus Christ of Latter-day Saints (LDS), which is also known as the Mormon Church, and moved the group from Nauvoo, Illinois, to the Great Salt Lake Valley in northcentral Utah, a semi-desert area that was being passed over by emigrants more interested in the gold fields of California. As an historical footnote, old-time Taos trapper Jim Bridger built "Fort Bridger" in southwestern Wyoming at this time to provide supplies for Mormons taking the cut-off from the Oregon Trail into Utah—a classic example of one mythic age meeting another. The Mormons initially wanted to create a separate, sovereign nation—a theocracy—in the West when the territory belonged to Mexico (which included the Great Basin and the port city of San Diego), but the Treaty of Guadalupe Hidalgo in 1849 transfered the land to the United States, which ended this dream. Therefore, it was the expansive Utah territory that the Mormons attempted to establish the "State of Deseret" (the word comes from *The Book of Mormon* and means "honeybee"). Brigham Young soon demonstrated that he was a capable leader in his plan to establish a Mormon state in the desert lands. Between 1847 and 1857, nearly a hundred towns and villages were formed across Utah, most based on the simple principle of self-reliance through communal agriculture—crop farming, fruit orchards, cattle and sheep ranches.

Like several other religious groups in American history—one thinks of the Amish people of Pennsylvania, the Hutterite communities of Montana, and even the pantheistic "Hippie" communes of New Mexico and California in the 1960s and 1970s—the Mormons sought, and are

Their collective myth has been a familiar one—that there is a utopian sanctuary in the Far West where the beehives overflow with honey, the apple branches hang low from the weight of the fruit, and the valley fields provide an abundance of crops for a peace-loving people.

The Mormons have played an active and powerful role in the mythologizing of the American West, particularly in portraying the valley, mountain, and desert regions of Utah as a new-found Eden.

still seeking, to create a distinct society for themselves in a world they see as wanting ethical order. In this attempt to forge a better way of life in a morally "fallen" environment they are also in keeping with some of the oldest myths of western civilization (as seen in the Puritan's flight to the New World to escape the "cesspool" of the Old World). The Mormons' unique perspective on the human condition has been explored on film (John Ford's 1950 feature film *Wagonmaster*) as well as in literature (from Mark Twain's 1869 travel narrative *Roughing It* to Wallace Stegner's 1950 prolabor novel *The Preacher and the Slave*). More recently, a new generation of Mormon writers have begun to reflect, sometimes in conflicted ways, upon the faith, as in the essays and books of Moab author Terry Tempest Williams (known for such works as R*efuge* [1990] and *Leap* [2000]).

The Mormons are perhaps best known for their close-knit communities that embrace one of the oldest myths of human experience—that an idyllic oasis can be found in the metaphoric desert. Their temples are often quite striking in design, and their missionaries (over fifty thousand strong) work in many countries worldwide. Their presence is widely felt in western America, both as a collective cultural entity and in the form of such celebrities as NFL quarterback

Steve Young (a direct descendent of Brigham Young), musical good-will ambassadors Donny and Marie Osmond, and political figures such as Utah Senator Orrin Hatch, currently one of the most outspoken conservatives in the Congress. Hatch and other prominent leaders from the state sometimes find themselves responding to questions on an array of issues, including paternalism, the status of women and minorities, polygamy, arranged marriages, and underaged unions (the latter of which have been the subject of several recent nationally-publicized court trials in Utah).

Ultimately, the Mormon mythic legacy has been the establishment of a series of communities—from small rural towns like Moab to major urban centers like Salt Lake City—that offer a way of life that is structurally different to souls weary of existence elsewhere. Much of the Mormon's sense of religious dedication and cheerful cooperation is captured in their traditional folksongs, as in the classic ballad "Some Must Push and Some Must Pull," a song familiar to music students across the land:

> For some must push and some must pull,
> As we go marching up the hill,
> So merrily on our way we go,
> Until we reach the Valley-O!

THE FRED HARVEY COMPANY AND THE SANTA FE RAILROAD
Visions of El Dorado

IN A NOW-OBSCURE (but once extremely popular) film entitled *The Harvey Girls* (1946) the twenty-two-year-old actress/singer Judy Garland (who had seven years earlier starred in *The Wizard of Oz*, 1939) portrayed a Fred Harvey Girl. Such was the cultural significance once assigned to these popular ambassadors of the Southwestern-based Fred Harvey Company, that such a major performer of the time was cast to play one of their own. Indeed, the Fred Harvey Company was one of the most aggressive and successful commercial mythmakers in the history of the American West. Their products were the arts and crafts, cultures, traditions, legends, natural beauty, and open spaces of the Southwest. Some have even gone so far as to say that the Fred Harvey Company "invented" the Southwest as the modern mythological realm it has become.

By using the Atchison, Topeka & Santa Fe Railroad across New Mexico and Arizona, the Fred Harvey Company brought hundreds of thousands of tourists to the Four Corners region. Their tours provided opportunities both for mass public education about the Southwest and for the sale of Native American baskets, pots, blankets, beadwork, leather goods, textiles, and jewelry. Among their clients in the early

Women selling pottery to Santa Fe Railway passengers at Isleta Pueblo in the early 1900s. Courtesy the Heard Museum, Phoenix, Arizona.

years were such luminaries as Douglas Fairbanks and Albert Einstein (whose visit to Fred Harvey's Hopi House at Grand Canyon was captured in a popular photograph). The only remotely close travel experience available at the current time would be a few of the better cruise-ship tours of Scandinavia, the Mediterranean, or the Caribbean, which are also designed to provide a group of visitors with an intimate and informed sense of unique local communities.

After arriving in the United States as an English immigrant and natural entrepreneur, Fred Harvey made a calculated decision early on (1876) to capitalize on the romantic senti-ments (now that the frontier was clos-ing) the nation felt for the West in general and for Native Americans in particular. Harvey began his empire with a series of restau-rants—staffed by Harvey Girls—along the rail lines. These popular rest stops became centers for the sale of Western merchandise, as well as for initiating infor-mal side-excursions to unique spots—pueblos, ruins, Indian villages—

Fred Harvey—self-made man and consummate mythmaker. Courtesy the Heard Museum, Phoenix, Arizona.

along the way. Eventually Harvey began to offer elaborate guided tours at such locations as the South Rim of the Grand Canyon and the various pueblo communities in the upper Rio Grande region. Rarely has a myth been so actively promoted as was the fable of the South-west as an exotic repository of near-extinct and threatened cultures.

Naturally, the Native Americans in the region were not entirely displeased with the development, for the sale of their crafts brought much-needed money into cash-poor reservation economies. The downside was that the influx of tourists tended to contaminate the purity of indigenous cultures. Over time, the Fred Harvey Company became an enormous, if unexpected, business success in the West, and no trip to the region was considered complete without one of their fascinating tours. At the time of his death in 1901, Fred Harvey had built over two dozen restaurants and sixteen hotels. He also owned twenty cars on the Santa Fe Railway.

Harvey relied on local experts such as J. L. Hubbell to act as scouts and locate fine local artisans, acquiring their work to sell in various trading posts. Hubbell, who was active as a regional trader from the early 1880s well into the twentieth century, operated a number of trading posts in the Four Corners Region. His famed trading post near Ganado, Arizona, in the heart of the beautiful Painted Desert region, is now a National Historic Site. Hubbell's posts were famed for their beautiful Hopi and Navajo pottery, blankets, textiles, kachinas, and jewelry. In a classic example of art following demand, the growing market for these objects caused a renaissance among the Hopi and Navajo artists and brought about a marked increase in both quality and productivity.

The Harvey family continued to operate the business after Fred Harvey's passing, and the company persists to this day. Perhaps most important, given a longer historical perspective, was the amazing collection of art that the Fred Harvey family assembled over the years. This unique collection of authentic artifacts and objects of art has proven to have lasting aesthetic and ethnographic value. This is not a bad legacy for a man whose first job in the United States was washing dishes, but who went on to introduce his adopted country to a landscape they did not know within their own borders. Fred Harvey left no novels or paintings to explore and celebrate the myths of the West, but he was just as powerful a mythmaker as any of those whose work is now found in the finest libraries and museums of the land.

DUDE RANCHES
Mama, Don't Let Your Babies Grow Up to be Cowboys

LONG AGO AND FAR AWAY, I worked college summers as a horse wrangler at dude ranches in Colorado and Wyoming. Coming from the flat, purgatorial landscapes of the Midwest, the high country was (and still is) a marvelous romance to me. As I led trail rides up into the north Absaroka wilderness near Cody, Wyoming, or took fly-fishermen in by pack horse to the Flattops wilderness near Glenwood Springs, Colorado, I felt as though I had been given free admission into some kind of paradise. My happiness could not be measured, at least by any instrument on earth. (It is amazing how time makes one forget the bad parts.) Over the course of those summers, I was transformed, as so many have been before and since, from complete city

Roy Underwood's CITY SLICKERS *(Columbia, 1991), starring Billy Crystal, featured three "dudes" or urbanites, on their first visit to the desert Southwest. Courtesy Photofest.*

slicker to compleat (sort of) cowboy—sharp-toed cowboy boots, well-worn leather riding chaps, dusty cowboy hat, perpetual sunburn, a certain swagger, a certain twang, a certain overstated insouciance.

Our instructions were to tell stories on the trail rides to entertain the dudes—pasty-faced wealthy folks mostly from Philadelphia, New York, and Boston, all looking for outdoor adventure. Quite often, we would simply invent these stories as we rode along: "That's the ridge where Jessie Van Cleve and the Stinking Water Gang finally caught up with Old Bobcat Bill. He was hung from that big lightning-struck cottonwood over yonder." Or, "About ten years ago there was a confirmed Bigfoot sighting in that canyon. No, I'm serious, there actually was. I saw the report and the photographs down at the Forest Service office in Buford. Of course, they keep it secret. Otherwise there would be a general panic." Or, "No, no. That's an old Shoshone burial ground. We can't camp on that spot. I know a better place about two miles ahead. Yes, I know you're all a bit saddle sore and tired, but it's just a little further. And the view up there of the back range is much more spectacular, I promise."

For the past century, the mythological creature known as the cowboy has been kept artificially alive through films, novels, paintings, songs, and—as if by primitive life support system—through Western dude ranches. Here people from outside the region can still ride tall in the padded saddle, chase and rope a terrified steer, and get drunk by a trail fire as pirate-eyed coyotes sing up the moon (as in the movie *City*

Slickers [1991]). Afterwards, everyone can safely return to their homes in the suburbs and cities. The dude ranch phenomenon—unique to the West—began in the 1880s and 1890s as one biblical disaster after another (blizzards, droughts, financial panics, declining beef prices, changing laws and regulations) beset the cattle industry. Gradually, word began to reach the East through such books as Theodore Roosevelt's *Ranch Life and the Hunting Trail* that the American West was a giant playground with horseback riding, camping, fishing, hunting, photography, wildlife watching, sightseeing, and general relaxation for the young at heart. Meanwhile, ranchers discovered that they could easily supplement their income during the short summer season by allowing city dudes to come along for the ride. (In other words, people would actually pay good money for the chance to work beside illiterate, bean-eating cowboys on the range.) It all seemed too good to be true, and it prospered as do all enterprises that are fueled by good humor and a classic myth.

A dude ranch is its own self-contained world—a log headquarters building (which normally includes the kitchen and dining hall), dude cabins, bath house, blacksmith shop, tack cabin, saddle shed, hay barn, chicken coop, pig yard, milking shed, corrals, bunkhouse for the wranglers and field hands, and dormitory house for the cabin girls (from which the wranglers can often be seen exiting early in the morning). The dude ranch can be thought of as an immense mythmaking machine. Here people come to escape the exquisite boredom of a

The dude ranch can be thought of an an immense mythmaking machine. Here people come to escape the exquisite boredom of a hotel, or the manufactured comfort of a bed-and-breakfast, and experience the real West (whatever that is).

hotel, or the manufactured comfort of a bed-and-breakfast, and experience the real West (whatever that is). Part of what they do find, ordinarily, is simple hospitality—lots of old-fashioned warmth and friendship—as well as wide-open spaces and real live cowboys (or at least what appear to be). The dude ranch is all a lie in part, all a re-creation of a thing that never really was. If the experience is partially false on the surface, though, it is at least wholly true at the core—and because of that the families keep returning, decade after happy decade.

Quite often, a trip to a dude ranch involves participating in a rodeo—either an informal barrel-racing competition or roping exercise in the saddling corral, or an off-ranch trip to a nearby county or state fair. In 1974, while working at the 7-D Ranch in Wyoming, I was somehow persuaded by the ranch foreman, Don Hicks, to ride a range bull (something I'd never done before). Slammed against the corral fence, I was awarded with a beautiful bruise and a separated shoulder. Across the West, rodeos are big business, and among cowboys, working members of the rodeo circuit are treated as celebrities and cult figures. Once an obscure sport, professional rodeo competi-tions—featured in towns like Denver and Las Vegas—are now often seen on cable channels. Rodeos have also served traditionally as fodder for the film industry, as in *The Misfits* (1961), in which the broken-down cowboy played by Montgomery Clift, is nearly pulverized by a half-wild horse in the rodeo ring (only to be attended by a kind-hearted Marilyn Monroe).

Another favorite diversion on dude ranches is a trail ride to a ghost town or old mining camp. The mountains and deserts of the West, from Canada to Mexico, are littered with these often-scenic remnants of a by-gone age. In Colorado, many of the old mining towns are clustered in the San Juan Mountains—especially in the high country around Telluride and Silverton—and are a favorite among landscape painters and photographers (Ansel Adams worked this country during the 1940s with his large format camera, as does local master John Fielder to this day). Elsewhere, in southern Arizona and New Mexico, relic ghost towns and hard rock mines abound.

Even after all these years I can still

A nineteenth-century mining camp in the high country of Colorado. Courtesy John Murray.

remember those distant summers working on the dude ranches: the beauty of the high mountain landscapes, the warm comradery, the hilarious misadventures (a runaway dude horse, with me attached sideways by one hand to the saddle horn), the hard work (forever shoeing horses when things got "slow"), the summer nights at our secret swimming hole. I can remember how the hay fields smelled after the first cutting, and how the peaks rose calm and blue in the distance, and how the rain rattled softly on the roof of the deer-hunting tent, and how lovely the crags were after the first snows. It all remains forever clear. It was a great time, a wonderful romance, falling deeply in love with the landscape and with the legend of the cowboy. As a little boy growing up in Ohio, I often pointed to the old black-and-white television set when my favorite afternoon show, *The Lone Ranger*, came on and said, "When I grow up, I will go there." Like so many before and since, the Western dude ranches provided this perpetual little boy with the opportunity to live, if only for a little while, one of the most beautiful myths ever created on Earth.

COMMERICIAL ADVERTISING
The Selling of the West

STEAK SAUCE. SPORTS CARS. Cosmetics. Hair products. Clothing. Beer. Bicycles and sports equipment. Timex watches. All have been effectively marketed using Western landscapes and mythology in very focused and creative ways. While commercial advertising initially tended to represent the landscapes of the West as a marketable product in and of themselves (as with the posters and pamphlets of the Fred Harvey Company), matters in this respect began to change early in the twentieth century. Over the course of the next several decades, the West was consciously promoted as a legendary background—a realm of adversity and adventure, legend and fable, heroes and villains. Businesses cleverly used the landscapes, history, and people of the West to sell products on television, in newspapers and magazines, and through billboards and other mass-market media.

These commercial representations contributed to the mythology of the West in both subtle and not-so-subtle ways. For example, most people have not a clue as to where the Fisher Towers are located (along the Colorado River near Moab in southeastern Utah), and yet tens of millions of consumers around the world have seen these distinctive rock formations in advertisements for everything from automobiles to suntan lotion, and would recognize the formations instantly. Similarly, automobile commercials featuring the monoliths of Monument Valley have regularly helped promote the fable of the West as a vast desert (though most of the West is definitely not). In addition to the use of the landscape in commercials, automobile makers have also relied on Western-sounding names to capture America's adventurous spirit: Cherokee, Ranger, Mustang, Montana,

Pathfinder, Explorer, Tahoe, Yukon, Bronco, Rodeo, Frontier, Wrangler, and Ram to name a few. Elsewhere, images of the vineyards of Sonoma County, or of the orchards of the Central California Valley, have been skillfully used by wine-makers and fruit-growers to evoke the old Western myth of Edenic fertility (which, taken back all the way in our culture, leads to the Egyptian legend of the western isle of Atlantis cited in Plato's dialogues).

Several areas in the West are intensively used by commercial production crews. One of the most popular is the Painted Desert in southern Utah and northern Arizona. Here, commercial-makers find vast expanses of open space, much of it public land, as well as strikingly beautiful formations of red, orange, tan, and cream-colored sandstone. A further attraction is that the federal agencies charge very little for commercial filming on the lands they manage (as contrasted with private land owners). Local communities in the region are also supportive of commercial activities, (which frequently hire nearby residents—river rafters, rock climbers, security guards, kitchen help, wranglers, carpenters, electricians, and so forth—to help on the shoots).

In recent years, a number of successful mass-market commercials have been shot along the Colorado River as it transits the area around Moab, Utah. Specifically, the Castle Rock formation in Castle Valley was used in 1985 by Isuzu, the Japanese car manufacturer, for one of its amusing David Leisure commercials, in which the comedian/actor, impersonating a car salesman, says with a straight face, "Honest, I drove it all the way up here." The formation was also included by Miller Brewing Company in an innovative beer commercial. (The spire was chipped away to reveal a beer bottle hidden within.) In nearby Arches National Park, the Clairol cosmetics company shot a variety of television and magazine advertisements in the 1980s, featuring models out in the desert environment. The park, particularly the spectacular Courthouse Wash landscape (eroded monoliths in the redrock country of southeastern Utah), has also been used for automobile commercials. In nearby Monument

Monument Valley is often featured in commercial advertising. Courtesy John Murray.

Valley, the French Government recently shot an anti-smoking television commercial, parodying the 'Marlboro Man' ads commonly shot in the red rock country of southeastern Utah. Monument Valley is also regularly used by automobile manufacturers, especially in the Redlands Pass area on U.S. 163 just south of Mexican Hat, Utah.

No discussion of Moab and Monument Valley would be complete without mention of the irrepressible entrepreneur Harry Goulding, who pioneered the commercial use of the area (on the Navajo Reservation) by bringing the unique landscapes and people to the attention of railroad-based tourists and, later, Hollywood. Goulding first saw the scenic area (which had already been featured in the 1925 George Seitz film *The Vanishing American,* based on the Zane Grey novel) in the late 1920s. He later settled in the valley (which is actually a high plateau) and built a small trading post at the base of Oljeta Mesa. After enticing director John Ford to Monument Valley in 1939 to shoot *Stagecoach,* Goulding worked tirelessly both to attract more films to the park and to develop a stable trading business that, in turn, helped the local cash-poor economy. Goulding is emblematic of many other local leaders across the West who have been instrumental in attracting business to their respective home regions.

In recent years, Monument Valley and Moab have become increasingly popular as background locations for production teams shooting music videos that are then seen on VH-1 and MTV. A number of major stars (ranging from lounge lizard Michael Bolton to country-western crooner Clint Black to rock singer Jon Bon Jovi) have recorded music videos in the Moab–Monument Valley canyon country, as well as at Lake Powell near Page, Arizona. Other areas in the West also popular for music videos include the Algodones Dune Field east of San Diego, California (seen in the *Wayne's World* music video), and the Mojave Desert east of Los Angeles, featured by the Irish rock group U2 in the video for their landmark *Joshua Tree* album.

Fifty years from now, one hundred years from now, the West will still be used to sell commercial products. Production crews will still come out to shoot background tape, and the landscapes and legends will be just as lovingly (or crassly, depending on perspective) exploited. Some may find the whole process of making commercials in the West unseemly, and perhaps it is from a purist standpoint, but the commercial exploitation of the region is no different, in the final analysis, from the extraction of lumber or minerals. In fact, it is far less damaging to resources and people. Above all, the commercialization of myths provides helpful insights into both the advertisers who make the commercials and the consumers who then buy the products. In any event, these commercials underscore the pervasiveness of legend in American culture, and the often-provoking ways myth is used as metaphor.

In any event, these commercials underscore the pervasiveness of legend in American culture, and the often-provoking ways myth is used as metaphor.

ARIZONA HIGHWAYS
The Transcendent Landscape

FOR THE PAST FIVE YEARS, on the nightstand beside my bed, there has been a stack of about a dozen vintage *Arizona Highways* magazines. On many a restless, or lonely, or cold winter night they have transported me to a warm, sunny landscape I dearly love. The oldest dates from June 1951, with a cover photograph featuring a magnificent late-afternoon rainbow over the South Rim of the Grand Canyon. The issue includes articles on the Arizona Strip country and Lake Mojave, various nature poems, and among other things, the stellar photography of Josef Muench. The most recent dates from September 1963 and commemorates Arizona's "new" wilderness areas—Superstition, Pine Mountain, Blue Range, Sycamore Canyon, Chiricahua, Galiuro, Mazatzal, Mt. Baldy. Coincidentally, this issue also features a lengthy article on Northland Publishing, the publisher of the book you are currently reading.

These mid-twentieth-century issues of *Arizona Highways* differ from those in the early twenty-first century only superficially, primarily in the coarse paper quality (which sometimes caused even four-by-five photographs to appear as though they were grainy four-hundred-speed snapshots). Editorially, the magazine has remained remarkably consistent over the past half-century, with a focus primarily on the picturesque aspects of the Arizona mountain, canyon, and desert country. The spectacular natural images can still instantly convey a reader weary of life in the city and regions far from the Southwest to a place where the landscapes are largely untouched by humankind, dark clouds are rare, and the sky is always an impossible shade of chromium blue.

In a world in which popular culture magazines, ranging from *Outside* to *Sports Illustrated*, are often so filled with gaudy advertising that it is difficult for the reader to discern an editorial focus, let alone to follow an article, *Arizona Highways* has over the years remained refreshingly unencumbered by advertising. Decade after decade, the magazine has persistently remained true to the purity of its inspiration—the landscapes and people of Arizona—and has steadfastly resisted the passing vagaries and vicissitudes of changing fashion. Founded in 1925, just as the automobile was beginning to bring increasing numbers of tourists into the Old Southwest, *Arizona Highways* has become an influential, albeit quiet, mythmaking source in the American West. First conceived of as a marketing aid to promote good roads and state tourism, the magazine has grown to become something far more. It has gently but powerfully shaped public perceptions of Arizona

ARIZONA HIGHWAYS *features the legendary landscapes of one of the West's most beautiful states. Courtesy Brad Melton Collection. Photo by Klaus Kranz.*

in particular, and of the Southwest in general, as an Edenic sanctuary of nature. For many people around the country and the world, the images of Arizona seen in its pages are as much an epiphany of an earthly utopia as they are magazine illustrations.

Nearly four hundred thousand people each month buy *Arizona Highways*. Many more read it in libraries or office waiting rooms. It is relaxing. It is diverting. It is inspiring. It is educational. And it is romantic, quietly evoking the sublime, while never crossing the line into the sentimental. The magazine shows, in its words and images, that a myth does not have to be a lie, a legend does not have to be untrue, and a fable does not have to be fiction. The mythological country known as Arizona, a place of public land and culturally diverse, friendly people, is not a realm from the imagination of Samuel Johnson *(Rasselas)* or Voltaire *(Candide)*. The Grand Canyon, the Sonoran Desert, Sedona, the

Sunsets in the Sonoran Desert have inspired many ARIZONA HIGHWAYS' *photographers. Courtesy John Murray.*

Painted Desert, and the Mogollon Rim really do exist. And they are all waiting, come next summer vacation, to be discovered.

The most recent issue, as I wrote these lines (April 2000), celebrated the magazine's seventy-fifth anniversary and included the photographs and writings of a man who spent 108 days below the North Rim of the Grand Canyon (something I've always wanted to do, though perhaps the biblical forty days would suffice), while undertaking a number of extended loop trails west of the North Rim lodge. The issue also featuredstriking aerial images of Monument Valley and other classic Arizona landscapes. One of the founding editors of the magazine was also remembered. Fifty years from now, on a nightstand somewhere, a man or a woman will perhaps have this very issue, and turning its pages, will remember the good old days at the turn of the century. Such is the quiet legacy of this enormously successful mythmaker.

ROUTE 66
"Get Your Kicks, On Route Sixty-Six!"

EVERY HIGHWAY HAS ITS OWN HISTORY, its own unique passage over the cultural landscape, its own fables and legends. One thinks of the ancient stone road to Colonus, Greece, on which a young traveler named Oedipus met and slew his father (and went on to unwittingly marry his mother). Or of the medieval highway to the cathedral at Canterbury, England, on which a group of mythical pilgrims walked, telling amazing and sometimes bawdy stories that a poet named Geoffrey Chaucer would assemble into a wonderful book entitled *Canterbury Tales*. Or of our own Route 66, which has spawned a Pulitzer-prize winning novel (*The Grapes of Wrath*, 1940), a hit television series *(Route Sixty-Six)*, an Oscar-winning film (*Easy Rider*, 1969), and a popular song ("Route Sixty-Six," written in the 1950s by Bobby Troup and recorded by performers as diverse as Nat King Cole and the Rolling Stones). Only a few other thoroughfares in America—such as the Old Natchez Trace in Mississippi, or the Oregon Trail, or the Pacific Coastal Highway (101)—have seen as much national legend-making.

To his dying day at ninety-two, my grandfather told the colorful story of how he drove the family on an epic journey from Cincinnati, Ohio, to Yellowstone National Park in the summer of 1929. The roads were all dirt and gravel, reliable maps were nonexistent, and his old Studebaker developed a flat tire "at least once a day." Had he made the pilgrimage to the American West just a few years later, he could have driven all the way from Chicago to, among other places, Grand Canyon National Park on a nicely paved highway, Route 66. Formed as part of the 1926 National Highway System, U.S. Highway 66 was a much-needed response to the rapid growth of automobile use during the Roaring Twenties. It was built to link interstate travel and commerce between the Midwest and the Pacific Coast. Running twenty-two-hundred miles, the road coursed south through the cornfields of Illinois, crossed the broad

Entire books have been devoted to the amazing cultural entity that is Route 66. Courtesy Terrance Moore.

Mississippi River at St. Louis, passed over the sunflower-filled expanses of the Great Plains, spanned the austere deserts of the Southwest, and finally stopped at the Santa Monica Pier on the shores of the Pacific in southern California.

Much of Route 66 followed historic roads and trails that had first been pioneered by surveying parties before the Civil War, when the government was searching for the best southern rail route. In California, for example, the highway followed the old Beale wagon road, which had first been surveyed by Edward Fitzgerald Beale, the Indian Commissioner to California, in 1857. This wilderness route, roughly along the thirty-eighth parallel, traversed the Mojave Desert and linked Los Angeles with that much older travel system, the Colorado River. Route 66 in Arizona and New Mexico followed the northerly path established by Captain Lorenzo Sitgreaves in 1851. Through Texas and Oklahoma it adhered to the trail of Captain Marcy in 1849. What all this meant from a mythic standpoint is that the road, in a sense, was physically linked to a deeper period of history in the West, that fabled time when a loaded gun was as necessary on a trip as a full canteen, when trail horses were the only means of conveyance, and there were real dangers— outlaws and so forth—to contend with.

By the time the highway was fully paved, in 1938, the American West had changed dramatically, at least in its outward appearance (automobiles and airplanes having all but replaced horses and trains). Inside, though, its mythic core remained much the same. Travelers along

Route 66 shared a common geographic and cultural heritage with the traders and emigrants who had passed along the early Santa Fe Trail (which linked Santa Fe to Kansas City) and Oregon Trail (which linked Kansas with the promised land of Oregon). The Far West was still seen as an Arcady, a realm of hope and regeneration, a landscape filled with the promise of a better life. The highway's mythic quality was given brilliant expression in John Steinbeck's 1939 novel *The Grapes of Wrath:*

> Tom [Joad] drove slowly and carefully in the traffic, and then they were [suddenly] on 66—the great western road, and the sun was sinking on the line of the road. The windshield was bright with dust. Tom pulled his cap lower over his eyes, so low that he had to tilt his head back to see out at all…. Tom said, "We stay on this road right straight through [to California]."

These few lines capture all the excitement and promise of this new paved road to the West— toward a bright future that awaits all who leave behind the lost, decayed world of the East.

The accomplished filmmaker John Ford, who had recently directed the Oscar-winning Western *Stagecoach* (1939), soon signed on to produce a film version of *The Grapes of Wrath*. With the plain-speaking, mild-mannered Henry Fonda cast as Tom Joad, and with considerable location-shooting along Route 66, the film closely followed the characters, plot, and story line of Steinbeck's work. One of the most moving scenes occurred at the Colorado River, when the Joad family crossed the bridge that finally and fully separated them from the East, and entered that legendary province of the country and of the spirit, California. Sadly, all the Joads would find at the end of Route 66 was more injustice and heartache, although the family, so symbolic of the larger family of America, had remained intact, bound by unbreakable love and loyalty, through their travels and travails.

Three decades later, in 1968, Henry Fonda's son, Peter Fonda, produced a film that also followed Route 66. This film, like *The Grapes of Wrath*, was also destined to win an Oscar. Interestingly enough, the film included a scene at the same Colorado River bridge (in Needles, California) as Peter Fonda (Captain America) and Dennis Hopper (Billy) ride their motorcycles east to the Mardi Gras. The wide-angle camera lens pans over the same desert mountains (the Chemehuevi Mountains) that appeared thirty-eight years earlier in *The Grapes of Wrath.* In the earlier film, the protagonists were traveling west on Route 66 from the wasteland of the East to the hope-filled Arcady of California. In *Easy Rider*, the journey is reversed, as the characters travel east into the dark heart of America.

Easy Rider is throughout a celebration of the motorcycle, which over time has come to rival, if not replace, the traditional horse in the American West. Whereas John Wayne was always mounted on a sixteen- or seventeen-hand quarter horse, the characters of *Easy Rider* are mounted on massively powerful Harley Davidsons. The West of actor/director Peter Fonda is not the West of Tom Mix or Gene Autry, John Wayne or Ward Bond. It is an anti-world, with anti-heroes engaged on an inscrutable mission. The American flag is not waving from a cavalry guidon but is stitched to the back of a leather jacket. The Indians are the "good guys" and the "bad guys" are the police. The desert is a place not of pitched battles but of quiet revelation. Through it all they roar along on their Harleys, looking for a mythical place (as at the Taos Pueblo in northern New Mexico) where people can live, if not in peace, at least with some measure of tolerance.

A considerable amount of American history has journeyed down Route 66. In *The Grapes of Wrath*, Steinbeck described the landscape along Route 66 as "the terrible desert, where the distance shimmers and the black cinder mountains hang unbearably in the distance." The arid expanses of the West are terrible only to those who do not understand the region's myths, who do not recall the lessons of history, and who have failed to learn the principles of nature. Bits and pieces of Route 66 still can be found, and are worth seeking out—such as the stretch that runs through the Mojave Desert near Amboy, California. Here, standing by the nearly abandoned road in the great silence of the open desert, one can begin to appreciate how powerfully landscape has shaped myth, which in turn has shaped culture.

Henry Fonda portrays displaced farmer Tom Joad in John Ford's THE GRAPES OF WRATH *(20th-Fox, 1940). Courtesy Photofest.*

AFTERWORD
Only the Earth Endures

Although human life is fleeting, the myths of the American West will always endure. Courtesy John Murray.

When I think of these times, and call back to mind the grandeur and beauty of those almost uninhabited shores: when I picture to myself the dense and lofty summits of the forest, that everywhere spread among the hills, and over-hung the margins of the stream, unmolested by the axe of the settlers...when I see that no Aborigines are to be found there, and that the vast herds of elks, deer and buffaloes which once pastured on these hills and in these valleys... have ceased to exist, when I reflect that all this grand portion of our Union, instead of being a state of nature, is now more or less covered with villages, farms, and towns... and that the woods are fast disappearing.... When I remember that these extraordinary changes have all taken place in the short period of twenty years, I pause, wonder, and, although I know all to be fact, can scarcely believe its reality.

—John James Audubon (1831)

The Americans who poured through the Cumberland Gap, who explored the Upper Missouri, who homesteaded the Kansas prairie, who filled to overflowing the Arcady of California, and who raised bright cities like Los Angeles and Phoenix, brought with them both the natural human propensity to fictionalize reality—to invent myths—and the Old World myths that formed the foundation of their civilization. This book has been an attempt to chronicle the relationship between the human imagination and the American West. More specifically, we have examined how the myths of the region—the heroic myth, the utopian myth, the eternal youth myth, the agrarian myth and others—have helped to shape the human experience. In case after case, we have seen how the diverse creations of the imagination have exerted as much of an influence on history as political movements, economic develop-ments, transcendent leaders, or even those twin mythmaking forces of nature—environmental changes and natural selection.

Myths shape our lives in ways large and small. They can produce harm or good, and their effects can be noted at the scale of the province or at the level of a small provincial family. In the months following my mother's passing in Denver, for example, my father, like many widowers, rendered his loss more acute by mythologizing the past. Had he dealt with the fullness of reality instead of the fragment that is myth, his suffering would have been diminished. On the other hand, the story of their first meeting was a pleasant fable that enlivened many a dinner party in their suburban home. It was, by any accounting, a good myth, a creation legend that strengthened the bonds of love in an ordinary middle-class family of the modern West. The same myth-making process has continually exerted itself at the level of society across the region. In some cases these cultural myths have been quite positive in their effects, as in Theodore Roosevelt's skillful resurrection of the Greco-Roman heroic myth, or in Edward Abbey's evergreen myth of the West as a natural paradise that needs to be preserved. In others, though, as in the racist treatment of the Native Americans in the nineteenth century or in the forced internment of many Japanese-Americans during World War II, the mythmakers have inflicted lasting harm upon large numbers of innocent people.

The line between reality and myth is not always easy to discern. The artist George Catlin, for example, is normally considered a reliable source of information about the early West. Not only was he a representational painter whose works exhibited considerable fidelity to nature, he was also an attorney who attended law school with future Vice President John C. Calhoun and noted world-explorer John Lloyd Stephens—in other words, a person trained to respect fact and report accurately. In May 1832, while traveling on the Upper Missouri, Catlin observed that "a party of five or six hundred Sioux Indians" arrived at the fort with "*fourteen hundred fresh buffalo tongues* [Catlin's italics]" which they then exchanged for a "few gallons of whiskey." He continues, "This profligate waste of the lives of these noble and useful animals...fully supports me in the seemingly extravagant predictions that I have made as to their extinction, which I am certain is near at hand." If true, this observation challenges popular myths about the Native Americans of the northern plains, especially the Sioux, living in strict, near-religious equilibrium with the environment. Based on Catlin's account, a significant number of the tribe were capable of killing prodigiously with little regard for their traditional beliefs.

On the other hand, though, we have, just eleven years after Catlin, the comments of another trusted Western source of the Western frontier, the artist John James Audubon. In his journal entry for June 11, 1843, Audubon states that "We have seen much remarkably handsome scenery [along the Upper Missouri River] but nothing at all comparing with Catlin's descriptions; his book must, after all, be altogether a humbug. Poor devil! I pity him from the bottom of my soul; had he studied, and kept up the old French proverb that says, *Bon renomme vaut mieux que ceinture dore* [A good, well-earned

Myths shape our lives in ways large and small. They can produce harm or good, and their effects can be noted at the scale of the province or at the level of a small provincial family.

fame is better than gold], he might have become an 'honest man'—the quintessence of God's works." In cases like this—where one credible observer directly calls into question the general veracity of another—it falls upon the reader to sort fact from fiction, history from histrionics, disinterested reportage from self-serving manipulation, reality from myth. Only in this way can the past be intelligently navigated, the present be clearly understood and the future be successfully predicted. Quite often, as with this example, the historical reality is probably a paradoxical mixture of several opposing points-of-view, each of which has nurtured its own myth.

The myth-making urge is deeply rooted in the human consciousness. It is part of the way the human brain—that radiant darkness of perception and self-interest—interprets reality. Myths inspire us to higher endeavors, defend us from what we fear, and render complex events more comprehensible. Just as the hermit crab wears a borrowed shell to protect itself, so does the human mind carry its own armor—an array of myths that form, as it were, a functional exoskeleton. Because of the universal, and therefore timeless, nature of this facility, the myths of the American West are not merely the antique stuff of frost-bitten prospectors and sun-burned cowboys. To the contrary, new myths are being spawned and nurtured every day across the region. In Roswell, New Mexico, for example, contemporary mythmakers would have the credulous believe that the experimental mannequins aboard a downed weather balloon were space aliens. Further to the west, other members of the same guild have spun elaborate stories of captured alien spacecraft being furtively tested at the government's secure aircraft zone—Area 51—near Las Vegas, Nevada. In both cases, the respective local chambers of commerce have been quite happy to support these myth-makers in their hilarious and often profitable endeavors.

The epigraph for this essay from John James Audubon refers to the original West—the Ohio

The Cliff Palace Ruins in Mesa Verde National Park offer a quiet warning to modern civilization. Courtesy John Murray.

River Valley—and to the manifold changes Audubon witnessed there, in the Old Northwest of George Rogers Clark (older brother of William Clark) before the artist explored the Upper Missouri. Since the beginning, change has been a central constant in the history of the American West. The axiom that has governed all myth-makers, from the French *coueur-du-bois* to the producers of contemporary films such as *Dances With Wolves* (1990), is that those who resist change are annihilated and those who accept it are liberated. For well over two centuries now the West has offered the hope of change to an eastern world that is often governed—as Thoreau noted in his 1861 essay "Walking"—by conventional modes of thinking and living, and that early on lost the majority of its public land to private ownership. The unique myths of the West—so connected to the liberating presence of open space and public land—have over time transformed the world. The region has become a realm unto itself, a shining territory where the sun goes every day, and restless people move instinctively in search of health, happiness, and freedom.

In the end, we have seen that the most wonderful creation of nature in the American West is not the Grand Canyon or the Yellowstone Plateau or the Big Sur Coast, but the human imagination. It is more powerful than a river, more magnificent than a herd of wild horses thundering over the prairie, more destructive than a tornado, more inscrutable than the trail back to deer hunting camp in a blizzard. Its potent Edenic myth inspired a lost and broken man, as we saw with the story of John Muir, to become an influential advocate. On the other hand, Custer's mad pursuit of fame (the old quest myth), helped the Colonel find an early and ignoble grave. The agrarian myth led ingenious farmers to transform a parched desert, in California's Imperial Valley, into a fertile paradise; but another more dangerous myth—the utopian myth of unlimited progress—nearly destroyed the region during the Great Depression. Seen in this context, the ultimate value of any inquiry such as this is that it reminds us to beware of destructive myths, and the venal souls who would perpetrate them upon us, and, conversely, to enjoy those beneficial myths that enrich our world.

Over time every reader of this book will grow old and die. Every generation that inhabits the West will in turn vanish quietly from the earth. These myths, however, like the landscapes that inspired them, will always endure. They are the cultural DNA, as it were, from which each successive generation forms a new civilization. They create us as much as we create them, and we live and die according to the ideas they embody. We inhabit a world in which symbol is as important as fact; a world in which the most difficult story to tell is, quite often, what actually happened; a world in which what we appear to be is regularly taken to be more important than who we are. Let us resolve that in the future we will each respect truth as much as legend, and that we will embrace no myth that visits harm upon anything in nature, be that wild nature or human nature.

In the end, we have seen that the most wonderful creation of nature in the American West is not the Grand Canyon or the Yellowstone Plateau or the Big Sur Coast, but the human imagination.

A CHRONOLOGY OF THE AMERICAN WEST

1540	Coronado begins two-year expedition to explore the Southwest
1680	Pueblo revolt in northern New Mexico
1692	de Vargas retakes northern New Mexico
1734	Birth of Daniel Boone (1734–1820), first mythic western frontier figure
1769	Spanish begin establishing missions along the California coast north of San Diego
1803	Louisiana Purchase doubles the size of the United States
1804	Lewis and Clark commence their two-year mission of discovery up the Missouri River
1805	Zebulon Pike explores Colorado and New Mexico
1819	Beginning of two-year expedition to Colorado by Major Stephen Long
1820s	Age of fur trappers
1822	Jedediah Smith begins western explorations in Rocky Mountains
1831	Publication of James Ohio Pattie's *Personal Narrative*
1832	Artist George Catlin journeys through the Far West
1835	Establishment of Republic of Texas
1835	Publication of Washington Irving's *A Tour on the Prairies*

1842	Fremont begins his western expeditions (report published in 1845)
1843	Artist John James Audubon explores the Upper Missouri
1843	Oregon Trail established
1845	Texas becomes a state
1846	Oregon is established south of Canada
1846	Francis Parkman journeys through the West, later writes *The Oregon Trail*
1846	Mormons begin to leave Illinois for Utah
1846	Mexican-American War rages for two years
1848	California gold rush
1848	Treaty of Guadalupe Hidalgo greatly expands U.S. presence in Southwest
1857	Establishment of Overland Mail Company
1858	First stagecoach and mail service from Missouri to California
1859	Albert Bierstadt joins the expedition of General Lander through the Rockies
1859	Gold discovered in Colorado, Nevada, and Idaho
1860	Pony Express begins
1861	First telegraph connects East and West coasts, permitting real-time communication across the country
1861	Civil War begins, a four-year conflict that will tem-

	porarily slow western expansion
1861	Samuel Clemens (later known as Mark Twain) journeys west to Nevada
1862	Homestead Act
1864	Sand Creek Massacre in Colorado
1865	Beginning of Sioux Wars, which will last until 1876
1867	Purchase of Alaska
1869	First transcontinental railroad joins at Promontory Point, Utah
1869	Major Powell explores Green and Colorado Rivers, later publishes narrative in 1875
1869	John Muir's first summer in the High Sierra
1870s	Massacre of buffalo across the Great Plains
1871	Thomas Moran joins expedition to explore Yellowstone headwaters
1872	Mark Twain publishes *Roughing It*
1872	Yellowstone National Park formed
1876	Colorado becomes a state
1876	Battle of the Little Bighorn
1877	Retreat of Chief Joseph and Nez Percé
1880	Charles Russell begins work on Montana ranch
1881	Frederic Remington begins to paint the Far West
1881	Helen Hunt Jackson

publishes *A Century of Dishonor*, a book whose thesis will influence later works such as the film *Cheyenne Autumn* (1964)

1881 The gunfight at the OK Corral takes place in Tombstone, Arizona

1883 Theodore Roosevelt arrives in the West, establishes cattle ranch

1886 Geronimo surrenders

1889 Oklahoma land rush

1890s Vast areas in the public domain are withdrawn from development by the federal government and designated as forest reserves

1890 Massacre at Wounded Knee marks the end of the frontier

1891 Publication of John Bourke's *On the Border with Crook*

1892 Sierra Club formed by John Muir

1893 Historian Frederick Jackson Turner announces the death of the American frontier

1894 Publication of John Muir's *The Mountains of California*

1895 John Ford born

1896 Utah becomes a state

1897 Gold rush in Alaska

1898 Artists Ernest Blumenschein and Bert Geer Phillips first visit Taos, New Mexico

1900 Publication of Jack London's *The Son of the Wolf*, his first book

1900 Both Carmel, California, and Taos, New Mexico, emerge as important art colonies

1900 Frederic Remington paints historic scenes of the American frontier that will later inspire filmmaker John Ford

1901 Theodore Roosevelt becomes first president to have lived on the western frontier

1901 Publication of John C. Van Dyke's *The Desert*

1902 Owen Wister's novel *The Virginian* becomes a national best-seller

1903 *The Great Train Robbery*, often cited as the first narrative Western film, is released

1903 Publication of Mary Austin's *The Land of Little Rain*

1903 Publication of Jack London's *The Call of the Wild*

1907 John Wayne born

1908 President Theodore Roosevelt designates Grand Canyon National Monument

1909 Publication of Enos Mills' *Wild Life on the Rockies*

1912 Publication of Zane Grey's *Riders of the Purple Sage*

1912 Arizona and New Mexico become states

1912 Western artist Maynard Dixon decides to stop illustrating and begin painting the "real" West

1913 Publication of Willa Cather's first farming novel, *O Pioneers!*

1915 Taos artists formally organize themselves as a society

1915 Publication of Willa Cather's *The Song of the Lark*

1916 Establishment of National Park Service

1916 General Pershing enters Mexico in pursuit of Pancho Villa

1918 Publication of Willa Cather's *My Ántonia*

1919 Georgia O'Keeffe travels to Taos, New Mexico

1923 Willa Cather awarded Pulitzer Prize for *One of Ours*

1925 William S. Hart stars in *Tumbleweeds*

1924 John Ford films *The Iron Horse* on location in Nevada

1925 *The Vanishing American* is filmed by George B. Seitz in Monument Valley

1927 Willa Cather publishes *Death Comes for the Archbishop*

1929   *In Old Arizona* becomes the first Western to win an Oscar (Best Actor)

1929   J. Frank Dobie publishes *A Vaquero of the Brush Country*

1930s   Songwriter Woody Guthrie recognized as important folk-artist

1930s   Bob Wills and his Texas Playboys build following in Texas, Oklahoma, and the Southwest

1930s   Photographer Dorothea Lange documents the effects of the Dust Bowl and the Great Depression on the southern Great Plains

1930s   Emergence of f/64 Group photographers, especially Ansel Adams and Edward Weston, as influential Western mythmakers

1930s   Photographer Imogen Cunningham explores the human form and natural Western landscapes in several projects

1930   John Wayne stars in his first major picture, *The Big Trail*, shot in Jackson, Wyoming

1931   Nobel Prize in literature is awarded to Sinclair Lewis (first American)

1931   Gary Cooper stars in *The Virginian*, based on the Owen Wister novel, and the first sound Western

1933   *The Lone Ranger* begins as a radio program from WXYZ Radio in Detroit

1934   Gene Autry makes his first film appearance in a film entitled *In Old Santa Fe*

1936   *The Texas Rangers*, starring Fred MacMurray, shot in Santa Fe, New Mexico

1936   Publication of John Steinbeck's *In Dubious Battle*

1937   Wallace Stegner publishes his first novel, *Remembering Laughter*

1936   *The Petrified Forest*, with Humphrey Bogart, Leslie Howard and Betty Davis, appears, based on the Broadway production of Robert E. Sherwood's play

1939   John Steinbeck publishes *The Grapes of Wrath*; the book is awarded the Pulitzer Prize

1939   *Stagecoach* wins two Oscars

1939   What has come to be known as the "Old Tucson" film set is built west of Tucson, Arizona, for the film *Arizona*; it recreates 1860s Tucson and will eventually be used as the backdrop for over three hundred films, television episodes, and commercials

1940   *The Grapes of Wrath*, with Henry Fonda, is filmed in California and New Mexico (Santa Rosa and Pecos River); Fonda's performance is awarded an Oscar

1941   *High Sierra*, with Humphrey Bogart, is filmed in Alabama Hills near Lone Pine, California

1941   U.S. enters World War II, will include internment of Japanese-Americans in the West

1943   Publication of Wallace Stegner's *The Big Rock Candy Mountain*

1945   Publication of John Steinbeck's *Cannery Row*

1945   Atomic bomb exploded in New Mexico

1946   *My Darling Clementine*, with Henry Fonda and Walter Brennan, filmed in Monument Valley

1947   Publication of A. B. Guthrie's novel of mountain men, *The Big Sky*

1947   *The Sea of Grass*, with Spencer Tracy and Katherine Hepburn, is filmed in central New Mexico

1947   *Fort Apache*, with John Wayne, Henry Fonda, and Shirely Temple, is filmed in Monument Valley and near Mexican Hat, Utah

1948   *The Treasure of the Sierra Madre*, filmed in Mexico, wins three Oscars

1948 *The Hopalong Cassidy Show*, one of the first television Westerns, appears

1949 *She Wore A Yellow Ribbon*, with John Wayne and Ben Johnson, is filmed in Monument Valley and near Mexican Hat, Utah

1949 *Wagonmaster*, with Ben Johnson and Harry Carey, Junior, is filmed in Professor Valley and Spanish Valley near Moab, Utah

1950 *Rio Grande*, with John Wayne, Maureen O'Hara, and Ben Johnson is filmed in Professor Valley near Moab, Utah

1952 Publication of Joseph Wood Krutch's *The Desert Year*

1953 Publication of John Steinbeck's *East of Eden*

1952 *High Noon*, filmed in California, wins four Oscars

1953 Mari Sandoz publishes *Cheynne Autumn*

1953 Louis L'Amour publishes his first successful western novel, *Hondo*

1954 *Salt of the Earth,* filmed in Silver City, New Mexico

1954 Publication of Wallace Stegner's *Beyond the Hundredth Meridian*

1955 *Bad Day at Black Rock*, with Spencer Tracy, is filmed near Lone Pine, California

1950s Beat poets—Gary Snyder, Allen Ginsberg, Kenneth Rexroth—form in San Francisco

1955 *East of Eden*, with James Dean, is filmed in California; based on the John Steinbeck novel, it will win an Oscar

1956 *The Searchers*, with John Wayne and Natalie Wood, is filmed at Monument Valley

1956 Edward Abbey publishes *The Brave Cowboy*

1958 Alaska becomes a state

1958 Twenty-eight-year-old Clint Eastwood begins acting in television show, *Gunsmoke*

1959 Hawaii becomes a state

1959 *Sergeant Rutledge*, one of the first films to feature an African-American in a starring role, is filmed by John Ford in Monument Valley

1960s Los Angeles bands—the Beach Boys, the Doors, the Mamas and the Papas, and so forth—transform national musical scene

1960 *The Alamo*, with John Wayne, is filmed near Brackettville, Texas

1961 *The Comancheros*, with John Wayne, is filmed at Professor Valley near Moab

1961 Larry McMurtry publishes

Horseman, Pass By (later serves as the basis for the film *Hud*)

1961 *The Misfits*, with Marilyn Monroe, Montgomery Clift, and Clark Gable, is filmed in and around Reno, Nevada

1962 *Lonely are the Brave*, with Kirk Douglas, is filmed in the Albuquerque vicinity

1962 Edward Abbey publishes *Fire on the Mountain*

1962 Publication of Ken Kesey's *One Flew Over the Cuckoo's Nest*

1962 John Steinbeck awarded the Nobel Prize

1963 *Hud*, with Paul Newman, Melvyn Douglas and Patricia Neal, is filmed in Texas and wins three Oscars

1963 *How the West Was Won* wins four Oscars

1963 *Cheyenne Autumn*, John Ford's last western, is filmed in Monument Valley

1964 Congress passes the Wilderness Act

1966 Publication of Larry McMurtry's novel *The Last Picture Show*

1966 *A Fistful of Dollars*, the first European-made Western appears (starring Clint Eastwood)

1967 *Bonnie and Clyde*, wins an Oscar

1967 Historian William Goetzmann awarded Pulitzer Prize in history for his book *Exploration and Empire: The Explorer and the Scientist in the Winning of the American West*

1968 *Hang 'Em High*, with Clint Eastwood, is filmed at White Sands National Monument, New Mexico

1968 *Butch Cassidy and the Sundance Kid*, with Paul Neumann and Robert Redford, is filmed in Utah, Colorado, and New Mexico

1968 The San Francisco–based band the Grateful Dead emerges as an important alternative musical voice for the West

1968 *Easy Rider*, filmed in Mojave Desert, Flagstaff, Monument Valley, and Taos

1968 Publication of Edward Abbey's *Desert Solitaire*

1969 *True Grit*, filmed in southern Colorado, garners a Best Actor Oscar for John Wayne

1970s L.A.-based bands such as the Eagles and Fleetwood Mac dominate national music

1970 *Chisum*, with John Wayne, filmed at Eaves Movie Ranch in New Mexico

1971 *The Last Picture Show*, with Ben Johnson, Cloris Leachman, and Cybil Shepard, is filmed in Texas and wins two Oscars

1971 Wallace Stegner's novel *Angle of Repose* awarded Pulitzer Prize

1972 *Joe Kidd*, with Robert Duvall and Clint Eastwood, is filmed at the Alabama Hills in California and at the Old Tucson film set

1972 *The Cowboys*, with John Wayne, filmed in southern Colorado and in northern New Mexico (Bonanza Creek Ranch, Chama Basin, Galisteo basin)

1972 *Jeremiah Johnson*, with Robert Redford, is filmed in Utah

1974 Country/Folk/Pop singer John Denver named unofficial "Poet Laureate of Colorado" by Governor Richard D. Lamm

1974 Country-western singer Willie Nelson begins to play a revolutionary new form of country-western music, aimed at younger audiences

1973 *High Plains Drifter*, with Clint Eastwood, is filmed on location at Mono Lake, Calfornia

1974 *The Milagro Beanfield War* published

1975 Publication of Edward Abbey's *The Monkey Wrench Gang*

1975 Larry McMurtry publishes *Terms of Endearment*

1970s Emergence of Montana artist Russell Chatham as an influential regional tonalist

1970s Emergence of Kiowa painter T. C. Cannon as chief figure in "Indian Renaissance" artistic movement

1979 John Wayne receives a special lifetime achievement Oscar in March; dies of cancer in August

1979 *The Electric Horseman*, with Jane Fonda and Robert Redford, is filmed in Nevada and Utah

1980 Alaska Lands Bill doubles national park system and triples national wilderness system

1980 *The Urban Cowboy*, with John Travolta, is filmed in Houston, Texas

1980s Emergence of western nature writers Rick Bass and Terry Tempest Williams

1980s Emergence of Phoenix artist Ed Mell, who paints in the tradition of Maynard Dixon

1981 *Fire on the Mountain*, based

on the 1962 Edward Abbey novel and starring Buddy Ebsen, is filmed in southern New Mexico

1983   Western novelist Louis L'Amour awarded National Gold Medal by Congress

1983   Robert Duvall awarded Best Actor Oscar for his performance in *Tender Mercies*, filmed in Waxahatchie, Texas

1985   *Silverado*, with Kevin Costner, Danny Glover, and Scott Glen, is filmed in northern New Mexico at various sites including the Cook Ranch, The Eaves Movie Ranch, and the Ghost Ranch

1985   Larry McMurtry's *Lonesome Dove* is awarded the Pulitzer Prize

1986   *Three Amigos!* with Steve Martin, Chevy Chase, and Martin Short shot partly at the Old Tucson film set

1988   *The Milagro Beanfield War*, based on the John Nichols novel, is filmed by Robert Redford near Taos, New Mexico

1989   *Lonesome Dove* is filmed partly in New Mexico at Bonanza Creek Ranch, Cook Ranch, San Ildefonso Pueblo, Santo Domingo Pueblo, and at Angel Fire

(Black Lake)

1990s   Emergence of south Texas artist Cesar Martinez as major figure in Western art

1991   *Bugsy*, with Warren Beatty and Annette Benning, is filmed in southern California

1991   *City Slickers* filmed in Utah at Goblin Valley State Park, Arches National Park, Deadhorse Point State Park, and in New Mexico at Ghost Ranch, Nambe Pueblo, and Plaza Blanca

1993   *Geronimo*, with Gene Hackman and Robert Duvall, is filmed at Professor Valley near Moab, Utah

1993   *Tombstone*, with Val Kilmer and Glenn Ford, shot in southern Arizona

1993   *Maverick*, with Mel Gibson, James Garner, and Jodie Foster, filmed near Page, Arizona

1994   *Wyatt Earp*, with Kevin Costner, Gene Hackman, and Dennis Quaid, is filmed in northern New Mexico

1995   President Clinton designates 1.5 million-acre Grand Staircase–Escalante National Monument in Utah

1995   Los Angeles band No

Doubt releases album entitled *Tragic Kingdom*

1999   *The Hi-Lo Country*, starring Woody Harrelson, Patricia Arquette, and Willie Nelson, is filmed in northern New Mexico

1999   *The Wild Wild West*, starring Will Smith, is filmed in northern New Mexico

1999   *All the Pretty Horses*, a film based on the Cormac McCarthy novel, is shot in New Mexico by Oscar-winning actor Billy Bob Thornton

1999   Annual Harris Poll reveals that the second most popular film star of all time is John Wayne (behind Harrison Ford and in front of Mel Gibson)

2000   President William Jefferson Clinton designates several large national monuments in the American West

2000   George W. Bush elected; first president born in the West since Lyndon Johnson

2001   Major exhibit of western art from Anschutz Collection at Denver Art Museum

SELECTED BIBLIOGRAPHY

Among those [people] I have known the love of books and the love of the outdoors, in their highest expressions, have usually gone hand in hand. Usually the keenest appreciation of what is seen in nature is to be found in those who have also profited by the hoarded and recorded wisdom of their fellow men. Love of outdoor life, love of simple and hardy pastimes, can be gratified by men and women who do not possess large means, and who work hard; and so can love of books.

—Theodore Roosevelt,
Autobiography (1913)

A lifetime could be spent reading primary and secondary works on Western mythology and culture. Here are a few of the titles that have been helpful to me over the years, and whose reading has enriched these pages. Most of these books can be found in your local public library. If not, they can always be ordered through Interlibrary Loan. Many can be found at your local chain or independent bookstore or on Amazon.com. All make for delighting reading.

Abbey, Edward. *Abbey's Road* (New York, 1975).

———. *Desert Solitaire* (New York, 1969).

———. *The Brave Cowboy* (New York, 1956).

———. *The Monkey Wrench Gang* (New York, 1975).

Adams, Ansel. *Autobiography* (New York, 1979).

Austin, Mary. *The Land of Little Rain* (New York, 1903).

Bass, Rick. *The Deer Pasture* (New York, 1985).

Betzinez, Jason. *I Fought With Geronimo* (Lincoln, Nebraska, 1987).

Bird, Isabella. *A Lady's Life in the Rocky Mountains* (available in reprint).

Black Elk. *The Sacred Pipe: Black Elk's Account of the Seven Rites of the Oglala Sioux* (New York, 1953).

Bogdanovich, Peter. *John Ford* (Berkeley, 1978).

Bourke, John Gregory. *An Apache Campaign in the Sierra Madre* (available in reprint).

———. *On the Border with Crook* (available in reprint).

Brown, Dee. *Bury My Heart at Wounded Knee: An Indian History of the American West* (New York, 1971).

Burnside, Wesley. *Maynard Dixon, Artist of the West* (Provo, 1974).

Castenada, Carlos. *The Teachings of Don Juan* (New York, 1973).

Cather, Willa. *O Pioneers!* (New York, 1913).

Catlin, George. *Letters and Notes on the Manners, Customs, and Conditions of North American Indians* (Dover reprint, New York, 1973).

Chatham, Russell. *One Hundred Paintings* (Livingston, Montana, 1989).

Connell, Evan. *Son of the Morning Star* (San Francisco, 1984).

Corn, Wanda M. *Grant Wood: The Regionalist Vision* (New Haven, 1983).

Costner, Kevin and Michael Blake. *Dances with Wolves, the Screenplay* (New York, 1990).

Crampton, Luke and Dafydd Rees. *Encyclopedia of Rock* (New York, 1996).

Devoto, Bernard. *The Course of Empire* (Boston, 1952).

Dobie, J. Frank. *A Vaquero of the Brush Country* (New York, 1929).

Dutton, Clarence. *Tertiary History of the Grand Cañon District* (Washington, 1882, available in reprint).

Ferguson, Harvy. *Wolf Song* (New York, 1927).

Frederick, Joan. *T. C. Cannon: He Stood in the Sun* (Flagstaff, 1995).

Fremont, John. *Narrative of the Exploring Expedition to the Rocky Mountains in the Year 1842* (available in reprint).

Gaar, Gillian. *She's a Rebel: The History of Women in Rock and Roll* (Seattle, 1992).

Ginsberg, Allen. *Howl* (San Francisco, 1956).

Goetzmann, William H. *Exploration and Empire* (New York, 1966).

———. *The West of the Imagination* (New York, 1985).

———. *Karl Bodmer's America* (Lincoln, Nebraska, 1984).

Greeley, Horace. *Overland Journey* (available in reprint).

Gregg, Josiah. *Commerce of the Prairies* (available in reprint).

Grey, Zane. *Riders of the Purple Sage* (New York, 1912).

Guthrie, A. B. *The Big Sky* (New York, 1952).

———. *The Way West* (New York, 1956).

Haiship, Neil. *Giants of Country Music* (New York, 1995).

Harrison, Jim. *Legends of the Fall* (New York, 1978).

Horan, James D. *The Life and Art of Charles Schreyvogel* (New York, 1969).

Horgan, Paul. *Lamy of Santa Fe* (New York, 1975).

Irving, Washington. *A Tour on the Prairies* (available in reprint).

Hagerty, Don. *Ed Mell: Beyond the Visible Terrain* (Flagstaff, 1998).

Hassrick, Peter. *Frederic Remington, The Late Years* (Denver, 1981).

Hendricks, Gordon. *Albert Bierstadt, Painter of the American West* (New York, 1974).

Inge, William. *Picnic* (New York, 1953).

Jackson, Donald, editor. *The Letters of the Lewis and Clark Expedition* (Urbana, 1962).

Jackson, Helen Hunt. *A Century of Dishonor* (available in reprint).

James, Edwin. *Account of an Expedition* (chronicle of Long expedition, available in reprint).

Jeffers, Robinson. *Flagons and Apples* (New York, 1912).

Kerouac, Jack. *On the Road* (New York, 1957).

Kesey, Ken. *One Flew Over the Cuckoo's Nest* (New York, 1962).

———. *Sometimes a Great Notion* (New York, 1964).

King, Clarence. *Mountaineering in the Sierra Nevadas* (available in reprint).

Kittredge, William. *Owning It All* (Minneapolis, 1987).

Krutch, Joseph Wood. *The Desert Year* (New York, 1952).

L'Amour, Louis. *Hondo* (New York, 1953).

Lewis, Meriwether and William Clark. *History of the Expedition* (available in reprint).

London, Jack. *The Son of Wolf* (New York, 1900).

Lyle, Laurie. *Portrait of an Artist, a Biography of Georgia, O'Keeffe* (New York, 1980).

Maclean, Norman. *A River Runs Through It* (Chicago, 1979).

McCloud, Barry. *Definitive Country Music* (New York, 1995).

McCracken, Harold. *The C. M. Russell Book* (New York, 1957).

McGuane, Tom. *Nobody's Angel* (New York, 1982).

McMurtry, Larry. *Horseman, Pass By* (New York, 1962)

———. *The Last Picture Show* (New York, 1966)

———. *Lonesome Dove* (New York, 1985).

Meltzer, Milton. *Dorothea Lange, a Photographer's Life* (New York, 1978).

Momaday, N. Scott. *House Made of Dawn* (New York, 1969).

Mills, Enos. *Wild Life on the Rockies* (New York, 1909).

Morand, Anne. *Thomas Moran: The Field Sketches, 1856–1923* (Norman, 1996).

Muir, John. *My First Summer in the Sierras* (available in reprint).

———. *Our National Parks* (available in reprint).

Neihardt, John G., editor. *Black Elk Speaks* (New York, 1932).

Newhall, Beaumont. *William Henry Jackson* (Fort Worth, 1974).

Nichols, John. *The Milagro Beanfield War* (New York, 1974).

Norris, Frank. *The Octopus: A Story of California* (New York, 1901).

O'Dair, Barbara, editor. *The Rolling Stone Book of Women in Rock* (New York, 1997).

Pattie, James O. *The Personal Narrative* (available in reprint).

Parkman, Francis. *The Oregon Trail* (available in reprint).

Pike, Zebulon. *An Account of the Expedition* (available in reprint).

Porter, Katherine Anne. *The Collected Stories* (New York, 1966).

Powell, John Wesley. *The Exploration of the Colorado River and its Tributaries* (available in reprint).

Quirarte, Jacinto and Carey Clements Rote. *Cesar A. Martinez: A Retrospective* (Austin, 2000).

Redford, Robert and Richard Friedenberg. *A River Runs Through It, the Screenplay* (Livingston, Montana, 1992).

Renner, Frederic G. *Charles M. Russell* (New York, 1974).

Rexroth, Kenneth. *In What Hour* (San Francisco, 1941).

Roethke, Theodore. *The Lost Son and Other Poems* (New York, 1948).

Rogers, Will. *Roger-isms, From The Cowboy Philosopher* (New York, 1919).

Rölvaag, Ole. *Giants in the Earth* (New York, 1927).

Roosevelt, Theodore. *Ranch Life and the Hunting Trail* (available in reprint).

Rusho, W. L. *Everett Ruess: A Vagabond for Beauty* (Layton, Utah, 1983).

Russell, Don. *The Lives and Legends of Buffalo Bill* (Norman, 1960).

Russell, Osborne. *Journal of a Trapper* (available in reprint).

Ruxton, George. *Life in the Far West* (available in reprint).

Samuels, Harold. *Frederic Remington, a Biography* (Garden City, New Jersey, 1982).

Sandoz, Mari. *Old Jules* (New York 1935).

Schulteis, Rob. *The Hidden West, Journeys in the American Outback* (San Francisco, 1983).

Seton, Ernest Thompson. *Wild Animals I Have Known* (available in reprint).

Snyder, Gary. *Riprap* (New York, 1959).

———. *Turtle Island* (New York, 1975).

Stegner, Wallace. *The Sound of Mountain Water* (New York, 1969).

———. *Where the Bluebird Sings To The Lemonade Springs, Living and Writing in the West* (New York, 1992).

Steinbeck, John. *The Grapes of Wrath* (New York, 1939).

Sweeney, Edwin R. *Cochise: Chiricahua Apache Chief* (Norman, 1991).

Thrapp, Dan L. *The Conquest of Apacheria* (Norman, 1967).

Tillet, Leslie. *Wind on the Buffalo Grass; The Indians' Own Account of the Battle at the Little Bighorn and the Death of Their Life on the Plains* (New York, 1976).

Twain, Mark. *Roughing It* (available in reprint).

Tyler, Ron. *Alfred Jacob Miller: Artist on the Oregon Trail* (Fort Worth, 1982).

Van Dyke, John. *The Desert* (New York, 1901).

Waters, Frank. *Pike's Peak* (New York, 1971).

Weston, Edward. *The Daybooks* (New York, 1973).

Wilder, Laura Ingalls. *Little House on the Prairie* (New York, 1935).

Wilkins, Thurman. *Thomas Moran, Artist of the Mountains* (Norman, Oklahoma, 1966).

Williams, Terry Tempest. *Refuge* (New York, 1990).

Wills, B. Rosetta. *The King of Western Swing: Bob Wills Remembered* (New York, 1998).

Wister, Owen. *The Virginian* (New York, 1902).

INDEX

Note: italic page numbers indicate pictures.

Abbey, Clarke, 106
Abbey, Edward, 69, 72, 95, 100, *104*, 165
    life and work, 104–106
Aberbach, Joaquin, 43
Abiquiu, New Mexico, 39
Across the Borderline, 139
Adams, Ansel, 5, 13, 24–25, 32–36, 41
    and San Francisco, 130
    and San Juan Mountains, 155
Alfred Stieglitz Collection, 40
Algodones Dune Field, 158
Allison, Jerry, 121
Almanac Singers, 119
Amboy, California, 163
American Beauty, 131
Amor Prohibido (album), 141
"Amor Prohibido" (song), 141
Anasazi, 3–4
Anthem of the Sun, 131
Apache, 78–83
An Apache Campaign in the Sierra Madre, 82
An Old Fighter, 27, *27*
Apacheria, 83, *83*
Arches National Park, *105*, 106, 157
Area 51, 155
Arikara, 74
Arizona Highways, 144, 159–160, *159*
Arizona Strip, 159
Arthur, Jean, 103
Artist's Point, 18
Aspen trees, 6, *135*
Aspevig, Clyde, 28
Atchison, Topeka & Santa Fe Railroad, 151
Audubon, John James, 164, 165, 166–167
Austin, Mary, 94–96
Autry, Gene, 54, 59, 112, *112*
Axis: Bold as Love, 133

"Back in the Saddle Again," 112
Badlands, 66, 87, 147
Baez, Joan, 118
Baker, Carroll, 92
Baker, Gladys Pearl, 57
Barrow, Bonnie and Clyde, 137
Bass, Rick, 47
Bass, Sam, 137

Battle of the Little Bighorn, 6, 92. *See also* Little Bighorn National Battlefield
Beach Boys, 122, 124–126, *124*
Beale, Edward Fitzgerald, 162
Beale wagon road, 162
Bean, Roy, 147
Beatles, 122
Beatty, Warren, 47
The Belmonts, 121
Berninghause, Oscar, 24
Bernstein, Elmer, 50
Berry, Chuck, 124
Betzinez, Jason, 69, 80, 81
Beyond the Hundredth Meridian, 100–101, *100*
Bierstadt, Albert, 12–13, 16–19
Big Bend National Park, 118
The Big Bopper, 121, 122
Big Foot, 147
The Big Sky, 8, 71, *100*, 102–103
Big Sky Journal, 144
The Big Trail, 4, 5, 52
The Big Valley, 55, *55*
Billy the Kid, 137
The Birth of a Nation, 52
Black, Clint, 158
Black Hills, 6, 66
Blackfoot Indians, 31, 102
Blake, Michael, 65
Blood Tribe, 15
The Blue Hotel, 97
Blumenschein, Ernest, 23–25
Bob Wills and His Texas Playboys, 116–117
Bodmer, Karl, 6, 12, 66
Bogart, Humphrey, 50–51
Bolton, Michael, 158
Bon Jovi, Jon, 158
Bonanza, 55
The Book of Mormon, 149
Bound for Glory, 119
Bourke, John Gregory, 69, 81–82
Boyd, William, 54
Brady, Mathew, 75
Bradley, Ed, 47
Brando, Marlon, 45
The Brave Cowboy, 105–106
Breck, Peter, *55*

Bridal Veil Falls, *86*
Bridger, Jim, 23, 73, 149
Brigman, Anne, 37
Brokaw, Tom, 47
Broken Arrow, 78
Bronson, Charles, 50
Brower, David, 90
Brown Palace Hotel, 18, 104
Brown, Dee, 65
Brunswick records, 116
Bryce Canyon National Park, *101*
Brynner, Yul, 50
Buckingham, Lindsey, 128
Buddy Holly and the Crickets, 121–122
Buffalo Bill Museum, 22, 28
Buffalo Bill's Traveling Wild West Show, 15, 143–144. *See also* Cody, Buffalo Bill
Buffalo Bull's Backfat, Head Chief, Blood Tribe, 15, *15*
"The Buffalo Skinners," 114
Bull moose, *88*
Burns, George, 137
Burns, Robert, 134
Burroughs, John, *89*, 90
Bury My Heart at Wounded Knee, 65
Bus Stop, 56
Busey, Gary, 120
Butch Cassidy and the Sundance Kid, 51, 56, 62–63
Byrds, 122

Cabeza de Vaca, 140
Calhoun, John C., 165
California, 162–163, 164, 167
"California Dreamin'," 123
The Call of the Wild, 56
Camer Obscura Photographic Gallery, 38
Campbell, Glen, 111, *112*
Camus, Albert, 130
Cannon, Mamie, 42
Cannon, T. C., 13, 41–45
Cannon, Walter, 42
Canterbury Tales, 161
Canyon de Chelly, *7*
Carey, Harry, 22
Carlson, Ken, 28
Carson, Kit, 23, 73
Castle Rock and Valley, 157

Cather, Willa, 91–94, *93*
Catlin, George, 5, 12, 14–16, 66, 165
A Century of Dishonor, 75
Chad Mitchell Trio, 134
Chama Valley, 33–34
Chandler, Brian "Chas," 133
Charbonneau, 74
Charles Russell Museum, 22
The Chasm of the Colorado, 18, *19*
Chatham, Russell, 13, 34, 45–47
Chaucer, Geoffrey, 161
Chemehuevi Mountains, 163
Cheyenne Autumn, 53, 71, 91, *91*, 92
Cheyenne tribe, 7
Chicago Herald, 143
Chief Watching, 43, *44*
Children of the Mountain, *12*
Chinatown, 50
Chisum, 59
Chivington, John, 5
Church of Jesus Christ of Latter-day
        Saints. *See* Mormons
Cirque of the Towers, *26*
City Slickers, *153*, 154
Clairol, 157
Clapton, Eric, 133
Clark, George Rogers, 166–167
Clark, Walter Van Tilburg, 97
Clark, William, 11, 14, 167. *See also*
        Lewis and Clark expedition
Cliff Palace Ruins, *166*
Clift, Montgomery, 56, 57, 155
Coburn, James, 50
Cochise, 78, 82–83
Cody, Buffalo Bill, *142*, 143. *See also*
        Buffalo Bill Museum, Buffalo Bill's
        Traveling Wild West Show
Cody, Wyoming, 153
Coe, Phil, 146
Cole, Nat King, 161
The Collected Stories, 92
Colonial West. *See* Manifest Destiny period
Colorado, *135*, 136–137
Colorado Plateau, *101*
Colorado River, 156, 157, 162, 163
Comic books, *70*
Commercial advertising, 156–158
Conjunto music, 140–141
Connell, Evan, 7

Connors, Chuck, 55
Conrad, Robert, 55
Cooper, Gary, 49, *50*
Coral-Brunswick recording company, 121
Costner, Kevin, 65–67, *65, 66*
Country-western music. *See* Cowboys:
        music; Nelson, Willie; Wills, Bob
Courthouse Wash, 157
Couse, E. Irving, 24
Cowboys,
        music, 113–115, *113*
        myth of in *Dr. Strangelove*, 49
        and Remington and Russell, 11, 20
Crane, Stephen, 97
Crazy Horse, 91, 92
Crazy Horse, 71, 91, 92–93
Cream, 122
Crook, General, 69, 81–82
Cultural periods, 70–72
Cumberland Gap, 164
Cunningham, Imogen, 13, 35, 36–38
Curtis, Edward, 36
Curtis, Sonny, 121
Custer, George Armstrong, 6–7, 42, 69, *70*
        book by, *70*, 78
        as follower of outdated myth, 167
        and Wild Bill Hickock, 146

Dallas, 56
Dances With Wolves, 51, 65–67, *65, 66*
de Young Memorial Museum, 37
Death Comes for the Archbishop, 91–92, *93*
Death Valley, 35
Death Valley Days, 54
Delicate Arch, 106
Denver, John, 8, *8*, 70, 134–137, *136*
Desert Solitaire, 104, 106
Desert Southwest, 31
DeVoto, Bernard, 102
Dexter, Brad, 50
Los Dinos, 140–141
Dix, Richard, 97
Dixon, Maynard, 9, 10, 13, 29–32, 41, 130
Dodge City, Kansas, 145–146, *146–147*
The Doors, 122, 126–127
Douglas, Kirk, 106–107
Dow, Arthur, 39
Downhill Racer, 62–63
Dr. Strangelove, *48*, 49

Dreaming of You, 141
Duchamp, Marcel, 42
Dude ranches, 153–156
Dunes Oceano, *35*
Dunton, W. Herbert, 24
Dust Bowl Ballads, 119
Dutton, Clarence, 91, 100
Duvall, Robert, 79
Dvořák, Antonín, 25
Dylan, Bob, 117, 122, 123, 131, 139
        and Woody Guthrie, 118, 119

The Eagles, 103, 111, 127–128, *128*
Earp, Morgan, 146
Earp, Virgil, 146
Earp, Wyatt, 145–146, *146*
Earth First!, 104–105
Earth Knower, 29–31, *29*
East of Eden, 98
Eastwood, Clint, 49–50, 55, 59–61, *59*
Easy Rider, 161, 163
Edison, Thomas, 144
Einstein, Albert, 151–152
"El Paso," 111
The Electric Horseman, 62–63, 138
Electric Ladyland, 133
Emerson, Ralph Waldo, 90
The End of the Innocence, 128
Entre a Mi Mundo, 141
Erickson, Leif, 55
Evans, Dale, 54
Evans, Linda, 55, *55*

Fairbanks, Douglas, 151–152
Fielder, John, 155
Film Und Foto, 38
Films, 49–51. *See also* Television westerns
Fire on the Mountain, 105
The First Traveling Saleslady, 60
Fisher Towers, 156
A Fistful of Dollars, 60
Fleetwood, Mick, 128
Fleetwood Mac, 127–129
Folk legends, 145
Fonda, Henry, 53, 162–163, *163*
Fonda, Jane, 47
Fonda, Peter, 47, 163
The Fool's Progress, 104, 106
For a Few Dollars More, 60

Ford, Francis, 52
Ford, Harrison, 47
Ford, John, 15, 51–53, *51*, 60, 76, 150, 162
    and Monument Valley, 8, 52–53,
        92, 158
Fort Apache, 51, 52
Foster, Stephen, 134
Four Corners Region, 152
Francis of Assisi, Saint, 106
Frazier, Luke, 28
Fred Harvey Company, 151–153, 156
Freeman, Morgan, 60–61
Frey, Glen, 128
From the Faraway Nearby, 40–41, *40*
Frontier cultural periods. *See* Cultural
    periods
Frontier Marshall, 145
f/64 Group, 31, 32–33, 35, 36, 38

Gable, Clark, 56, 57–58, *57*
Garcia, Jerry, 130–132, *131*
Gardner, James, 50
Garland, Judy, 151
The Gene Autry Show, 54
General Grant National Park, 90
Geronimo, 69, 78–83, *78*
Geronimo: An American Legend, 79
Geronimo, His Own Story, 79–81
Ghost Dance, 147
Ghost Ranch, 39
Ghost towns, 155, *155*
Gila River, 80
Gila River Wilderness, *79*
Gilcrease Museum, 22
Ginsberg, Allen, 130
"Git Along Little Dogies," 115
Glacier National Park, 31
Glen Canyon, 72
Glenbow Museum, 28
Glenwood Springs, Colorado, 153
Gold miners, *85*
The Good, the Bad, and the Ugly, 60
Goulding, Harry, 158
Graham, Bill, 131
Graham, Martha, 119
Grand Canyon, 18, 88, 159, 160, 161
Grand Canyon, 1908, viii, 1–2
Grand Gulch, 2–3
Granger, General, 82

Grant, Ulysses S., 16, 18, 82
The Grapes of Wrath, 53, 98–99
    and Route 66, 161, 162–163
Grateful Dead, 130–132, *131*, 133
The Grateful Dead, 131
Great Depression, 13, 116, 118–119, 167.
    See also The Grapes of Wrath
Great Northern Railroad, 31
Great Plains, 162
Greeley, Horace, 85, 120
Greene, Graham, *66*, 67
Greene, Lorne, 55
Grey, Lina Elise Roth, 96
Grey, Zane, 69, 96–97, *96*
Grunge bands, 111, 134
Gunfight at the O.K. Corral, 145. *See also*
    OK Corral legend
Gunsmoke, 56
Guthrie, A. B., 8, 9, 71, 100–103
Guthrie, Arlo, 119
Guthrie, Marjorie, 119
Guthrie, Woody, 118–119, *118*

Hackman, Gene, 60–61, 79
Hagman, Larry, 55
Harris, Richard, 61
Harrison, Jim, 47, 61, 69, 71, 72
Hart, William S., 22
Harte, Bret, 94
Harvey, Fred, 152–153, *152*. *See also* Fred
    Harvey Company
The Harvey Girls, 151
Hatch, Orrin, 150
Hayden Expedition, 18
Hayes, Gabby, 54
Head Chief, 15
Heflin, Van, 103
Helena Mayer, Canyon de Chelly, 37
Hemingway, Ernest, 69, 145
Hendrix, Al, 133
Hendrix, Jimi, 122, 127, 132–134, *132*
Henley, Don, 47, 111, 127–128
Hennings, E. Martin, 24
The Heritage of the Desert, 96–97
Hetch Hetchy Valley and Dam, 88, 90
Hickock, Wild Bill, 146
Hicks, Don, 155
Higgins, Victor, 24
The High Chaparral, 55

High Noon, 56
High Plains Drifter, 60
High Sierra, 50–51
Hinman, Eleanor, 92
Hole (band), 134
Holliday, John H. ("Doc"), 146
The Hollow Men, 49
Holly, Buddy, 8, 120–122, *120*
Honeysuckle Rose, 138
Hopalong Cassidy, 54
Hopi, 6, 152–153
Hopper, Dennis, 163
Horn, Tom, 137
The Horse Whisperer, 9, 51
Horseman, Pass By, 72, 107–108
Hotel California, 128
How The West Was Won, 51
Howard, Leslie, 49
Howard, O. O., 78, 82–83
Hubbell, J. L., 152–152
Huckleberry Finn, 9
Hud, 107
Huston, John, 50
Huston, Walter, 49, *50*

I Fought with Geronimo, 80, 81
In Dubious Battle, 99
"Indian Renaissance," 41
Indian Wars, 78
Institute of American Indian Arts, 42
The Iron Horse, 52
Irving, Washington, 74–77, *75*
Isleta Pueblo, *151*
Isuzu, 157

Jackson, Helen Hunt, 5, 75
Jackson, William Henry, 19
James, Jesse, 147
"James Dean," 123
Japanese-Americans, 5, 165
Jardine, Al, 124, 125
Jefferson, Thomas, 20, 72
Jeffords, Tom, 78
Jennings, Waylon, 117, 121–122, 137
Jeremiah Johnson, 62, 62–63
Jimi Hendrix Experience, 122, 133
Joe Kidd, 60
Jonathon Troy, 105
Joplin, Janis, 127, 130, 133
Joshua Tree, 158

The Journals of Lewis and Clark, 72–74, *73*
Jury for Trial of a Sheepherder for Murder, 25

Kansas, 164
Kicking Bear, 147
King, Clarence, 91
King of the Cowboys, 54
Kinks, 122
Kiowa Five, 42
Kokopelli, 11, 144
Kreutzmann, Bill, 131
Kristofferson, Kris 137
Krutch, Joseph Wood, 95
Kubrick, Stanley, 49
Kuhn, Bob, 28
Kuhnert, Wilhelm, 27
KVOO radio, 116–117

"L.A. Woman," 112
"La Bamba," 111
Ladd, Alan, 50, 103
Lady Godiva, 60
Lake Mojave, 159
Lake Powell, 158
Lamm, Richard, 136
The Land of Little Rain, 95, *95*
Lander, Frederic, 16–17
Landon, Michael, 55
Landscape. *See* Nature
Lange, Dorothea, 13, 31–32
Las Vegas, New Mexico, 166
The Last Picture Show, 107
Leadon, Bernie, 128
Leap, 150
"Leaving on a Jet Plane," 134
Led Zeppelin, 122
Ledbetter, Huddy (Leadbelly), 119
Legends of the Fall, 69, *71*, 72
Leigh, William R., viii, 1–2, 12–13
Leisure, David, 157
Lennon, John, 122
Lennon, Julian, 123
Leone, Sergio, 60
Lesh, Phil, 131
Lewis, Meriwether, 11, 102. *See also*
    Lewis and Clark expedition
    as writer, 73–74
Lewis and Clark expedition, 6, 11, 70
    journals of, 72–74

Library of Congress Archive of Folk
    Song, 119
Limit of Deseret, 10
Little Bighorn National Battlefield, *6.*
    See also Battle of the Little Bighorn
Little House on the Prairie, 55
Little Missouri River, 71, 87
Lomax, John, 114
London, Jack, 97
The Lone Ranger, 54, 56, 156
Lonely Are the Brave, 106
Lonesome Dove, 107, 108
The Long Valley, 99
Long, Richard, *55*
Long, Stephen, 6, 11–12
Long's Peak, *18*
Lopez, Jennifer, 141
Los Angeles County Museum, 37
Los Angeles music, 123–130
Love, Mike, 124, 125

Maclean, Norman, 9, 62, 63, 64, 91
The Magnificent Seven (film), 50
The Magnificent Seven (TV series), 56
Majors, Lee, 55, *55*
*Mama and Papa Have the Going Home to
    Shiprock Blues*, 42
The Mamas and the Papas, 123
The Man Who Shot Liberty Valance, 60
Mandan, 6, 14–15, 74
Manifest Destiny period, 6–7, 59, 70–71
    and Theodore Roosevelt, 88
Manzarek, Ray, 127
Marcy, Captain, 162
Marin, John, 41
Martinez, Cesar, 8, 45
Masterson, Bat, 146–147, *146*
Mauldin, Joe, 121
Mayer, Helena, *37*, 38
McCartney, Paul, 126
McDonnell, Mary, 67
McGuane, Tom, 9, 45, 47
McKernan, Ron "Pigpen," 131
McMurtry, Larry, 8, 72, 100, 107–108, *107*
McQueen, Steve, 50
McVie, Christine Perfect, 128
McVie, John, 128
Meisner, Randy, 128
Mell, Ed, 32

Melville, Herman, 75
Mesa Verde National Park, *166*
Metropolitan Museum of Art, 40
Mexican Hat, Utah, 158
Mexican-U.S. border country, *122*, 141
    as cultural region, 139
Milagro Beanfield War, 71–72, *71*
Miller, Alfred Jacob, 6, 12
Miller, Arthur, 56, 57
Miller Brewing Company, 157
Mining towns, 155, *155*
Mint, A Pretty Girl, 15
Mis Mejores Canciones, 141
The Misfits, 56, 57–58, *57,* 155
Mississippi River, 162
The Missouri Breaks, 45
Missouri River, 72, 102, 164, 165, 167.
    See also Little Missouri River
Mitchell, Joni, 123
Mitchell, Mitch, 133
Mitchum, Robert, 56
Mitten Buttes, 2, 9
Moab, Utah, 156, 157–158
Mogollon Rim, 160
Mojave Desert, 31, 33, 94, *94*, 158
    and Route 66, 162, 163
Momaday, N. Scott, 1
Modotti, Tina, 35, 37
The Monkey Wrench Gang, 72, 105
Monroe, Marilyn, 56–58, *56, 57,* 155
Montana, *9*, 51, *102*
Monterey Bay, 98
Monterey Pop Festival, 133
Montgomery, Bob, 121
Monument Valley, 2, 9, 97, *157*, 160
    and John Ford, 8, 52–53, 158
    as scene of commercials, 156, 157–158
Moon, Morning Star, Evening Star, 25
Moonrise Over Hernandez, 33–35, *34*
Moore, Clayton, 54
Moran, Thomas, 12–13, 16–19, 89, 104
Mormons, 148–150
Morrison, Jim, 112, 127, *127*
Morrison, Pamela, 127
Mount Moran, 18
Mount Toro, 45
Mountain men, 73
The Mountains of California, 91
Movies. *See* Films

Moyers, Bill, 139
Muench, Josef, 159
Muir, John, 5, 8, 76, 89–91, *89*, 104, 167
The Mural, 42
Murie, Margaret, 69–70
Murray, Don, 56
Museum of Western Art, 27
Music, 111–112. *See also* Cowboys:
    music, Pacific Coast music
My Antonia, 93
My Darling Clementine, 60, 145
My Life and Experiences Among Our
    Hostile Indians, 78
My Life on the Plains, *70*, 78
Myths, 4
    agrarian, 167
    Anasazi, 4
    and *Arizona Highways*, 159–160
    bad, 4, 5, 8, 165, 167
    California myth of eternal youth,
        123, 126, 130
    and change, 167
    and commercial advertising, 156–158
    and cowboys, 20, 49, 113–114
    dude ranches as mythmaking
        machine, 153–154
    Edenic, 70, 73, 77, 101, 106,
        159–160, 165, 167
    of the family, 63–64
    and films, 49–51
    folk legends, 145
    Fred Harvey's Southwest, 151–153,
        156
    function in interpreting reality, 166
    good, 4–5, 8, 165, 167
    Greco-Roman heroic myth, 165
    McMurtry's challenging of, 108
    Mormon utopianism, 148–149
    and music, 111– 112
    mythmaking periods of the West, 6–8
    outlaw, 137, 139
    and Route 66, 161–163
    of San Francisco freedom, 131
    shaping of human experience,
        164–165
    of space aliens, 166
    and visual arts, 12–13
    West as source for, 5–6, 8–9
    of the West in popular culture, 144,

147
    and writers, 69–72

Napoleon, 72
National Museum of Wildlife Art, 28
National Parks. *See* Catlin, George;
    General Grant National Park;
    Glacier National Park; Muir, John;
    Roosevelt, Theodore; Sequoia
    National Park; Yellowstone National
    Park; Yosemite National Park
Native Americans. *See also* Ghost Dance,
    "Indian Renaissance," Indian Wars,
    tribal names
    arts and crafts sold through Fred
        Harvey Co., 151–153, *151*
    conflicting accounts of equilibrium
        with nature, 165–166
    encountered by Lewis and Clark
        expedition, 74
    and Manifest Destiny period, 70, 71
    of Missouri River drainage, 14
    myths about, 5, 74, 165
    Washington Irving on, 75
Nature, 11–13, 51, 56, 58, 72, 167
    as muse and healer, 136
    Stegner on, 101
    Washington Irving on, 75–76
Navajo, 6, 152–153, 158
Needles, California, 163
Nelson, Willie, *110*, 117, 137–139, *138*
New Mexico, 79
New West, 58
Nichols, John, 69, 71–72
Nicholson, Jack, 45–46, 50
Nicks, Stevie, 128
"Night Life," 138
Nirvana, 111, 134
No Doubt, 129–130
No One Gets Out of Here Alive, 127
Nobel Prize, 98, 99
The North American Indian, 36
Nude Descending a Staircase, 42

O Pioneers, *91*
Oakley, Annie, 143, *144*
Ochs, Phil, 118
Of Mice and Men, 98, 99
Oh God!, 136

Ohio River Valley, 164, 166–167
OK Corral legend, 145–146
O'Keeffe, Georgia, 11, 32, 38–41
"The Old Chisholm Trail," 114–115
Old Natchez Trace, 161
Olijeta Mesa, 158
On the Border with Crook, 82
One Hundred Paintings, 46
One Life at a Time, Please, 106
One of Ours, 92
One of These Nights, *128*
Ordinary People, 63
Oregon Trail, 149, 161, 162
The Oregon Trail, 76 , *76*
Osmond, Donny and Marie, 150
O'Sullivan, Timothy, 19
The Outlaw Josie Wales, 60
Overland Monthly, 94
The Ox-Bow Incident, 97

Pacific coast, *123*
Pacific Coast music, 123–134
Pacific Coastal Highway, 161
Paint Your Wagon, 60
Painted Desert, 152, 157, 160
Paintings. *See* Visual arts
Pale Rider, 60
Palo Duro Canyon, 39
"Pantheistic sublime," 13, 33
Parkman, Francis, 74–77
Partridge, Roi, 38
Partridge, Ron, 38
The Pastures of Heaven, 99
Pawnee, 74
Paxton, Tom, 118
"Peaceful, Easy Feeling," 111
The Pearl, 98
Pearl Jam, 111, 134
Pecos Bill, 147
Penn, Arthur, 45
Pet Sounds, 126
Peter, Paul, and Mary, 134
Peterson, Roger, 122
The Petrified Forest, 49, 50
Petroglyphs. *See* Rock art
Petty, Tom, 129
Phillips, Bert, 23, 24
Photograpy. *See* Visual arts
Piazzoni, Gottardo, 45
Picasso, Pablo, 38

Pickens, Slim, *48*, 49
"Piece of My Heart," 130
Pike, Zebulon, 6, 11
Pindar, 134
Pine Butte Grizzly Bear Preserve, 103
Pitt, Brad, *64*
Poems, Prayers, and Promises, 136
Porter, Katherine, 92
Portrait 1876–1976, 7, 42
Postcolonial West, 71–72
The Preacher and the Slave, 150
Precolonial West, 70
The Professor's House, 91–92, 93
Pueblos, 6

Quintanilla, A. B., 140
Quintanilla, Abraham, 141
Quintanilla, Suzette, 140
Quintanilla-Perez, Selena. *See* Selena

Raitt, Bonnie, 139
Ranch Life and the Hunting Trail, 87–88, 154
Rawhide, 55, 60
Ray Price Band, 138
Reagan, Ronald, 54
The Real McCoys, 56
Realism, 98
Red Cloud, Nebraska, 93
Red-Headed Stranger (album and film), 138
Redding, Noel, 133
Redding, Otis, 133
Redford, Robert, 9, 62–64, *62*, 138
Redlands Pass, 158
Refuge, 150
Las Reinas del Pueblo, 141
Reiner, Carl, 136
Remington, Frederic, 8, 12–13, 19, 20–22, 29, 71, 88
Reno, Major, 7, 69
Return of a Blackfoot War Party, 21–22, *21*
Return to Saturn, 130
Ricketts, Ed, 98
The Rifleman, 55
Rio Grande, 52
Ritter, Thelma, 57–58
River of No Return, 56
A River Runs Through It (film), 62, 63–64, *64*

A River Runs Through It and Other Stories (book), 63–64
Robards, Jason, 92
Robbins, Marty, 111
Robinson, Edward G., 92
Rock art, 1, *3*
Rocky Mountain Front, 72, 101–102
The Rocky Mountains, Lander's Peak, 17–18, *17*
Rodeos, 155
Rogers, Roy, 54
Rolling Stones, 117, 122, 161
Roosevelt, Theodore, 20, 76, *86*, 104, 147
    and Geronimo, 79
    life and literary works, 70–71, 86–89, 154
    and myth, 4, 69, 86–87, 165
    naming of Rough Riders, 144
Roswell, New Mexico, 166
Rough Riders, 144
Roughing It, 75, 84–86, 150
Route 66, 161–163, *161*
"Route Sixty-Six" (song), 161
Route Sixty-Six (TV series), 161
The Roy Rogers Show, 54, 56
Ruess, Everett, 69
Rumours, 128–129
Rungius, Carl, 9, 12–13, 26–28
Russell, Charles, 8, 12–13, 20–22, 71, 89

Sacajawea, 74
Salinas Valley, 98
Salt Lake City, *148*, 150
San Francisco music, 130–132
San Juan Mountains, 155
San Juan River, 11
Sand Creek Massacre, 5
Sandoz, Mari, 8, 71, 91–94
Sangre de Christo Mountains, 25
Sangre de Cristo Mountains, 33–34
Santa Fe Railway, 151, 152, *151*
Santa Fe Trail, 162
Sasquatch, 147
Schmit, Tim, 128
Scholder, Fritz, 7, 41, 42, 43
The Scouts, 22
The Sea at Pacifica, 46–47, *46*
The Sea of Cortez, 99
The Searchers, 52–53

Seattle music, 132–134
Sedona, Arizona, 160
Seeds of Man, 119
Seeger, Pete, 119
Seitz, George B., 97
Selena, 139–141, *140*
Selena Live, 141
Sequoia National Park, 90
7-D Ranch, 155
Sgt. Pepper's Lonely Hearts Club Band, 126
Shakespeare, 134
Shane, 50, 103
Sharp, Joseph Henry, 23, 24
She Wore a Yellow Ribbon, 52
Sheffer, Craig, *64*
Sheldon, Charles, 27
Sierra Club, 89
Sierra Nevada Range, 33
Silent Hour, 30
Sioux, 6–7, 74, 147
Sitgreaves, Lorenzo, 162
Sitting Bull, *142*, 143, 147
Skerritt, Tom, *64*
Slade the Terrible, 85
Slick, Grace, 130
Smiley, Jane, 92
Smith, Hyrum, 149
Smith, Joseph, 149
Smith, Tucker, 28
"Some Must Push and Some Must Pull," 150
Son of the Morning Star, 7
The Song of the Lark, 93
The Songwriter, 138
Sonoran Desert, *83*, 160, *160*
Sons of the Pioneers, 54
The Sound of Mountain Water, 100–101, *100*
Space aliens, 166
"Spaghetti Westerns," 60
Spector, Phil, 124
Springsteen, Bruce, 123
St. Louis, 73, 162
Stagecoach, 52, *52*, 144, 158
Stanford University, 98, 100, 107
Stanwyck, Barbara, *55*
Star Road and White Sun, 25, *25*
Starr, Belle, 137
Stefani, Gwen, 129

Stegner, Wallace, 69, 95, 107, 118, 150
    life and work, 100–103
Steinbeck, Carol Henning, 98
Steinbeck, John, 98–99, *99*
Stephens, John Lloyd, 165
Stewart, Jimmy, 78, 92
Stieglitz, Alfred, 32, 39. *See also* Alfred
    Stieglitz Collection;
    O'Keeffe, Georgia
Stovepipe Wells, 35
Strand, Paul, 32
Strasberg, Lee, 58
"Streets of Laredo," 111
Study for the Earth Knower, 29
Sudden Impact, 49–50
Sullivan, Ed, 121
Sullivan, Niki, 121
Summer Fields Near the Yellowstone River,
    46, 47
"Summer in Algiers," 130
Sundance Film Festival, 63
Synthetic symbolism, 41

Taos (New Mexico) art colony, 13, 23–25
Taos Society of Artists, 23–24, *24*
Tejano music, 140–141
Television westerns, 54–56
Tender Mercies, 8
Terry, Blind Sonny, 119
Teton Mountains, 51
Texas, *108, 115*
Thompson, Hunter S., 70
Thoreau, Henry David, 20, 90, 120, 167
A Thousand Acres, 92
*Through Another Lens, My Years with
    Edward Weston*, 35
To a God Unknown, 99
Tombstone, Arizona, 145–146
Tortilla Flat, 98–99
A Tour on the Prairies, 75, 76
Townsend, Peter, 133
Tragic Kingdom, 129–130
Treaty of Guadalupe Hidalgo, 149
Trevor, Claire, *52*
Troubadour tradition, 134
Troup, Bobby, 161
True Grit, 49–50, 51
Tsatoke, Lee, 42
Tsatoke, Monroe, 42

Tumbling Tumbleweeds, 54
Tusk, 129
Twain, Mark, 9, *68*, 75, *84*, 130, 150
    life and work, 84–86
Twain, Shania, 117
Two Mules for Sister Sara, 60
"Two Painters," 43

Ufer, Walter, 24
Unforgiven, 59, 60–61, 144
Union-Pacific Railroad, 52
Utah, 148, 149
Utopian movement, 20
U2 (band), 158

Valens, Ritchie, 111, 121, 122
Van Dyke, John, 95
The Vanishing American (film), 158
The Vanishing American (novel), 97
Vaughn, Robert, 50
Ven Conmigo, 141
Villon, François, 134
The Virginian (film), 49, *50*
The Virginian (novel), 97
Visual arts, 11–13

Wagner, Robert, 47
Wagonmaster, 53, 150
Walker, Texas Ranger, 56
Wallach, Eli, 56, 57–58
Walsh, Joe, 128
Walsh, Raoul, 52
Wanted: The Outlaws, 138
War Soldier, Billy Soza, 41
Warner, Barbara, 43
The Way West, 8, 71, 103
Waylon and Willie, Highwaymen, 138
Wayne, John, 4–5, *4*, 49–50, *52*, 59–60
    life and work, 51–53
Wayne's World, 158
"We Built This City," 130
Weir, Bob, 131
Welles, Orson, 51
West. *See also* New West
    archetypes, 8
    and change, 167
    conflicting myths of precolonial
        period, 74
    contemporary interpretations, 7–8

cultural periods, 70–72
Francis Parkman on, 76
as landscape of hope, 69
Manifest Destiny period, 6–7, 59,
    70–71, 88
and myth, 5–6, 8–9
mythmaking periods, 6–8
settlement of, 164
Stegner's definition, 118
as virgin paradise, 6
Zane Grey interpretation, 97
Weston, Edward, 13, 32–36, 38, 41
*Where the Bluebird Sings to Lemonade
    Springs*, 100–101, *100*
The Who, 122, 133
"Wichita Lineman," 111
Widmark, Richard, 92
Wild West Show. *See* Buffalo Bill's
    Traveling Wild West Show
The Wild, Wild West, 55
Williams, Terry Tempest, 150
Wills, Bob, 116–117, *116*, 138
Wills, Johnnie Lee, 116
Wilson, Brian, 111, 124–126, 140
Wilson, Carl, 124, 125, 126
Wilson, Charis, 35, 37
Wilson, Dennis, 124, 125, 126
Wilson, Lois, 97
Wind River Range, 18, 26–27, *26*
Wister, Owen, 49, 97
Wood, Natalie, 52–53
Workingman's Dead, 131
Wounded Knee, 7, 147
Writers, 69–72
Wyatt Earp, 145

Yellowstone National Park, 15–16, 18, 161
Yellowstone River, 18
Yosemite National Park, *86*, 88
Young, Brigham, 149
Young, Steve, 150

Zappa, Frank, 123
Zevon, Warren, 129
Zwinger, Ann, 95
Zwinger, Susan, 95

JOHN A. MURRAY, one of America's best-loved writers, combines his passion for the Western landscape with his knowledge of popular culture in *Mythmakers of the West*. Over the last fifteen years he has authored and edited over forty books, which include such popular works as *The Colorado Plateau, Cinema Southwest*, and *Desert Awakenings*. He holds degrees from the University of Colorado and the University of Denver, and was an English professor from 1988 to 1994 at the University of Alaska, Fairbanks, where he also directed the professional writing program. He lives in Denver, Colorado.